Historic Towns of South-East England

Also by David W. Lloyd

The Making of English Towns
The Buildings of Portsmouth and its Environs
Save The City: A Conservation Study of the City of London (General Editor)
(with Nikolaus Pevsner) Hampshire (*Buildings of England*)
(with Donald Insall) Railway Station Architecture

Kent
Surrey
Sussex
Hampshire

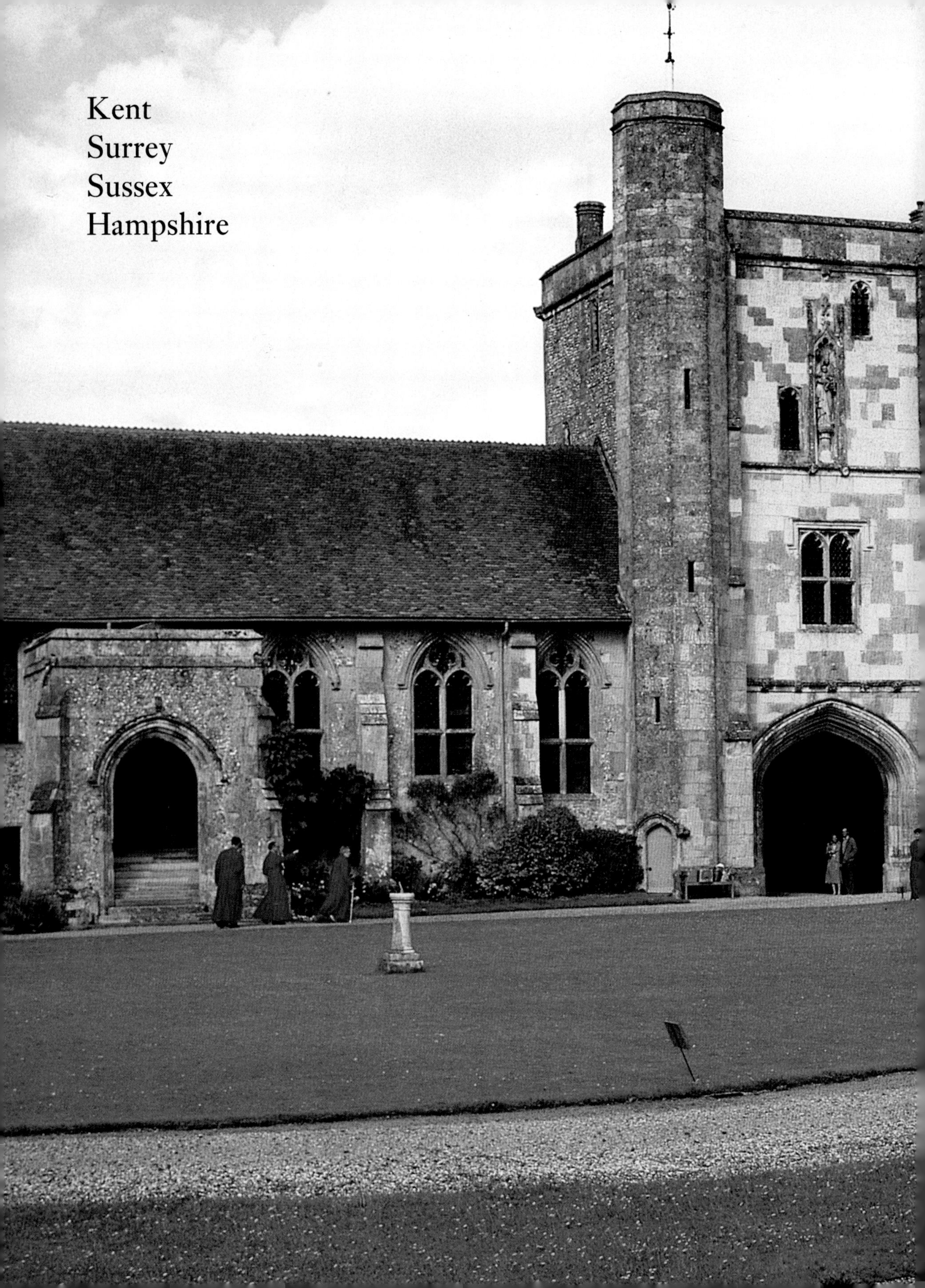

Historic Towns of South-East England

David W. Lloyd

Victor Gollancz Ltd
in association with
Peter Crawley
1987

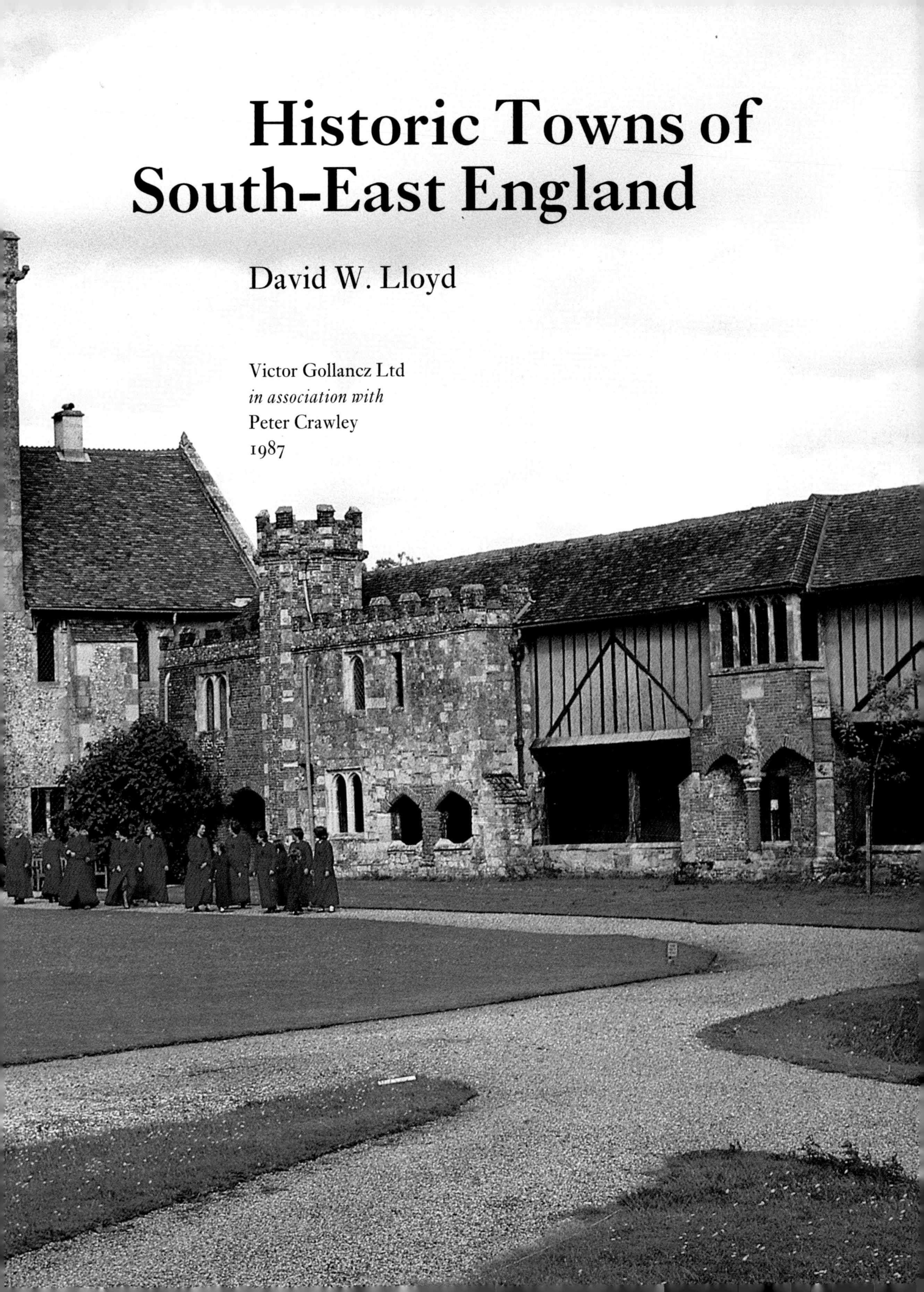

First published in Great Britain 1987
by Victor Gollancz Ltd,
14 Henrietta Street, London WC2E 8QJ

British Library Cataloguing in Publication Data

Lloyd, David
Historic towns of South East England.
1. Historic buildings——England——South East
2. Cities and towns——England——South East
I. Title
720'.9422 NA961

ISBN 0-575-03689-3

Designed by Harold Bartram
Filmset and printed by Jolly & Barber Ltd, Rugby, Warwickshire

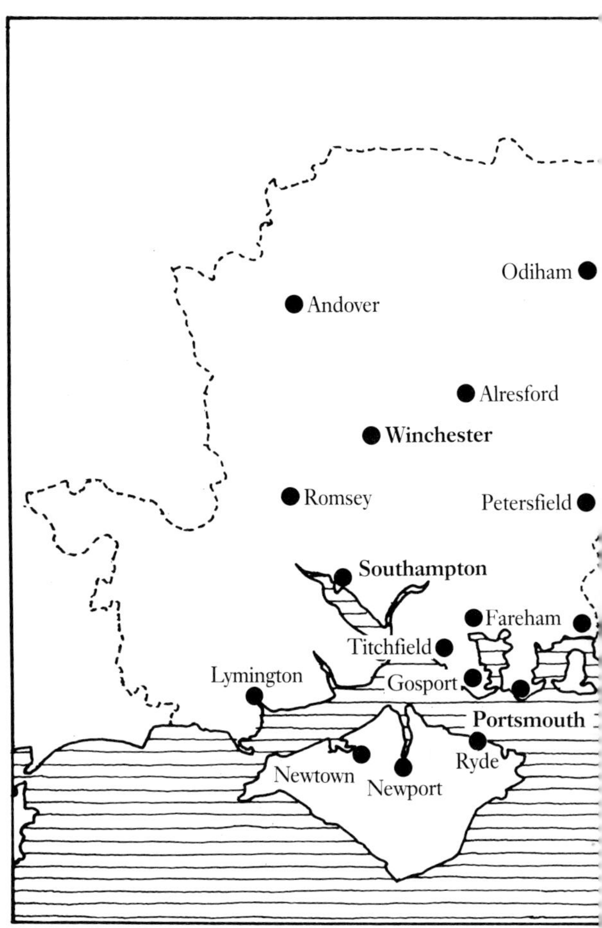

Previous page Hospital of St Cross, Winchester, founded 1136 as an almshouse; the gatehouse and hall date from *c.*1445

Contents

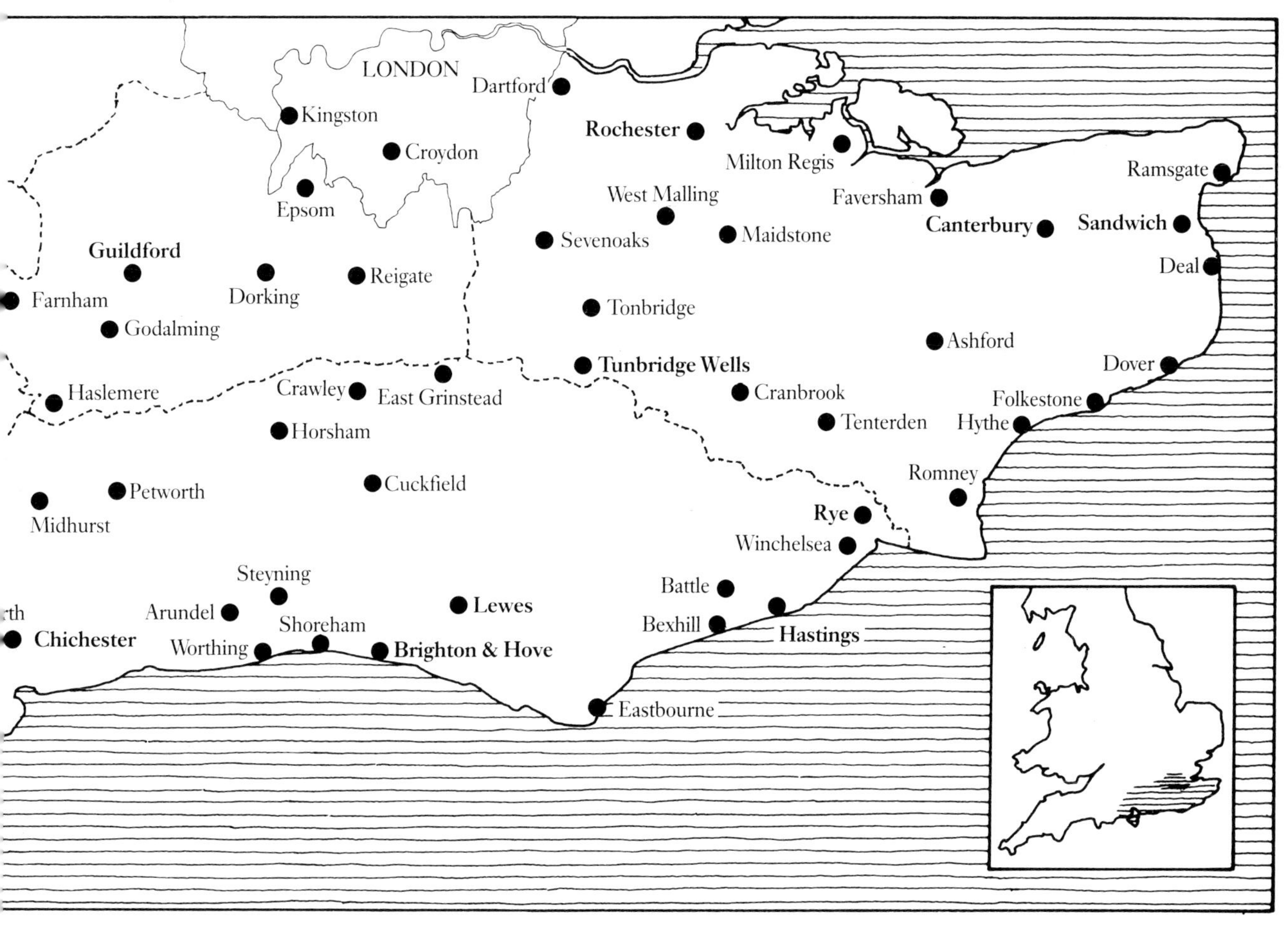
LONDON
Dartford
Kingston
Croydon
Epsom
Rochester
Milton Regis
West Malling
Faversham
Ramsgate
Canterbury
Sandwich
Sevenoaks
Maidstone
Deal
Guildford
Farnham
Godalming
Dorking
Reigate
Tonbridge
Ashford
Tunbridge Wells
Dover
Haslemere
Crawley
East Grinstead
Cranbrook
Folkestone
Tenterden
Hythe
Horsham
Romney
Petworth
Cuckfield
Midhurst
Rye
Winchelsea
Steyning
Battle
Arundel
Lewes
Shoreham
Bexhill
Hastings
Chichester
Worthing
Brighton & Hove
Eastbourne

Illustrations

Colour

Black and white

Maps

Preface

This book follows *The Making of English Towns*, published in 1984, which traced the evolution of cities and towns from their beginning to the present century. Because of its enormous scope, that book had to be very selective – often arbitrarily – in its coverage of individual places.

This book, by contrast, gives individual coverage to towns in a defined region – Hampshire, the Isle of Wight, Sussex, Surrey and Kent. The scope is still huge, including great maritime towns like Portsmouth and Brighton; cathedral cities such as Canterbury and Chichester; medium-sized towns as varied as Farnham, Dartford and Faversham; places hardly more than villages like Steyning and Cuckfield, and even a hamlet shrunken from former town size – Newtown on the Isle of Wight. Inevitably, because of pressure on space, some towns are not included which might have been, especially seaside resorts, and descriptions of the places included have to be reasonably brief and selective. I hope, none the less, that this book will be found to contain a great deal of interesting information unknown not just to visitors, but also to many people living in or near the towns described.

I was born in Southampton, lived there as a young child, and was at school at Charterhouse, Godalming, from which I was able to explore by bicycle the countryside, churches and towns of Surrey and the fringes of Sussex. This was not always strictly legitimate according to the school rules, but my enterprise was condoned, even quietly encouraged, by my housemaster – the great Walter Carruthers Sellar, author of *1066 and All That*, who, more effectively than anyone else, taught me to write English.

All the photographs (except that on p. 50, taken by myself) were taken by my publisher, Peter Crawley, whose encouragement and great patience I should like once again to extol. The maps in the main text are all taken from the early editions of the Ordnance Survey, dating from about 1860 to 1890. Their original scale was 25 inches to the mile with one exception (that of Alresford, which was at six inches to the mile), but they are not necessarily reproduced to the original scale. They are reproduced with the permission of the British Library. The photograph of Chamber Court, Winchester College, is published with permission of the Warden and Scholars.

David W. Lloyd
October 1986

Introduction

Many people think that most of south-east England is sprawling suburb and continuous seaside resort. Like many popular ideas of different regions of Britain this is far from the truth. There are large tracts of glorious countryside, and a fascinating series of towns. Many of these, as one would expect, are connected with the sea. The federation of the Cinque Ports – Sandwich, Dover, Hythe, Romney and Hastings – was formed before the Norman Conquest, originally to provide ships, when needed, for the king, who granted the towns special privileges. Rye and Winchelsea joined the federation later. Every one has suffered from the action of the sea, particularly through silting; Dover is the only Cinque Port which is still important. Shoreham, further west, suffered similarly; as elsewhere, a glorious church testifies former importance. Southampton was a giant of a port from Saxon to Tudor times; after a period of decline it developed again in the nineteenth century. Portsmouth succeeded Chatham as the country's most important dockyard in the eighteenth and nineteenth centuries.

Brighton, hitherto a fishing town, was one of the first successful seaside resorts, thanks to the Prince of Wales who started to visit it in 1783 and who, as Prince Regent, commissioned the architect Nash to design the Pavilion in its present fantastic form (1). The town reached its architectural climax when the Prince had become George IV. All along the coast other resorts developed in rivalry to Brighton; some were based on old small ports like Ramsgate, some on hitherto insignificant villages like Worthing; some were entirely new, like St Leonards west of Hastings. Eastbourne, Folkestone and finally Bexhill were the last resorts to be developed on an ambitious scale, all with aristocratic patrons.

The seaside resorts were preceded by two inland spas, Tunbridge Wells and Epsom, both deeply rural when first exploited in the seventeenth century. They appealed at first to people escaping the constriction of fashionable London life, and it was only in Victorian times that Tunbridge Wells' once raffish reputation gave way to one of utmost respectability.

Of the inland towns the two greatest are Canterbury and Winchester, both of Roman origin, with cathedrals whose history goes back to the beginning of English Christianity, that of Canterbury becoming a great centre of pilgrimage. Winchester was, in effect, the capital of England in late Saxon times, and remained so in some measure, with London gradually taking over, till the thirteenth century. Chichester and Rochester are smaller cathedral cities (though the latter is now part of a larger urban complex), both likewise of Roman origin. Monasteries dominated several small towns, notably Battle and Romsey – at the first only a few impressive parts survive, but in Romsey the abbey church stands entire. At Steyning part of a smaller but very impressive priory church remains.

Defence has always influenced the development of towns. Lewes exists because its hilly site was easy to defend (42). Castles were built at Rochester (51), Guildford and Tonbridge (73) to defend river crossings. Dover Castle, probably the finest in England after the Tower of London, is magnificently set above the cliffs and harbour, but Hastings Castle is fragmentary, because of erosion. Arundel Castle, of Norman origin, became the seat of a great aristocratic family. Farnham Castle was the fortified home of the Bishops of

Winchester (26). At Canterbury (13), Chichester, Rochester and, especially, Southampton (68) there are impressive stretches of city wall; Southampton and Canterbury, like Rye (colour illus. p. 107) and Winchelsea (77), preserve town gateways. At Portsmouth the town defences are later, formed in the age of artillery fire (47, 48).

Dozens of towns grew primarily as marketing centres. Some, situated on creeks or navigable rivers, were also small ports, like Maidstone (colour ills. p. 106), Dartford, Faversham, and Newport on the Isle of Wight. Medieval towns sometimes grew haphazardly, but very often they were planned, at least in parts, by their overlords, who might be churchmen or powerful barons. Alresford was founded anew and Farnham was developed from small beginnings by bishops of Winchester, both with T patterns of streets (Map I); Newport was laid out by the lord of the Isle, with a more complex street pattern (Map VIII). At Faversham a new wide street was formed, leading to the now vanished Abbey. Some smaller towns had little more than single wide streets, like Lymington (43), Crawley, Ashford, East Grinstead and West Malling (76) (Map XI); markets were held in the wider parts of those streets. At the last three, as at Maidstone, some market stalls became permanent and were replaced by substantial buildings, resulting on islanded blocks encroaching on what had been broad streets. Other towns were more complex, with rectangular market places, as at Petersfield (Map IX), or triangular ones, as at Romsey (57) and Kingston (Map VII). At the last two, as at Horsham (Map VI), once larger spaces have again been reduced by permanent buildings replacing the original market stalls. In striking contrast to the fascinating irregularity of most medieval towns is the rigid grid of the new port town of Winchelsea, started in the late thirteenth century but never finished as intended because of the retreat of the sea (Map XII).

Markets, whether for grain, livestock or general merchandise sold from stalls, were held on specified days in the streets or market places. Over the centuries, centralization and changing methods of trading have greatly reduced the number of markets, and many that survive, including all the cattle markets, have been moved to different sites. Nevertheless a few traditional stall markets still flourish at certain times on their original sites, as at Faversham, Petersfield, Lymington (43), Epsom and, most remarkably, Kingston and Croydon where the open markets, now held daily, take place on exactly the same sites where they did centuries ago.

South-east England has a rich variety of local materials. There were important limestone quarries on the Isle of Wight, providing the stone for Winchester Cathedral, many mainland churches, and the city walls of Southampton. Kentish ragstone, mainly from near Maidstone (and also from elsewhere on the 'ragstone ridge' parallel with the chalk North Downs) is a hard rough stone formerly shipped in quantity to London; Rochester Castle is built of it. Reigate stone, also once used in London, is soft and chalky, found locally mainly in churches. Sandstones were quarried in several areas, especially near Godalming (Bargate stone), and around East Grinstead and Tunbridge Wells, where it is soft and greyish, often with brown or orange tints. Horsham stone, quarried in hard slabs, was used for roofing in towns as far apart as East Grinstead (24), Cuckfield and Steyning. Flint was used on or near the chalklands for churches, defences and, occasionally, houses, as in Lewes (**40**), Brighton, Shoreham and Chichester. Fine Caen stone was imported for Canterbury Cathedral and a few other buildings.

Most houses were timber-framed until the middle of the seventeenth century, the panels within the timbering being filled with wattle and daub – tough interwoven sticks with lime-based plaster applied over them flush with the timbering. At first the timber was left exposed, perhaps lightly washed over – the fashion for blackening timber is very recent in this region. As elsewhere, houses usually had central open halls rising to the roofs, with smaller rooms at the ends or in wings, until the sixteenth century. From then, two-storeyed – or in towns often three-storeyed – houses became general, their upper floors often overhanging those below. The one type of timber-framed house specially associated with the area (though not peculiar to it) is the 'Wealden house' which had a central hall set back between two slightly projecting two-storeyed wings, the whole under a simple long roof with eaves extending continuously over the recessed central part. In nearly every surviving Wealden house, as well as others which originally had open halls, the halls have long since been subdivided into two storeys. A few open hall houses (not necessarily of the Wealden type) survive, variously altered but recognizable, in Southampton, Tonbridge (**74**), East Grinstead, Milton Regis, Battle, Crawley, Canterbury and elsewhere. Later timber-framed houses, usually with overhanging upper storeys, are found in some of these towns, as well as in Lewes, Winchester, Maidstone, Sandwich, Midhurst, Rye, Hastings, Rochester and other places. A few of the larger merchants' houses were stone-built, as at Southampton, and many had stone-vaulted cellars or undercrofts, even if timber-framed above; several of these survive in Southampton, Winchelsea, Canterbury and other towns, usually having long outlasted the original houses above.

Bricks began to be used in the sixteenth century (perhaps earlier in Sandwich, where they were imported from Flanders), especially, at first, for chimneys, and also for infilling within timber-framing (brick nogging), instead of wattle and daub. By the middle of the seventeenth century brick building was general; there then developed the 'Artisan' style, using classical motifs carved in bricks; there are examples in Dover (Maison Dieu House), Rye (the Old Grammar School), Sandwich, Dorking and elsewhere.

By the end of the seventeenth century the 'Georgian' type of house evolved, built to classical proportions, with sash windows becoming universal after about 1700. Every old town has its characteristic Georgian (or earlier classical) houses, usually of brick; among those with the finest collections are Chichester (**16**, **18**), Winchester (**84**), Lewes (**41**), Farnham (**27**), Fareham, Rochester (**55**), Epsom, Emsworth, West Malling (**76**), and, on a lower key, Odiham. Usually they front the streets directly, but are occasionally set back behind iron railings; there are fine examples at Chichester (**15**) and Petworth. Normally Georgian town houses had classical porches or doorcases, but many have been lost where shops have been inserted on ground floors. Fareham has an unrivalled collection of Georgian porches and door canopies. Georgian bricks were usually red, to varying hues depending on the qualities of local clays (colour illus. p. 23). Grey or purply headers – the ends of bricks burnt to those colours because of their positions in the kilns – were often used, especially in Hampshire and the Isle of Wight, with red bricks either as dressings (on corners or round windows) or in chequer patterns. Newport is especially notable for its variedly textured bricks. In later Georgian times buff or brownish bricks became fashionable; creamy buff bricks were produced on the Hampshire coast, while around Faversham, Milton Regis and Sittingbourne the production of brownish 'stock' bricks hugely increased in the nineteenth century, when they were sent by barge to help build the Victorian capital; they are also seen in coastal towns like Ramsgate.

Tile-hanging – the tiles being laid in overlapping courses on walls which might be timber-framed, or of rough stone or flint – was a great tradition in the region from at least the eighteenth century (colour illus. p. 22). Older timber-framed houses were sometimes covered in this way. Unfortunately hung tiles have recently been stripped from many houses, perhaps revealing timbering which had originally been exposed, but reducing the distinctive charm of towns like Godalming, Midhurst, Horsham and Steyning which used to be colourful through tile-hanging; Haslemere still has some. More deceptive than overlapping tiles are mathematical tiles, carefully formed and applied to walls to look like bricks. They are especially common in Lewes, but are found in many other towns, notably Tenterden and the earlier parts of Brighton – where they are usually grey or almost black (**2**), and sometimes have a glossy finish resulting from the use of salt water in manufacture.

Although oak-framed houses ceased to be built before 1700, houses were still constructed after that date, in certain areas, using imported softwood or deal for framing. Associated with this was the use of weatherboarding – similar to clapboarding in America – which was often, though not always, in deal. It is specially associated with the Medway and Thames estuaries (**54**), Epsom, and the Weald around Cranbrook and Tenterden (colour illus. pp. 47, 111).

Many older houses were modernized in Georgian times. Sometimes whole new brick fronts were added to timber-framed houses, the origin of which is evident only inside, at the backs or in the roofs: on other houses old façades were covered with tiles or weatherboarding. Many timber-framed houses were plastered over – the practice began in this region in the seventeenth century; Canterbury and Sandwich (**59**, **64**) have numerous houses where this happened. Older, small, windows were replaced by Georgian ones. In short, many of the oldest surviving houses have been altered and adapted, often many times over, to suit changing tastes and standards – and are not necessarily less interesting because of this. The practice, all too common recently, of removing accretions and 'making good' later alterations, so as to return buildings, supposedly, to their 'original' condition, usually results in their being falsified and looking like fakes, even if basically genuine.

Stucco, or hard plaster intended at first to resemble stone, became fashionable nationally after about 1810, and of nowhere is it more typical than Brighton. Stucco is especially associated with bowed frontages (**88**) – although the fashion for bow windows goes back well before that for stucco. Many bows were formed in late Georgian times, usually on first floors, but sometimes running through two or more storeys. The earlier ones were generally of wood, containing three sash windows following the curves, under carved cornices. Southampton and Portsmouth each developed a distinctive tradition; in the former they are bold, often almost semicircular (**67**), in Portsmouth shallower and more delicate. Other towns – notably Winchester (**83**), Chichester, Ryde, Newport, Lymington, Worthing (**88**) and Ramsgate have many varieties of bow window, including the common flat-fronted type with canted sides. In Brighton and Hove whole frontages were folded out in curves, most spectacularly in Brunswick Square (see colour illus. p. 26. Iron balconies often go with bow windows (**6**), e.g. Worthing and Brighton. (See colour illus. p. 27.)

Space is too short to summarize adequately the Victorian developments in southern towns. Some resorts, like Eastbourne and Folkestone, continued the Regency tradition of building for several decades, details becoming coarser and heavier. Terraced houses gradually became unfashionable, in favour of detached or semi-detached villas, pioneered in Decimus Burton's delightful Calverley Park at Tunbridge Wells. At the end of the century came the fashion for Flemish, Dutch and Baroque styles, together with a revival of rich red brick, produced in quantity in Sussex brickworks and seen, for instance, in some of the turn-of-the-century streets and villas of Eastbourne and Tunbridge Wells, where white-painted woodwork goes well with the bright red of bricks. Further west, the brick industry also expanded round Fareham, its products seen most impressively in the great Victorian forts which surround Portsmouth (**32**), and in the sometimes huge buildings of the Dockyard. Local stones were still used, notably at Godalming, where both Charterhouse and the railway station are built of rough Bargate stone.

The railway revived Southampton as a great port, helped the Regency resorts to develop further, and stimulated new resorts like Eastbourne. Appropriately Southampton, Brighton and Eastbourne have the best railway stations, the first (now superseded) is classical of 1839–40; the second has a great curved, iron-arched, train shed of the 1880s; the third has a florid frontage and lively skyline, recently well restored. The railways also encouraged what we now call commuting, first from Croydon, then from places further out like Dorking, Reigate and Sevenoaks, which have not lost their older character as market towns. Croydon grew from a small town into a suburban city; its Victorian town hall vies with those of Portsmouth and Dover, and the inter-war Civic Centre at Southampton, in its expression of municipal pride. These contrast with the earlier, more modest, guildhalls and market halls of which the best examples are at Guildford and Rochester (seventeenth century), Reigate (eighteenth) and Faversham (**30**).

Victorian churches contribute to the character and interest of many towns, notably Brighton (**4**) and Croydon, and also Dorking with its fine spire by Woodyer, although the area's most beautiful steeple (apart from that of Chichester Cathedral, rebuilt after collapse in Victorian times) is possibly the 'flying spire' of Faversham, dating from 1799 (**31**).

Of the 64 towns described, Southampton, Portsmouth and Brighton are big cities of complex and varied interest, not easily assimilated in short or single visits. Winchester and Canterbury are major historic cities with a huge number of buildings of absorbing interest apart from their main 'sights'; the same is true on a relatively – only relatively – smaller scale at

Chichester and Lewes. Rochester is well-preserved as the historic quarter of a larger urban complex, as is the old town of Hastings (35). Some towns have retained their historic centres cheek-by-jowl with crude new developments; Guildford is an outstanding example, Kingston and Fareham are others. Rye has been self-consciously picturesque, and much visited, for many years; Sandwich, another of the Cinque Ports, is at least as delightful to explore. Faversham is an outstanding example of an old town rescued from decline through the practical and persuasive powers of a local preservation society; more recently much the same has started to happen at Romsey. Farnham was the pioneer in what we now call urban conservation; eighty years ago a local businessman and architect together started to restore and improve historic buildings and to build new ones in conspicuous places which add to the character of the town (see colour illus. p. 50). On a smaller scale, there are many delightful places which today have the status of little more than villages, but which were regarded as towns in the past and have a compact urban quality. Among them are Tenterden, Cranbrook, West Malling, Alresford, Petworth, Steyning, Odiham, Titchfield, Cuckfield and, on a slightly larger scale, Midhurst. To this list can be added the old towns of Haslemere and Milton Regis, the latter surviving as an entity within the larger town of Sittingbourne. Nearly all the places so far mentioned have obvious and acknowledged historic quality. Perhaps more vulnerable, because they have grown a good deal and their qualities are not so obvious or so widely appreciated, are towns like Horsham, East Grinstead, Dorking, Sevenoaks, Petersfield, Ashford and Newport which are still very attractive in parts – but there is a danger that these parts may not be sufficiently strongly defended if and when they are threatened by development. Godalming may come into this category too; despite its charm, both it and its surroundings have been threatened – and stoutly defended – from time to time.

'Threatened' and 'defended' are appropriate words. It is not sufficiently realized how far the preservation of historic towns is dependent on planning control:- of their surroundings as parts of green belts and the like; of their individual buildings through 'listing'; of whole streets and squares as parts of conservation areas; and of their general character through control of new development. (Many architects object strongly to any controls over new development – but so many horrendous buildings have been designed in the last thirty years by qualified architects that such pleadings should not be heeded.) Planning authorities, at county, city or district levels, vary greatly in the qualities of their members, staff, policies, administration and resources. Some are good at urban conservation – the county authority in Hampshire and the city council of Rochester upon Medway (for what has been achieved in the old city there) are mentioned as two among many – but others are not so good. Nor are central government's decisions following appeals always enlightened. Fortunately there is a large number of civic and preservation societies which have achieved a great deal, through open battle, through behind-the-scenes persuasion, or through practical work, in stopping needless destruction and achieving visual improvements. Their work will be all the more needed with continuing uncertainties over the role of planning authorities, and the changing policies of individual authorities.

Alresford

Hampshire

Strictly New Alresford, this is a remarkable example of a planned medieval town. The Saxon village was Old Alresford, north of a small tributary of the River Itchen; the bishops of Winchester were its overlords. In 1200 Bishop de Lucy laid out the present town in the form of a T, the arms containing the main road from Winchester to London, the thick stem (Broad Street) the markets and fairs. Fires in 1689 and later destroyed the medieval fabric of the town but the street pattern survives. Most of the older houses are late seventeenth century or Georgian, but many of their brick façades have since been stuccoed or painted. Broad Street is delightful with its double line of trees; one of the best preserved earlier houses is on its west side near the bottom, with a façade of dark red and grey mottled brick, a wooden cornice and mullioned and transomed windows, characteristic of the end of the seventeenth century before sashes became universal. Beyond, the road narrows, twists and continues along an embankment, with a steep drop to the left and a lake on the right. This is really an earthen dam, built by de Lucy across the stream at about the same time as he founded the town. The lake so formed was almost certainly not intended as a headwater to help make the Itchen navigable, as is sometimes said, but to stock fish – an important item in a medieval bishop's household. Alresford was a major wool market in the fourteenth century, and the name Fulling Mill suggests a weaving industry. The town was static from the end of the Georgian period until very recently; now its small shops do a good trade, making a pleasant contrast with the stores and supermarkets of the larger centres, and the branch railway has been reopened by steam enthusiasts. (See colour illus. pp. 22/23.)

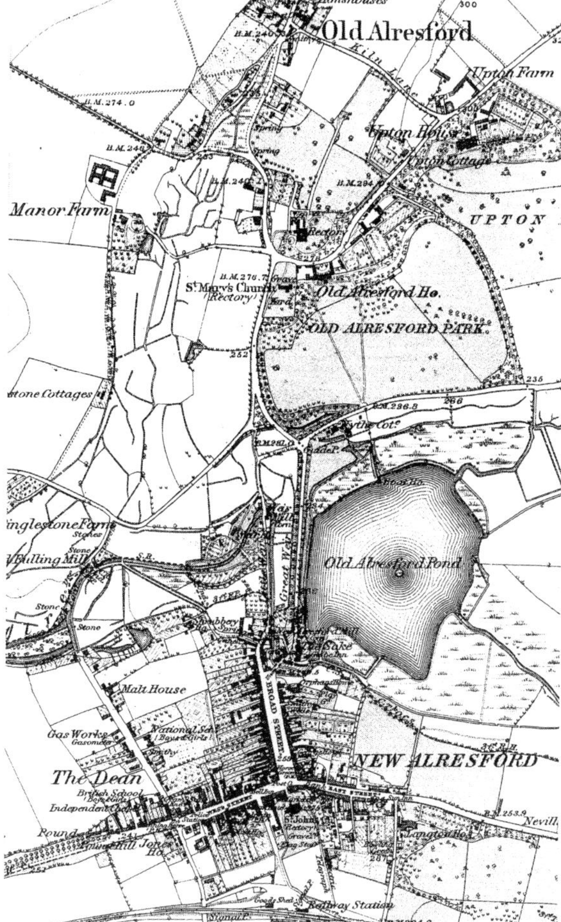

Map I **Alresford.** Bishop de Lucy founded New Alresford in 1200 south of the older village. He dammed a stream to form a large fish pond, and laid out the town to a T pattern, with Broad Street accommodating the market. The map is of 1870.

Andover

Hampshire

The name Andover is Celtic, the second part meaning water, as in Dover. The town had a guild merchant in 1175, unusual for so small a place, and was one of Hampshire's ancient corporate boroughs. It had a serious fire in 1434, and a few of the present buildings may date vestigially from the rebuilding. It was a major stage on the road from London to the south-west, and until recently the town centre looked much as it did at the end of the coaching era. In the 1960s the town was greatly expanded as part of the policy of dispersal from London; large housing estates were built, industries grew, and the shopping centre was enlarged. Some effort was made to keep the main shape of the old town, and to preserve the dominance of the two focal buildings, the Guildhall and the church. The classical Guildhall (1825) stands effectively at the head of the wide High Street which keeps most of its old frontages; they bulge slightly inward on either side and broaden at both ends, to good effect. The narrow Upper High Street, largely rebuilt, leads to the climax of the church, successor to a medieval building which was unnecessarily demolished in 1840–1. It was designed by the little-known Augustus Livesay of Portsmouth (architect also of Newtown church, Isle of Wight), although Sydney Smirke supervised its completion, after trouble with the structure. The interior is magnificent, with lofty arches, high make-believe plaster vaulting, and chancel seen through an elaborate screen. Georgian and older buildings surround the church pleasantly; one houses the museum, with material from Danebury, an Iron Age hillfort a few miles away. The Angel Inn opposite the church has a Georgian front added to a timber-framed structure evident from the yard behind. Old inns are still a notable feature of Andover; the former Star and Garter in High Street, renamed the Danebury Hotel, has a splendid stuccoed front of about 1830 with very broad bow windows; the Globe has a Georgian front and refurbished yard. Other former inn yards have been adapted as footways off the High Street. The fine Town Mills of 1764, spanning the small river Anton, is now a restaurant.

The new estates on the northern edge of the town were designed by the Greater London Council at the time when reaction was setting in against high-rise flats. The houses are mostly two-storeyed, sometimes three, grouped artily round greens, paved spaces or small courtyards, which are often linked by footways under arches as in the old inn yards. Trees planted at the time are now noticeably taking root. Each estate is tightly-knit, but is often separated from the next by a wide grassy space which is neither field nor park. For all the arty effects, which are sometimes good, this form of housing is less satisfactory than the better sort of garden suburb with larger individual plots and less excessive spaces.

Arundel

Sussex

No town in England – Windsor excepted – is more dominated by the works of a single family than Arundel. The Fitzalans were earls of Arundel from the thirteenth century; their heiress married a Howard, Duke of Norfolk, in 1557 (he was beheaded in 1572), and their descendants have owned the castle since. Most, though not all, of the dukes have been Catholic, and they are hereditary Earls Marshal of England – it is one of the pleasanter anomalies of the British constitution that a Catholic holds this important ceremonial office, close to the monarchy, while the monarch herself is head of the Anglican church.

The castle was first built in 1067 by Richard of Montgomery, Norman lord of Arundel and Shrewsbury; the lower part of the inner gate dates from not long after. The circular keep on Montgomery's motte was built in the twelfth century and the barbican in the thirteenth. The castle was ruined in the Civil War and remained so – the Howards living elsewhere – until the 1790s when the then duke made it habitable again. Most of his work was replaced from 1890 by the fifteenth duke on a grandiose scale, almost rivalling Windsor, to the design of an architect called Buckler. The result is a clumsy piece of neo-medievalism, not effectively romantic, nor impressive except for its sheer bulk; one wonders what earlier, better Gothic Revival architects would have made of such a commission, like Pugin, Salvin, Scott, Street or Burges – who did the same thing so effectively at Cardiff Castle. Inside, by far the most attractive room is the one that survives from about 1800 – the mahogany-pillared library with its brass-fronted balconies, in which Ian Nairn says in his idiosyncratic way in *Buildings of England: Sussex*: 'space seesaws and tiptoes from side to side. . . .' The fifteenth duke also built the great Catholic church, made a cathedral in 1965. Into it have been translated the remains of Philip Howard, who died in the Tower in 1595 after years of imprisonment, refusing to renounce the Catholic faith; he was actually canonized in 1970. The cathedral, designed by J.A. Hansom and largely completed in 1873, is French in character and comes into its own in the eastern part where the light is suffused through the very fine stained glass by Hardman, giving the authentic medieval effect – so different from the flooding of light through clear glass windows, which many people seem to prefer. It is a relief to go from the cathedral to the old parish church, rebuilt from 1380 as a collegiate church, but fairly unimpressive outside. The interior is splendid – restrained, spacious and well-proportioned. Most of the building is the Anglican church, but the east part – the collegiate choir – was severed at the Reformation and became the property of the Howards; it remains Catholic and has been the burial place of the family since the time of the medieval Fitzalans. Though now partly visible from the main church through a glass screen it is entered only through the castle grounds – rather like cutting off the choir of a cathedral and giving it a separate entrance.

Arundel is a charming town, built on the side of a hill and having something of the quality of Lewes, though the High Street hardly compares. This once broadened down to the river, but the lower part has long since been encroached by an island block of buildings leaving two narrow streets on either side. The middle part has handsome Georgian fronts, but the top was drastically curtailed in 1803 by the then duke who diverted the London road and pulled down numerous houses east and north of the church to enlarge the castle grounds – an act as high-handed as the removal of any small village by a landowner during that period. Two very attractive streets lead westward.

Maltravers Street runs along the hillside with an irregularly raised pavement on the upper side (as at Hastings) and a great variety of houses of which the most distinctive are Georgian; little streets of flint and stucco open off from the further end. Tarrant Street, lower down, is narrower and livelier with its interesting shops. It runs parallel to the river which was formerly navigable, and which has followed its present course since the seventeenth century. From afar, and especially from the roads and railway to the south, the town looks wonderful, piled up the hillside to the ebullient Catholic cathedral and more subdued medieval church, with Buckler's huge castle on the right and, beyond, the glorious park – an enhancement of the Downs with their huge rounded slopes tumbling to the river gap.

Ashford

Kent

Ashford is an underrated place. It was first a market town, then a railway centre, and is now growing fast. There was originally a very long street, widening in the middle to accommodate the markets, and tapering at the ends. Encroachment at an early date on what was the widest part has resulted in a dense cluster of buildings, medieval to modern, in the very centre of the town, to colourful effect. An alley threads through to the church, a substantial ragstone building with a slender pinnacled tower, hemmed in a churchyard like a miniature close, with varied old buildings, many of them tile-hung; the most interesting is the former grammar school of 1635 with a brick mullioned window. Elsewhere in the town centre some fine Georgian buildings survive, especially in the furthest tapering part of the original main street, East Hill, which has been cut off by a new cross road. Redevelopment so far has created muddled effects without the charm of the older parts. Could not the growth that would inevitably come with the Channel Tunnel result in something new that is really memorable, to contrast with the historic areas – which must be watched?

Battle

Sussex

Battle is of course where William defeated Harold; William founded the abbey, with its high altar on the exact spot where Harold fell. It was an awkward site at the brow of a ridge, and the abbey buildings had to spread downhill, with some difficulty. The town grew outside the abbey gate, and was important enough in its own right at the time of the Dissolution to survive; today it is a busy shopping centre. Fortunately the shops are small, and the long High Street has a delightful range of buildings (at least above fascia levels) of different dates, materials and scales. The oldest are low and timber-framed, usually tiled or plastered over; there are taller Georgian houses and a few ebullient Victorian insertions. Priory House of about 1700, with balconied first-floor window under a baroque hood, and the busily gabled National Westminster Bank next door, are examples of the last two types. They are compatible with each other and with their equally different neighbours.

The street widens into a green at the entrance to the Abbey; facing it is a medieval 'Wealden' house called Pilgrim's Rest. The abbey gateway, built in 1338, is an early example of the type with octagonal corner turrets, seen also in the gateways of St Augustine's Abbey, Canterbury, several colleges at Cambridge, and (a late example), Abbot's Hospital at Guildford, as well as at Knole and Cowdray. The abbey was taken over at the Reformation by Sir Anthony Browne, a courtier and also purchaser of Cowdray, page 89. He pulled down the abbey church, and enlarged the abbot's house for himself. This, remodelled in Victorian times, is now a school. The visitor sees the remains of some of the monastic buildings, especially of the thirteenth-century dormitory with its two beautifully vaulted lower rooms. The southern of these is taller because its floor is lower, a result of the fall in the ground; its effect is particularly beautiful with high slender pillars supporting the branching ribs. The parish church, on a downward slope outside the abbey wall, must have looked fairly insignificant while the abbey stood. It has a typical Sussex fifteenth-century tower, symbol of the town's modest assertiveness against the abbey. The interior is more impressive than the outside leads one to expect, as so often in Sussex (Steyning, Eastbourne, Horsham); there are long twelfth-century arcades, and significant remains of wall paintings once of high quality. Further down is the Gothic railway station of 1852 – it may seem odd that the architect, William Tress, did not design in Norman. There is a pointed booking hatch, making one feel that one should, perhaps, kneel for a ticket to St Leonards or Tunbridge Wells. The platforms retain their fine fretted canopies, of the sort that has disappeared from so many other stations.

Bexhill

Sussex

Bexhill was promoted by the aristocratic De la Warr family from the 1880s; it was the first place where mixed bathing was allowed – hitherto the sexes were segregated on beaches. It has an Edwardian patina, and that makes its best building all the more astonishing – the De la Warr (pronounced Delaware) Pavilion of 1933–6 by Mendelsohn and Chermayeff, one of the few stylish International Modern buildings of any size built in Britain between the wars. With its picturesque angular massing, its solid horizontal concrete walls contrasting with continuous glazing, and projecting rounded wing with flat canopies and iron balconies – a whiff of the Regency – it stands splendidly on a slightly elevated shoreside site. Pevsner wrote in 1965 in *Buildings of England: Sussex* 'it has aged very well', as if even he, arch-champion of International Modern, expected such buildings to wither after such a short time. Changes of fashion should not blind one to its merits. As at Eastbourne the old village is inland, but has lasted better than the Old Town at Eastbourne. Weatherboarded houses frame the church on a hillock, and the ruins of the medieval manor house are preserved in a public garden.

Brighton and Hove

Sussex

Brighton is the greatest, and almost the oldest, seaside resort. People were bathing there, for pleasure or as a stimulant, in the 1730s. But the town has a far longer history as a fishing port. In Tudor times fishermen from Brighthelmstone, as it was then spelt, sailed, like those from Rye and Hastings, to catch cod off Scarborough in the summer, and herring off Great Yarmouth in the autumn. For the rest of the year they fished in the Channel, or carried general cargo. The vessels were beached, for Brighton had no harbour, though the difficult one at nearby Shoreham was sometimes used. One Brighton boat owner, Captain Tettersall, carried the future Charles II over to France in 1651, after he had spent the night secretly in a local public house. (Sadly, for present-day brewers, the site of the pub is not known.) Tettersall could not have imagined how he was helping to ensure the future prosperity of the town through safeguarding the royal line.

Old Brighton was already starting to decline at the time Charles was rescued – due to sea encroachment, which had destroyed the seaward part of the medieval town. A hundred years later a new era was beginning; Dr Russell, a Lewes physician, published a book on the benefits of bathing, specially recommending Brighton. The first royal visitors were George III's brothers, the Dukes of Gloucester (from 1765), York and Cumberland. The Prince of Wales – the future Regent and then George IV – first stayed in Brighton with his uncle Cumberland in 1783. In 1785 he secretly married Maria Fitzherbert (constitutionally this was impossible because she was a Catholic), and in 1787 the first fairly simple Pavilion, with bow windows and balconies, was built for them, to the design of Henry Holland. The Pavilion was not on the coast but north-east of the old town, which at first grew in that direction; only later did it spread along the sea front. Fashionable – or would-be fashionable – visitors increased steadily. Between 1811 and 1821 Brighton was the fastest growing town in England in proportion to its size (Bradford was next), but the town's architectural heyday was in the 1820s when George IV was king. The routine of the resort was at first like that of Georgian spas. Bathing took place early, followed by visits to coffee houses, card houses or circulating libraries. In the afternoons people might shop, walk on the downs, go to the races if they were on, or simply drive conspicuously back and forth along the front. In the evening there were balls and assemblies, often in the rooms attached to the principal inns, the

Old Ship (where the Georgian ballroom survives), and the Castle. After the 1820s the Georgian routine no longer prevailed – people organized their holidays more independently. Whole houses were hired for weeks or even months. At first the season was from summer to autumn, but it gradually became later till by the 1820s it was in the winter. (By then sea bathing was less fashionable and no longer obligatory.) George IV came to Brighton less often as King than he did as Regent, but William IV visited it fairly frequently. So did Victoria till 1845 when, not finding the Pavilion or Brighton to her liking, she bought Osborne on the Isle of Wight as her retreat. She sold the Pavilion to the town in 1850.

Brighton's growth accelerated after the railway opened in 1841. Fashionable people continued to stay for the winter season – local high society was particularly exotic around 1848–50 when refugees from coups in Europe came to Brighton, including Prince Metternich. There was an Edwardian Indian summer when the King came to stay periodically with friends and relatives in Hove and Kemp Town. More important for the fortunes of the town were the Victorian middle classes who stayed – at first often in hired houses, but increasingly in hotels – in summer or early autumn, the bread-winners sometimes commuting to London during the holiday if it were long. Clerical workers and better-paid artisans became more numerous towards the end of the century, staying in boarding houses which were usually in Regency

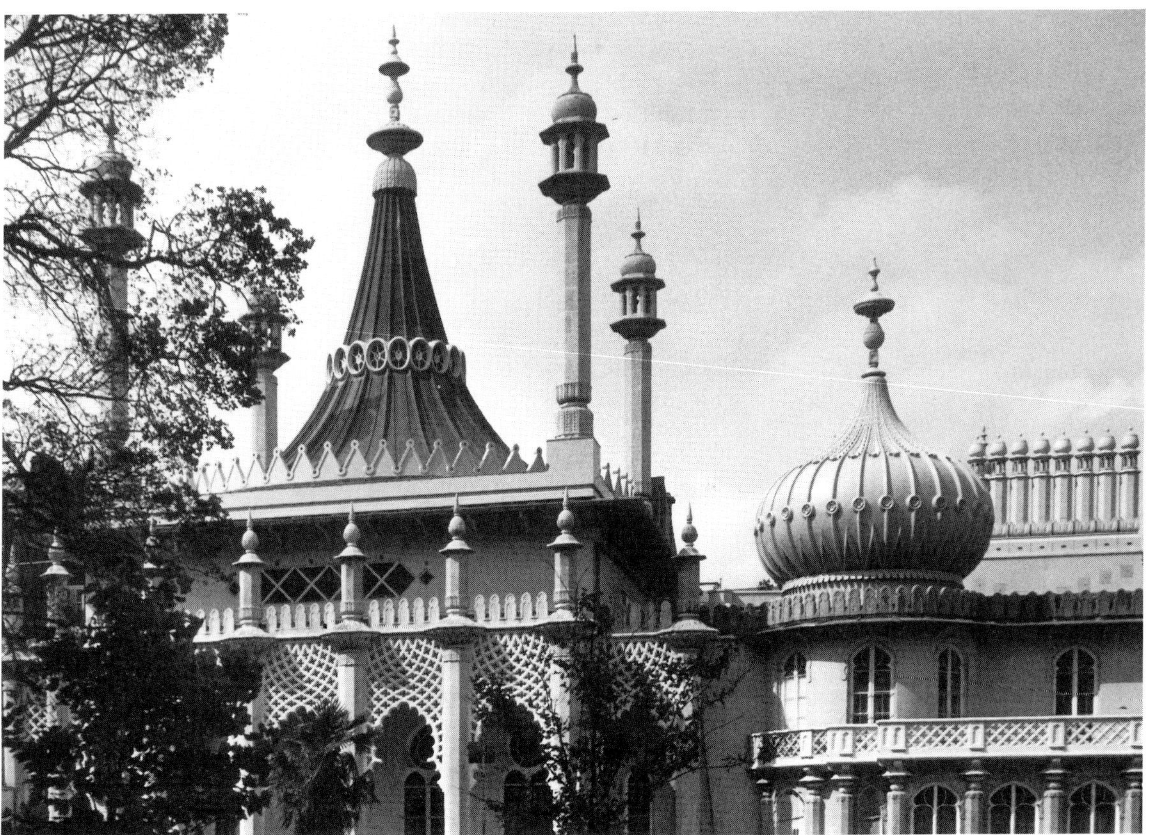

1 **Brighton Pavilion** – the fantasy of the Regency skyline, by John Nash.

terraces near the town centre. Day trippers arrived by train in thousands in high summer. So Brighton became a resort for all classes.

Despite some all too conspicuous redevelopment in the 1960s and 70s in sensitive parts of the town, Brighton is still a fascinating place to explore – not just the sea front, which many find disappointing, but the miles of older streets, lanes, squares and crescents inland, varying from the lively and intimate to the sedate and grand. Brighton had its own specific building traditions. The fishing town was largely built of pebbles from the beach and flint from the downs, bonded and framed by bricks, and this tradition lasted into the early years of the resort. Mathematical tiles were commonly applied to flint walls to look like bricks, often blue-grey and sometimes glossy through the use of seawater in manufacture. Stucco became fashionable after 1800, as in London; it was particularly suitable for Brighton as it afforded protection to buildings against the sea air. Bow windows were almost universal from the 1780s, when the Pavilion was built with prominent examples. They were usually rounded, running through all the main storeys of houses; sometimes they were flat-fronted with canted sides. From the Regency onwards many of the grander houses were built with their whole façades bulging out in curves. Iron balconies were nearly universal at first-floor level, rounding the bows, and very often they had blind-like canopies, forming verandahs, though fewer of these remain.

The town is described in sections: *The Old Town: The Pavilion and the Steine: Eastward to Kemp Town: Religion and Railways: Along the Front to Hove.*

The Old Town

Old Brighton was bounded by three streets, West, North and East, all now busily commercial, East Street having the most character. Within these is the dense network of 'Lanes', some simply narrow streets, others footways scarcely the width of two people, opening here and there into small irregular spaces. The pattern looks medieval, but in fact most of the area did not become densely built until the seventeenth century, after the buildings near the original seafront had been eroded away. As the fishing trade declined and the resort expanded, the historic heartland became more and more a mixture of poorer houses and small businesses, and then increasingly, from quite early this century, came to be appreciated as a place of raffish charm. Now the area is intensely self-conscious with its specialist shops, pubs, restaurants and other tourist magnets with décor varying from the brash and vulgar to the decorous and tasteful. The narrowest lanes are brick-paved; enough walls and frontages are of flint, pebbles or hung tiles to make the area still seem 'genuine' as well as self-consciously picturesque. In the last few years, odd bits of backland have been filled with new 'lanes', arcades, or 'squares', generally to good effect, making an even denser pattern than before. To many people this is the most appealing part of Brighton, illustrating in its manicured way the thoroughness of the transition between fishing town and sophisticated resort.

The Pavilion and the Steine

The Pavilion was built on the inland edge of the town, bordering – and, with its grounds, encroaching on – the Steine, originally a strip of common land extending far in from the shore. From the time it was first built – long before Nash gave it its fantastic form – fashionable houses spread sporadically along both sides of the Steine. Some of the earliest were built in the traditions of the old town, in dark pebbles framed in brick, but many of these were later stuccoed. Most have bow windows, rounded or flat, rising through all three, or occasionally four, storeys and many have iron balconies; some have roofed verandahs. Except where unsuitable new development has intruded, these houses, which were usually built singly and piecemeal, seldom quite matching their neighbours, make a fascinating rhythmic sequence; some are garishly painted, some decorously restored, some shabby. They face a noisy network of traffic lanes, enveloping a series of green spaces, which are the fragments of the original common. The spaces extend beyond the Pavilion, past Sir Charles Barry's sparkling white St Peter's church, to broaden out in the area called the Level, surrounded by stuccoed terraces and crescents of a somewhat later date. But for traffic, and some bad modern intrusions, this could be a wonderful linear space, penetrating far into the town, the oriental splendour of the Pavilion contrasting with the English Gothic of the church, set against the rhythmic background of the bow-fronted houses.

Eastward to Kemp Town

Brighton's medieval field system, with long narrow strips grouped in three large, originally open, fields, survived till the end of the eighteenth century. Communal farming was no longer practised; the strips were in varied private ownership. There was no systematic enclosure following an Act of Parliament, as happened elsewhere; the strips were simply developed piecemeal, and their pattern influenced the layout of the town. East of the town centre the strips were at right angles to the coast. Two or three strips, developed together, would produce the right width of land to form a street with houses on either side. The developers laid out the streets, but often leased plots, perhaps two or three at a time, to other builders, so that the formation of each street was a piecemeal process. In these ways bow-windowed streets were laid out in rapid succession east of the town centre from the 1790s – Charles Street, Broad Street, Madeira Place and many more. They are intermittently smart and shabby, though smartness has prevailed more and more in the old streets on this side of the town over the last few years. Further east is the Royal Crescent, far less grand than its counterpart in Bath of thirty years before; it perpetuated the traditions of old Brighton with its near-black glazed mathematical tiling, wrapping round the flat-fronted bows. Beyond the Crescent, development took place mainly after 1820, and is grander and more sophisticated – Regent's Park or Belgravia by the sea. The culmination is the area originally called Kemp Town – this name is now applied to a much wider area of eastern Brighton. Kemp Town was developed by T. R. Kemp, a local magnate and long-time M.P. for Lewes, where he owned the castle (page 85). He employed Charles Busby and Amon Wilds – an architect-builder partnership; Busby was an architect with American experience, Wilds a builder who had moved from Lewes. It

Above West Street, New Alresford, showing tile hanging

Opposite Georgian brickwork, Broad Street, New Alresford

81

is one of the grandest urban compositions in England, looking on the map like the neck and shoulders of a bottle, with the broad end open to the sea, two segments of a crescent (Lewes Crescent) forming the curves, and the elongated Sussex Square the spout. Wilds and Busby designed the façades only, the purchasers or lessees of the plots building the houses behind – a common practice in grand-scale development at the time, as around Regent's Park and in some of the later developments in Bath. It took over twenty years for the whole scheme to be completed. The result is not quite uniform – there are detailed differences particularly in roofline and balcony treatment and, while most of the houses are stuccoed, a few are partly of buff brick. The builder of Belgravia, Thomas Cubitt, took over about a third of the houses, and had his own seaside house in Lewes Crescent, just west of the rounded corner into Sussex Square. Flanking the crescent and facing the sea, are two fine terraces.

Religion and railways

As if in expiation for the behaviour of the Regency period, Brighton became a stronghold of the Anglican church in Victorian times. The revival was due initially to the Reverend Henry Wagner, vicar of Brighton from 1824. His parish included the whole of the town, and his original church was the ancient St Nicholas, standing on a hill outside the old town. This was thoroughly restored during his incumbency, but it keeps its ancient tower,

2 *Below left* **Charles Street, Brighton,** showing the bow windows and mathematical tiles characteristic of the town. The Palace Pier is in the background.

3 *Below right* **Upper Rock Gardens, Brighton,** one of the many streets leading inland east of the town centre.

its fifteenth-century arcades and screen and, particularly, its Norman font which is a masterpiece of Romanesque art. In the year that Wagner became vicar the young Charles Barry (later to design the Houses of Parliament) won a competition for the new church of St Peter, which was built on the Steine, as already described. In 1846 Wagner founded another church, St Paul's in West Street, where his son Arthur became curate. St Paul's was a model Victorian 'high church', designed by R. C. Carpenter, a disciple of Pugin (and the original architect for the great chapel of Lancing College). Externally it is in dark flint with white stone dressings – a refinement of the traditional pattern of building in the old fishing town. In 1858 another striking church was started – St Michael's in Victoria Road. The first part is an early work of G. F. Bodley, with some lovely glass by William Morris; the larger later part was a posthumous work of William Burges, who transformed Cardiff Castle into a Victorian fantasy. Externally, St Michael's is in full-blooded Victorian Gothic, with towering walls of deep red brick striped with layers of stone, in contrast to the stuccoed houses round it.

St Michael's stands in a hilly early Victorian part of the town, with houses in heavily detailed derivatives of the Regency style. Most are in terraces; the most charming, Montpelier Villas, are in semi-detached pairs, with bold bow windows enveloped in verandahs – on the ground floors, not the first. This is an early example of the new kind of middle-class housing – villas rather than terrace houses, either detached or semi-detached – which was

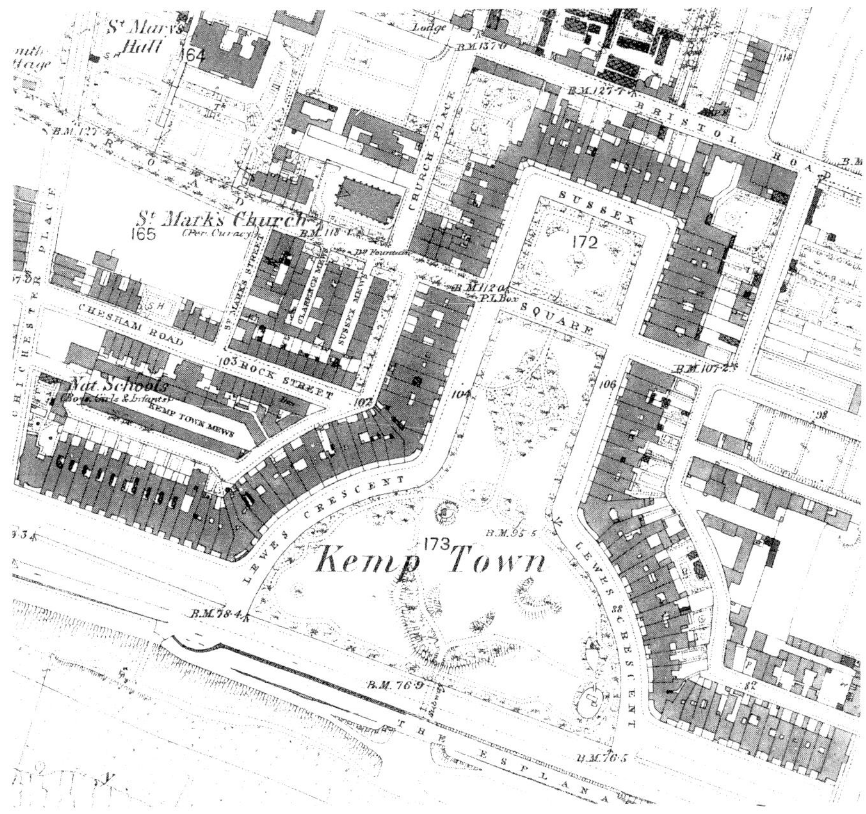

Map II **Kemp Town, Brighton** was laid out from 1823 by Amon Wilds and Charles Busby – an elongated square opening from a crescent which faces the sea. The map is of 1876.

Brunswick Square, Hove
(*see map* III)

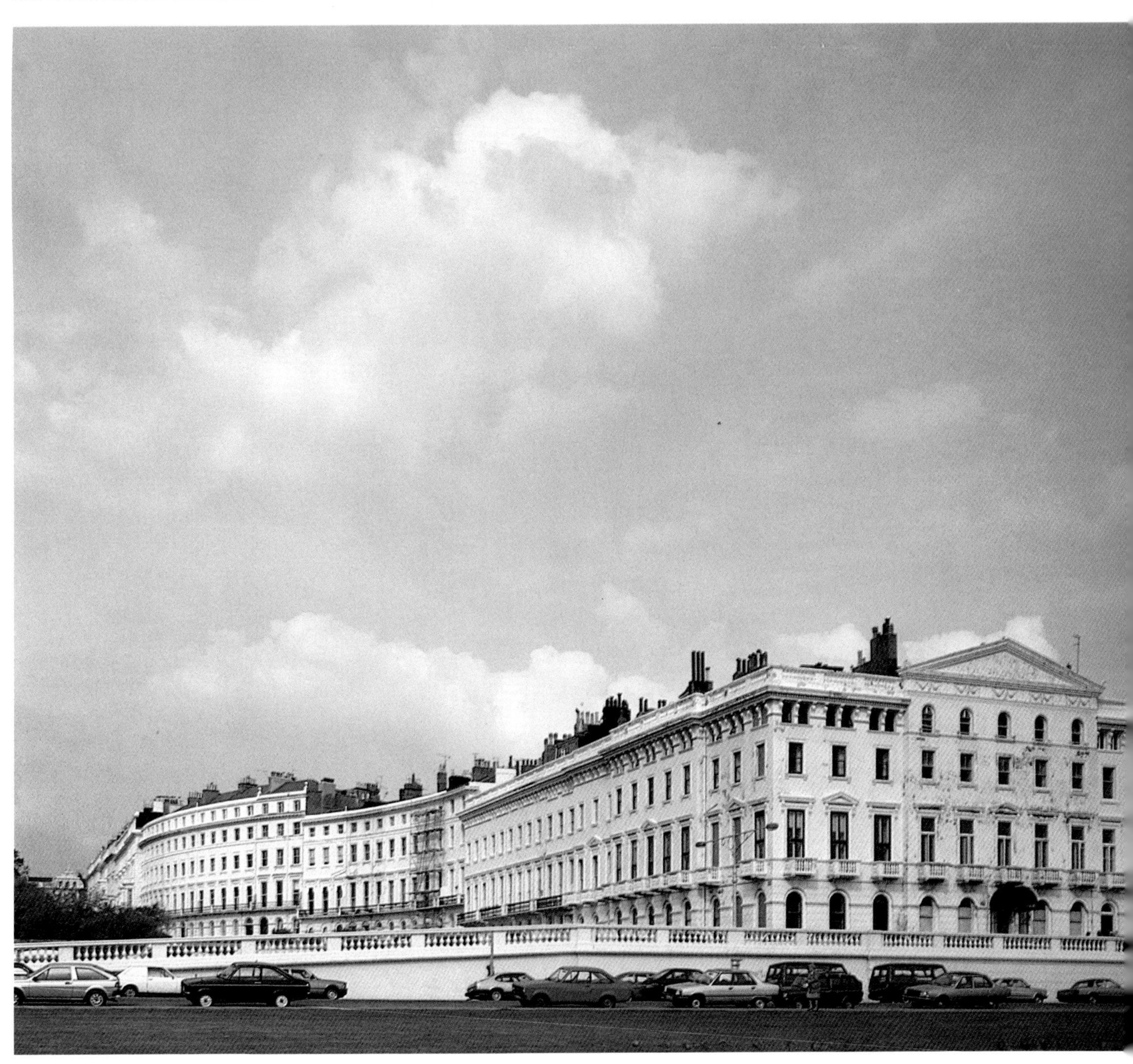

Adelaide Crescent, Hove
(*see map* III)

4 *Above left* **St Michael's Church, Brighton,** one of the many Victorian churches which make Brighton one of the best towns in England for the Gothic Revival. This is a late work of William Burges, with an earlier part by G.F. Bodley.

5 *Above right* **Camelford Street, Brighton,** another of the little streets east of the town centre.

usually preferred to terraced housing from the 1840s onwards (page 102). But fewer were built in Brighton than in most other towns through the Victorian period, partly because the terrace tradition was so well-established there, and partly because suitable land was in short supply. Much more typical of early Victorian Brighton is Powys Square nearby, with Regency-derived terrace houses, round-fronted and iron-balconied, set round a small garden; the 'square' itself is bottle-shaped. Clifton Terrace lies eastward – a fairly simple terrace magnificently set, with a view down plunging ground to the town centre, the sea now appearing between the unwelcome tall flats which rear below. Beyond is the big romantic churchyard of the ancient church of St Nicholas on a hillbrow. Northward from there, dense streets descend towards the station.

The London, Brighton and South Coast Railway was a company of strong individuality, and has impressive engineering works. The company's original engineer, J. U. Rastrick, and architect, David Mocatta, designed the beautiful Balcombe viaduct carrying the main line over a broad valley north of Haywards Heath. In Brighton itself another majestic viaduct of 1847 takes the sharply curving Lewes line high above the London road. The frontispiece of Mocatta's Brighton Station of 1841 survives but is hardly recognizable; much more impressive is the great train shed of 1883 with its rounded iron roofs and interplay of curves, one of the last of its type to be built.

South-east of the station, from Trafalgar Street down to Church Street, is a fascinating area developed from about 1800 onwards on what had been the northern open field of the town, with the street pattern influenced by the layout of the medieval strips, as in the area further east. All the houses were humble to middling, and were always interspersed with workshops, storage yards and shops. Twenty years ago parts of the area were cleared, and the rest was assumed to have no future, but since then the streets that survived have been upgraded, either as houses, as in Over Street, or as shops, as in Kensington Gardens, a long-established pedestrian thoroughfare. Many small shops flourish, and the area is probably much like the Lanes were fifty years ago, though the streets are straighter and not so narrow.

If one finds one's way north into Ann Street, which descends from the flank of the station to London Road, one sees an extraordinary tall brick building with sparse Gothic details, giving little indication that inside it is one of the most spectacular churches in southern England, St Bartholomew's. It was built in 1872 under the influence of Arthur Wagner the younger, by then a High Anglican priest of powerful renown, to the design of a little known local architect, Edmund Scott. The internal walls are of bare brick, inset by arches that emphasize its tremendous height – it is higher than Westminster Abbey. It was intended to be more ornate than it is, but resources available were concentrated on the sanctuary, where marble, and also metal work of superb quality in the Arts and Crafts tradition, was executed by Henry Wilson. The effect, with the elaboration of the eastern end contrasting with the austerity of the rest, is probably more memorable than what was originally envisaged would have been.

6 **Montpelier Villas, Brighton,** built *c.*1845, early examples of semi-detached houses, untypical of Brighton, but the bow windows with iron balconies and verandahs are utterly characteristic of the town.

This is not the end of the catalogue of Brighton's major churches. There are also St Mary's in Kemp Town, with a striking interior by Sir William Emerson, and St Martin's in Lewes Road, built as a memorial to the elder Henry Wagner, father figure of what was jocularly called 'London, Brighton and South Coast religion'.

Along the front to Hove

The former Chain Pier, opened in 1823 was an elegant structure built on the principle of a suspension bridge. It became the focal point of the seafront, and hence of Brighton as a whole, since the Pavilion is inland. Its main purpose was the berthing of ships from Dieppe and elsewhere – but from the start it was also a fashionable place to promenade: the first seaside pier to be used for recreation. It was swept away in a storm of 1896, but work was already starting on the new Palace Pier nearby, 'the grandest pier ever built' (S. Adamson: *Seaside Piers*), opened in 1899, with a concert hall at the end completed in 1901, and another half-way along in 1906. Piers were an extraordinary phenomenon of the Victorian, and still more the Edwardian, seaside – places where one could get some of the sensation of being at sea while being safely linked to land. Brighton's other pier, the West Pier, was opened in 1866; its entrance, shelters and concert hall at the end were added at different times in latter-day versions of the Brighton Pavilion mood. Unlike the Palace, the West Pier has been closed for many years because of deterioration, and has been the subject of continued efforts by conservationists to find the means to re-open it.

The seafront between the two piers is one of the most disappointing features of Brighton, neither grand nor picturesque, neither dignified nor vibrantly vulgar. But it has a series of hotels reflecting the history of the resort. First there is the Royal Albion of 1826, elegantly stuccoed and columned, overlooking both the sea and the Steine behind. Then the Old Ship, a rebuilding of one of the old town's inns, still preserving its ballroom of 1767. Then the Grand Hotel of 1864 (scene of the bomb outrage in 1984), solidly built to the design of John Whichcord, who came from Maidstone (page 89), and after that the Metropole of 1888 by Alfred Waterhouse, which with its rich terracotta and original ebullient skyline symbolized *fin-de-siècle* Brighton. Unfortunately its skyline has been simplified by the addition of more storeys. The main recent addition to the seafront, the Brighton Centre, has not added much to its visual character, still less its earlier neighbour, now called Kingswest. Behind these buildings is a once intricate Regency area now shattered by high-rise development. A rearing block of flats overwhelms the charming, small-scale Russell Square. Further inland is Churchill Square, not a square but a typical, and in some ways fairly satisfactory, shopping 'precinct' of the 1960s, integrated with high-rise flats and parking, which looms over the once attractive Clarence Square. Development like this is simply incompatible with the older, inner parts of Brighton with their tight-knit streets and little squares and spaces, and it is difficult to understand why the local council permitted, let alone encouraged it.

Map III **Brighton and Hove.** Bedford Square to the right, *c.*1810, was the first square in Brighton. Brunswick Square, started in 1825 by Wilds and Busby, is much grander, while Adelaide Crescent, of the 1830s to 1850s, is grander still; like Kemp Town it looks on this map, of 1876, like the top of a bottle. (See colour illus. pp. 26/27.)

Back to the sea: Regency Square, open to the front and with the West Pier on its axis, was begun in 1818. Bedford Square beyond is more modest; started in *c.*1810 it was the first square in Brighton, and outside the town proper when built. Some of the streets behind these squares, built in the 1820s and 30s, have raffish Brighton charm, especially Oriental Place and Silwood Place, designed by the younger Amon Wilds, son of the partner of Charles Busby. They have capitals with representations of fossil shells called ammonites – favourite devices of both the Amon Wilds as puns on their name. Alas, this area has been compromised by unsuitable new development.

At Waterloo Street, a typical thoroughfare of tall round-fronted houses leading in from the front, we have crossed the boundary into Hove. Hove was a separate ancient parish from Brighton, and it has preserved its separateness as a borough. In this street is St Andrew's, a charming small classical church of 1827 designed by Charles Barry – after his Gothic St Peter's in Brighton but before the Houses of Parliament. The unmistakably Italianate details of the bell turret are very early examples of this Victorian stylistic fashion. Intrepid explorers will find many interesting streets and alleys off and around Waterloo Street, some shabby, some smartened, mostly a bit of each.

Hove's architectural climax, Brunswick Square (see colour illus. p. 26), is a little further on, but before it is reached there is Embassy Court, a nice example of 1930s' International Modern style by Wells Coates, with its horizontal layers of windows and white concrete. Unfortunately it is out of scale with its Regency neighbours, but not so grossly as the 1960s tower blocks further east. Brunswick Square is the contrepiece of a grand scheme started in 1824 – contemporary with Kemp Town and as far to the west of central Brighton as the latter is to the east. Like Kemp Town it was designed by Wilds and Busby. The square, long and narrow and open to the sea, has an impressive rhythm of houses with bowed fronts, accentuated by stuccoed columns rising through two storeys between the windows. Oddly there are, at intervals, much narrower houses with sharply rounded fronts; these were built later in what were originally gaps giving access to mews behind. The square has no proper closure at its northern end; a street continues axially upwards, but is terminated only by a distant block of flats. Flanking the square, overlooking the front, are two fine stuccoed terraces very much in the manner of Nash, the best buildings along the whole of the western seafront.

The next scheme, including Adelaide Terrace and Crescent (see colour illus. p. 27), is more grandiose than Brunswick Square. It was originally designed by Decimus Burton, but the only part which is his work is Adelaide Terrace of 1833, partly facing the sea but mainly at right angles to it. The scheme was taken up again in the 1850s in a coarser style, and the result is Adelaide Crescent, really a huge bottle-shaped space with its broad end open to the sea, flanked by tall houses which make sweeping double curves, and penetrating into the heart of Hove.

That Hove is more than accidentally separate from Brighton is emphasized by the style of the seafronts in the two boroughs. The crowded confusion of Brighton's promenade suddenly ends at the boundary; in front of Brunswick Square, Adelaide Terrace and the buildings beyond are immaculate lawns with only a few shelters between them and the beach. Hove did not develop beyond Adelaide Crescent until the 1860s and 1870s, and the most prominent building in the further reach is a terrace of 1871, looking impressive with its solid buff brick walls which have recently been cleaned, but somewhat odd because of its two towers of unequal height. Till recently there was another block further on which made a pair, balancing the first block because the taller tower was at the opposite end. The architect was J. T. Knowles, best known for the Grosvenor Hotel at Victoria in London. Many Victorian villas in this area have recently been replaced by architecturally nondescript flats. But it is worth walking inland to Eaton Road and All Saints Church, built in 1891 by the greatest of Victorian church architects, J. L. Pearson. Externally it is not at first striking, partly because only the stump of the intended tower was built, and as a stump it is too prominent – a fault exactly paralleled in Pearson's other major church, St Michael at Croydon (page 52). Internally it is glorious, with a magnificent eastern climax.

In poignant and strange contrast is the old parish church of Hove, St Andrew's in Church Road, further west. Outside it is neo-Norman in flint and stone, the result of a renovation in 1836 by George Basevi, better known for his work in Belgravia. Again, the external appearance is deceptive, for internally the church is medieval. Hove in the early Middle Ages was quite a prosperous village, but erosion impoverished it and the church was reduced in size; the aisles were pulled down and the arcades blocked. With the growth in population Basevi enlarged the church again; he opened up the original impressive late Norman arcades, though all the capitals have had to be restored. The kingpost roof may be original, a rare survival from so early, and the stone flooring may be medieval too. It is very strange in the midst of Victorian Hove.

Canterbury
Kent

Canterbury is one of the oldest towns in England with a continuous history. There was probably a settlement on the site for two or three centuries before the Roman conquest, and the name of the pre-Roman tribe, *Cantii* in Latin, survives in the modern names of both the city and the county of Kent. Nothing of the important Roman town is now visible above ground, except for small parts of the city wall, but archaeologists have excavated the foundations of several Roman buildings, including those of a semi-circular theatre beneath what are now Watling and St Margaret's streets.

In the Dark Ages after the Roman withdrawal, the city within the wall was largely deserted, and may have been partly flooded. But settlement probably continued outside the wall to the east. In the sixth century Kent was a dominant Anglo-Saxon kingdom; King Ethelbert and his Christian wife Bertha (who came from the Paris region) received Augustine, the missionary sent by Pope Gregory from Rome, in 597. At first Augustine used the already existing St Martin's church which was Bertha's chapel – it survives still, with some of the Saxon fabric, on a hillside east of the city, the oldest church in England in continuous use. In 602 Augustine re-dedicated a deserted Roman building within the city wall which was said to have been previously a church; this was the precursor of Canterbury Cathedral. Soon afterwards another major church was founded outside the wall, which later became St Augustine's Abbey.

Canterbury became a centre of learning and was, for a time, like Winchester, famous for manuscript illustration. In 1070 Lanfranc, the Italian-born abbot of William the Conqueror's monastery at Caen, became Archbishop, and replaced the Saxon cathedral with a grander building resembling the still existing church at Caen. Lanfranc's cathedral was greatly enlarged by his successor Anselm, and it was in this building that Archbishop Thomas Becket was murdered in 1170. Four years later the cathedral was burnt, and from 1175 the eastern part was reconstructed in its present magnificent form, one of the first buildings in England in the new Gothic style which had developed in France. Unusually for England, it retains a great deal of its original stained glass, some of the best in Europe from that period, illustrating biblical scenes and miracles attributed to Becket.

Becket's shrine became the most popular destination for pilgrims in Europe, except Rome. Some came from the Continent via the Channel ports, but most must have travelled from London, like Chaucer's pilgrims, along Watling Street, through Rochester. (The 'Pilgrims' Way' which runs along the line of the North Downs is undoubtedly an ancient route, but its name and its connection with pilgrims are Victorian inventions.) The popularity of the pilgrimages lasted over two centuries, but after 1420 they declined, and dwindled to almost nothing by 1500. Meanwhile, from 1380, the cathedral nave was rebuilt under Henry Yevele in English Perpendicular, making with the earlier choir one of the most effective combinations of contrasting styles in any great church – unlike the effect in Westminster Abbey, where Yevele designed the nave in deliberate conformity with the older choir. Finally the great central tower was built about 1500 under John Wastell – designer also of the upper parts of King's College Chapel in Cambridge. It is easy to forget that most of the pilgrims would not have seen the nave completed, and very few would have seen the central tower. At the Reformation, Becket's shrine was smashed, but the cathedral survived as the chief church of the newly independent Church of England; Anglican canons replaced Benedictine monks. St Augustine's Abbey on the other hand was largely destroyed; little other than two gateways has survived above ground.

The city continued to prosper after the Reformation, as a marketing and, for a time, industrial centre. Flemish and Walloon refugees came in the 1570s and 1580s, as they did to Sandwich, Southampton, Norwich and other places. They brought weaving skills for 'New Draperies', light fabrics for which there were good overseas markets. In the later seventeenth century further refugees – Huguenots from France – developed silk weaving. The group of buildings called The Weavers by the river was certainly enlarged from an older house around the time of the first inflow of refugees, and may have been occupied by them, but the name is a fairly modern invention (and the furthest two of the picturesque gables seen from the bridge were added to the older buildings in the 1930s). In Georgian times both wool and silk weaving gradually declined.

Canterbury marked time in the Victorian period – despite the fact that it was a pioneer of the railway, with the early, and long dismantled, line to Whitstable. It still has two stations on different lines – the West station is a nice simple classical building. In the Second World War Canterbury was savagely bombed: the commercial heart of the city, with several historic buildings, was devastated. The cathedral escaped, but some buildings in the precinct were damaged. Now Canterbury is as busy a centre for visitors as it must have seemed at the height of the pilgrimages' popularity. It is also a university city, though the University of Kent, founded in 1962, is unfortunately on the half-rural outskirts instead of being near the city centre. But the centre itself has enjoyed a resurgence. As elsewhere – in Winchester, Southampton, Old Portsmouth and Chichester – there is increasing demand for houses within the line of the walls; old ones are refurbished and new ones have been built on some of the spaces, thus at last reversing the long-standing trend for people to move out of city centres to suburbs.

Except where it was badly bombed, Canterbury is well preserved as a historic city. Much of the city wall survives, mostly of fourteenth- and fifteenth-century date on the Roman alignment, and includes pieces of Roman fabric. It is much more conspicuous than it was before the war, as bombing or clearance (not always justified) of buildings which backed against it have revealed long stretches, faced in flint with stone bonding, with semi-circular towers at frequent intervals, much restored in recent years. Flint, with stone dressings, was also the main material for the smaller religious buildings in the Middle Ages; Caen stone was used for the cathedral. Most medieval houses were timber-framed, though some were partly of flint, and several stone-vaulted undercrofts survive, often, as at Southampton and Winchelsea,

7 *Opposite* **Canterbury Cathedral** seen through Christ Church Gate. English cathedrals are nearly always set in precincts, approached through gates from the city.

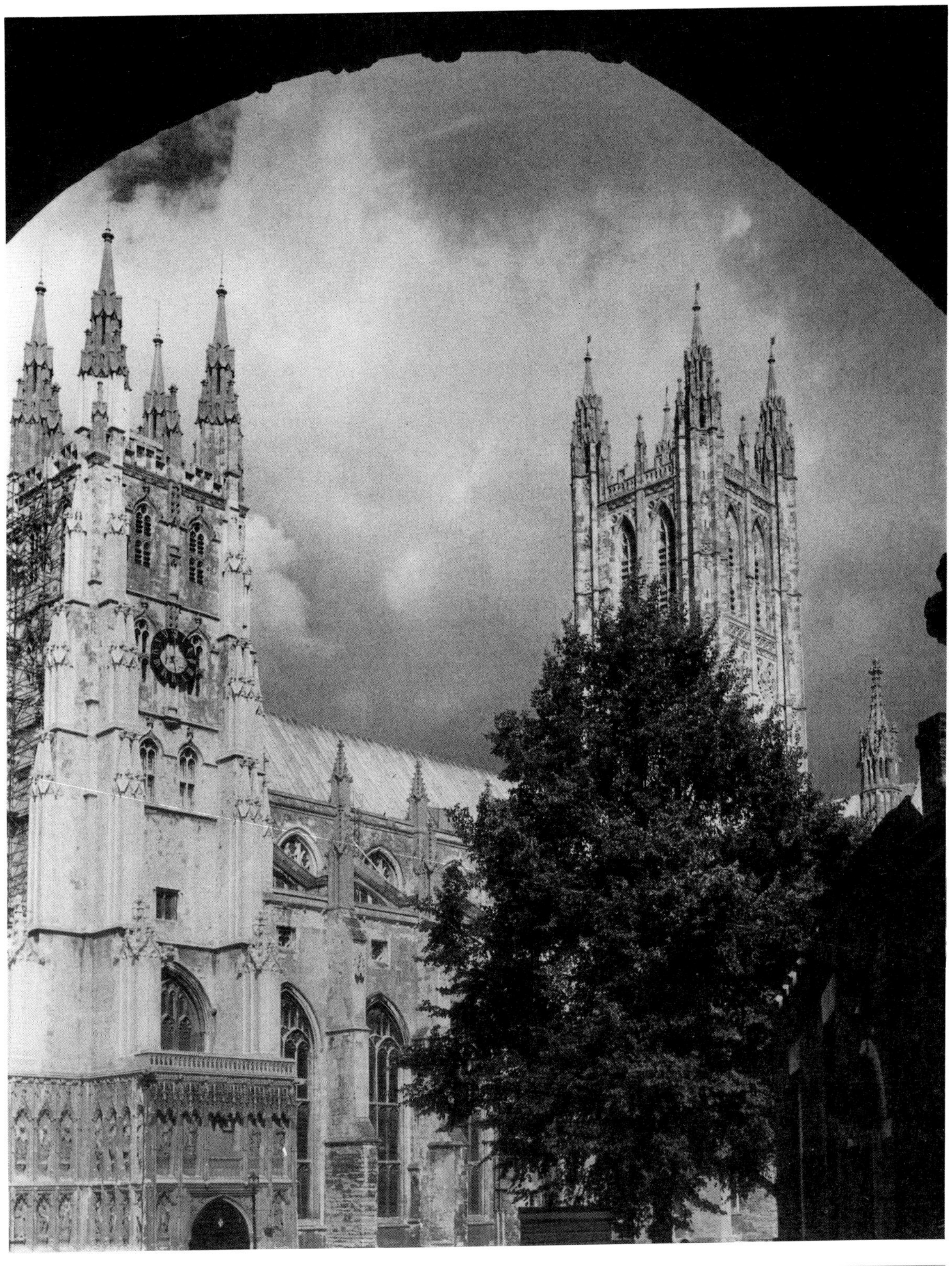

under later buildings. Numerous timber-framed buildings remain from the fifteenth to seventeenth centuries. In Georgian times there was the usual re-fronting of older houses, but the city was not then expansive enough for there to be any new formal streets.

There are miles of streets worth exploring in Canterbury, not all within the city walls – for these never contained the city; there were extensive suburbs outside even in the early Middle Ages. The four itineraries that follow – not precisely defined walks – all start at the junction of High Street, St Margaret's Street and Mercery Lane; they are *The cathedral and Palace Street: High Street and St Dunstan's: The castle and Greyfriars:* and *St George's Street and St Augustine's.*

8 **Mercery Lane, Canterbury**, leading to Christ Church Gate (9). The building on the left was the Chequers Inn, *c.*1390, at first accommodating pilgrims; the stone ground floor was always shops.

The cathedral and Palace Street

Mercery Lane is the *beau ideal* of a modernized medieval city lane, with overhanging buildings, a slight twist, and the cathedral towers seen at the end. The building on the west corner with High Street has jettied upper storeys (plastered and tiled in Georgian times) and a stone-arched ground storey. This was the Chequers Inn, where pilgrims stayed in the later part of the pilgrimage period, but the arches always contained shops, as they do now. The lane leads into the Buttermarket, a charming small *place* outside the cathedral gate. On one side there is a three-storeyed timber-framed building, interestingly treated. The upper storey is plastered, as many such buildings were in Georgian times, with sash windows. But on the first floor the plaster

9 **Christ Church Gate, Canterbury**, built 1517 and much restored 1931–7, leads into the cathedral and monastic precinct. In the background are plastered, Georgianized, timber-framed houses, typical of the city.

has been stripped, revealing the timber-framing and a medieval window within two panels of the frame. Christ Church Gate, built in 1517 in the English tradition with corner turrets (*cf* Battle Abbey), leads into the cathedral precinct. The setting of Canterbury Cathedral behind its lawn, withdrawn from the city and protected by the gate, is typically English – in contrast to Continental cathedrals which characteristically stand in the heart of their cities with streets or squares abutting, as at Rouen, Cologne, Antwerp, Seville and indeed St Paul's in London. The English tradition is explained partly – not wholly – by the fact that about half of the English medieval cathedrals, including Canterbury, Rochester and Winchester, were associated with Benedictine monasteries, where the bishop was titular abbot, with a prior under him. The monks used these cathedrals as their churches. However this is not the whole explanation for English cathedrals being withdrawn in this way, for others such as Salisbury and Exeter, which never had monasteries attached, are similarly set in closes.

After the Reformation the monastic precinct at Canterbury, as at Winchester, was transformed into an Anglican cathedral close. Some of the monks' buildings were demolished, others were converted into canons' houses or for other purposes, and new clergy houses were built. Anglican clergymen were in

10 **Castle Street, Canterbury,** a typical city street, with the slight curve and distant tower giving the perfect visual effect.

time allowed to marry, so that the typical cathedral close became a comfortable enclave with family houses; often lay people occupied some of them. At Canterbury there is a special factor: the King's School, refounded at the Reformation in a corner of the close, has expanded and now occupies much of the northern area of the precinct. However the main part of the precinct, including the courtyard in front of the school, is freely accessible to the public. It is best to start a walk in the cloister, built about 1400 in Caen stone, which has here weathered badly and is being drastically renewed – too thoroughly in the opinion of many preservationists. The chapter house is still used for its original purpose, and beside it a roofed passage leads into the heart of what were the monastic buildings. One of the most interesting buildings to survive is the Water Tower or Lavatory Tower (using the latter name in its original meaning of washing-place), which is octagonal with a complicated series of Norman arches on its open ground storey. Otherwise it is difficult to envisage the main part of the monastery, since some of the buildings were long ago pulled down or left as fragmentary ruins, like the monks' dormitory and 'necessarium' (what we understand as a lavatory). Even some of the post-Reformation buildings which partly replaced them were bomb-damaged, and the library, on the site of the end of the dormitory, is a post-war replacement. But there are compensations. If we follow the passage called the Dark Entry, and pass through a gate, we enter Green Court, once the service yard of the monastery, where there are spectacular views back to the cathedral, rising above the low buildings or sites of buildings in front. If the monastery were intact, these views would be much more restricted. The buildings of the King's School spread round Green Court; the most spectacular is the often-photographed one with the Norman staircase. Even though much of the building to which it leads is only neo-Norman, the staircase itself, with its protecting arches, is genuine.

We leave the precinct by the Court Gate near the Norman staircase and enter an interesting part of Canterbury. To the right is Northgate, the street crossing the site of the medieval city gate; to the left Palace Street, with a series of fascinating buildings on the west side. First there is the gabled seventeenth-century house, now the King's School shop, with its very prominent lean, emphasized by the upright door – it is perfectly stable. No. 17 has a modernized half-timbered front, but behind is a complex building with a Norman stone-walled cellar and a fourteenth-century timber-framed hall; the front part was added in the seventeenth century. The Crown Inn is more typical of Canterbury; it is three-storeyed and timber-framed with the top storey tile-hung, the first floor brick-faced, the ground floor with the façade of a Victorian pub. Beyond the small flint-faced former church of St Alphege is another over-restored-looking timber-framed house which was once the rectory; it dates from 1496 but contains thirteenth-century arches inside from its predecessor. How many other Canterbury houses are, perhaps unsuspectedly, much older and more interesting then they appear from outside?

High Street and St Dunstan's

Going along High Street westwards from Mercery Lane, we pass buildings of great variety and interest, only a few of which can be mentioned. The build-

11 **Greyfriars, Canterbury.** A delightful building, spanning a side stream of the River Stour, all that is left of the Franciscan friary built from 1267.

ing miscalled Queen Elizabeth's Guest Chamber is an old jettied house modernized in Restoration (not Tudor) times, with big bay windows glazed in small leaded lights, arched in their centre parts, typical of merchants' houses of their period – the most famous examples being on Sparrowe's House in Ipswich. On the top storey is pargetting, or plaster decoration in relief – a practice associated especially with East Anglia (as again on the house in Ipswich), but found elsewhere in Kent (page 88). The flint-walled Eastbridge Hospital, built over one of the branches of the River Stour, was founded about 1180 for poor pilgrims, expanded in 1342, and re-established after the Reformation as an almshouse. The old people now live in adjoining buildings, and the original parts are open to the public, including hall, chapel and undercroft. Then come the houses called the Weavers, already mentioned, by the main course of the Stour, and finally, passing much more of interest, the Westgate. This is the only Canterbury city gate to survive; together with Bargate at Southampton and the gates of York it is one of the finest town gates in England. It was rebuilt in 1380, possibly to the design of Henry Yevele, who was then supervising the rebuilding of the cathedral nave. There are a fine simple front on the city side, and two great rounded towers flanking the arch on the outside. It is built of Kentish ragstone, which must have come from at least twenty miles away.

Beyond the Westgate, St Dunstan's Street is broad and nearly straight – a wealthy suburban street by the seventeenth century. Several good houses remain from that century as well as older ones, some with Georgian fronts. The best is the three-gabled one called the House of Agnes, with more of the round-arched 'Ipswich' windows. At the far end is St Dunstan's church, one of several small flint-built parish churches – it was in such humble buildings that the ordinary people worshipped, not the cathedral. St Dunstan's is well-known because the severed head of Sir Thomas More was buried in the Roper chapel north of the chancel. More's daughter married William Roper who lived in a Tudor mansion on the other side of the street; its gateway survives.

The castle and Greyfriars

St Margaret's Street was partly bombed, and there is now an interesting jumble of old and rebuilt frontages. Past the irregular junction with Watling Street is Castle Street, with a typical mixture of altered timber-framed buildings and Georgian or later ones. Looking back there is a splendid view of the cathedral tower framed by the slightly curving street. It leads eventually to the castle – what survives is the lower part of the Norman keep. It takes imagination to picture anything comparable to Rochester Castle.

Short streets lead from Castle Street to the parallel Stour Street, which contains the Poor Priests' Hospital – built in the fourteenth century, converted after the Reformation to a workhouse and then to a charity school; it is now a museum. A narrow turning off Stour Street leads to the site of the Franciscan friary, or Greyfriars. Little is left except one charming small building spanning a side stream of the Stour on two arches; the use to which it was put is not known. Around is a market garden, a reminder that cultivation sometimes took place on backlands near the heart of historic cities.

12 *Top* **Poor Priests' Hospital, Canterbury,** a medieval charity with some of its original 14th-century buildings, later a workhouse, then a school and finally a museum.

13 *Above* **City Wall, Canterbury,** rebuilt in the 15th century on the Roman line, and much restored recently. Note the keyhole openings for primitive guns.

St George's Street and St Augustine's

St George's Street, the eastward continuation of High Street, was devastated by bombing. It was already the main shopping street, and its rebuilding as the centrepiece of what has become the biggest shopping centre in eastern Kent is not inspiring. Yet the reconstruction began in the early 1950s with some flair. The tower of the otherwise destroyed St George's church was kept as the centrepiece of a small and still attractive square, and beside it is what was originally Greig's grocery shop (now part of Woolworths) with a zigzag roof supported on slender columns, a stylistic reminder of the Festival of Britain era. Alas, later rebuilding was not in the same spirit. It is best to go through to the parallel Burgate Street where an even earlier post-war rebuilding was done in unashamed William-and-Mary style; it has now mellowed and seems entirely acceptable, although derided when it was built in 1950 for not being modern. Burgate Street passes through the line of the wall – one of the best preserved stretches is on the left. Then, across the roaring ring road, is the district east of the wall which was probably inhabited in early Saxon times when the walled city was largely deserted, and where St Augustine's Abbey (originally called St Peter and St Paul) was founded by Augustine himself. It came to rival the cathedral in grandeur, but was all but destroyed after the Reformation; what one sees today are the well-displayed foundations of successive buildings, and the shell of what was always a separate church, the Saxon St Pancras. Some of the domestic buildings survived, to be incorporated into a Victorian Anglican college designed by William Butterfield. By far the finest feature still intact is the great gateway, built from 1300, a prototype perhaps of the English gateways of which there is a slightly later example at Battle (page 17) and a much later one at the entrance to the cathedral precinct. Not far away is a smaller gateway of similar type, the Cemetery Gate. Finally, beyond the remains of the abbey, is St Martin's church, where the story started.

Chichester
Sussex

Chichester has been since Roman times – except for a break in the Dark Ages – the social and administrative centre of the western part of Sussex. Its form is fundamentally Roman – its surviving walls, often repaired, follow the Roman line, and its street pattern is partly that of the Roman town. The cathedral was started about 1080 to replace the Saxon one at Selsey, where the sea was encroaching. Chichester had the status of a port, though the quays were two or more miles away on the expansive harbour. Trade fluctuated,

but was vigorous in the eighteenth century, when much of the agricultural produce of the region was exported coastwise. Merchants and others built fine town houses, and the city became an amalgam of Georgian red brick and medieval stone, with some flavouring of flint. There was not much change in Victorian times; today Chichester is prosperous and fashionable with its theatre and well-stocked shops.

Chichester has undergone the pedestrianization treatment. Till recently the four chief streets, called simply North, South, East and West, were busy with both traffic and shopping, while the side streets, with many delightful buildings, were quiet. Now the main streets are either exclusive to pedestrians or have little but servicing traffic, while some of the side streets have become busy as accesses to car parks. A ring road was built outside the walls to allow this to happen, sadly disturbing the fields to the south-west. All this, understandably, caused fierce controversy, but when one goes to towns like Dorking, Epsom, Maidstone or Godalming which are still plagued in their central streets with traffic, one realizes what Chichester has gained.

The cross form of Chichester's main streets is not quite regular, thanks to slight deviation from the Roman pattern in late Saxon times, when the town was repopulated. North Street is not continuous with South, though East runs through to West. At the intersection is the marvellously appropriate Cross, an octagonal open-sided shelter, built by a bishop in 1501, with Georgian top, closing the views along all the main streets except North. The cathedral stands to the south-west, open on one side to the city – an arrangement unusual among English cathedrals, since they are usually set in closes. Chichester has its Close, but it is smaller than most and does not have an internal green space to set off the cathedral as at Salisbury, Exeter and Durham. The Close is entered casually, on either side of the cathedral, by footways that lead into the informal cloister – which is really a series of covered ways linking the cathedral with some of the canons' houses. From the cloister, a short straight path, lined with flint and brick walls, aligns directly on the Deanery, providing the one formal element in the Close. The Deanery was built in classical taste in 1725 – about eighty years after its predecessor had been sacked by Roundheads who had broken through a gap in the city wall behind.

The main thoroughfare of the Close is Canon Lane, which begins under an archway from South Street and ends at the gateway to the bishop's palace. Chichester was not a monastic cathedral like Canterbury or Winchester (page 146); it had a hierarchy of dean and canons in the Middle Ages, as now, but of course they were celibate. With the establishment of the Church of England they were allowed to marry, and by the eighteenth century the old celibate canons' houses had been transformed into, or replaced by, comfortable family residences. Several show a patchwork of medieval stone, flint, and Georgian brick; others were restored or rebuilt in Victorian times. The most striking group is Vicars' Close, a conversion of one side of the medieval quadrangle where the Vicars Choral, who sung at the services, were accommodated; they make a delightful picture with the cathedral spire rising obliquely behind. The medieval Vicars' Hall, seen at the end, is now a restaurant and entered from South Street.

14 *Opposite left* **Canon Gate, Chichester,** in local flint, leading into the Close. The cathedral spire is a replica of the original which collapsed in 1861.

15 *Opposite right* **Pallant House, Chichester,** built *c.*1712 by Henry Peckham, a merchant, with beautiful iron railings and curious representations of ostriches, the family emblems; it is now an art gallery. In the background are the houses in East Pallant (**16**).

South Street is the narrowest of the four main streets; apart from the Georgianized end of the Vicars' Hall it has – further down on the opposite side – a fine flint-faced house of about 1820 with a bow window on the first floor. Flint, long used locally as a humble alternative to stone or brick, became fashionable in its own right in the early and middle nineteenth century because of its striking texture; many villas as well as churches were then faced with it. An insignificant lane nearly opposite the Close Gate leads into the Pallant – the most surprising of the many delightful enclaves tucked away behind the main streets of Chichester. It was almost a town within a city – it was, for some ancient reason, a 'palatinate' under the Archbishop of Canterbury's jurisdiction, hence 'Pallant'. In the eighteenth century it was a fashionable quarter; Georgian houses were built along the four streets of the Pallant which make an irregular cross – a miniature of the plan of the city. The finest is Pallant House, built in 1712 by a merchant, and now an art gallery, set back from the street behind a superb iron screen. From it there is a splendid view along West Pallant, with the cathedral spire rising beyond the houses.

North Pallant leads into East Street, which would be the dullest of the four main streets but for the wonderful western view closed first by the Cross and then by the cathedral's distinctive detached bell tower. Opposite, a lane leads into another backwater, St Martin's Square. This is an irregular *piazza*, with Georgian houses facing different ways. The most intriguing composition is on the south-east, where two similar Georgian houses in deep red brick make a double corner; both have prominent Venetian windows, and one also has smaller windows with pointed curves in the gables – all part of a deliberately contrived and subtle piece of town scenery. Ian Nairn called the square 'as wayward and casual as one of the little scenographic squares of Rome'

16 East Pallant, Chichester. The Pallant is a curious enclave, which became fashionable in Georgian times; the houses are in deep red local brick.

(*Buildings of England: Sussex*). To one side is the unassuming entrance of St Mary's Hospital, one of the most remarkable buildings of its kind in England. It was a medieval hospital, originally with a 'nave' or hall, where the inmates lived, and a 'chancel' or chapel – as existed also at Portsmouth (page 100) and in the Maison Dieu at Dover. After the Reformation it became an almshouse, and in the seventeenth century eight tiny dwellings, each for an individual resident, were built of brick within the hall, with chimneys rising through the roof. Externally it is best seen on the south side, from a car park – which, partly occupying the sites of town house gardens, is all too typical of Chichester today. Another lane leads from St Martin's Square into North Street, the most complex and, for shopping, the busiest of the four main streets. It is the only one without a view of the Cross, but it has its own subtle shape, broadening and slightly curving towards the south, a legacy, no doubt, of the late Saxon re-forming of the decayed Roman city. Its oldest landmark is St Olave's, one of several tiny city churches which formerly existed (two others survive within the wall), with a flinty west wall and bellcote over; it is now a bookshop. Nearby is the Market Hall, its original columned ground storey designed by, of all people, John Nash, but given a sympathetic second storey in 1900. Beyond, projecting over the pavement, is the Council House or town hall, a Palladian design of 1733. Behind the pavement arcade is a broken, but restored, Roman stone which was discovered when the Council House was built – with an inscription recording that it came from a temple of Neptune and Minerva (the exact site of which is not known), built by Cogidubnus. He was the Celtic ruler of the area at the time of the Roman conquest, and, as he co-operated with the Romans he was allowed to retain his status and much of his autonomy; he lived in the palace at Fishbourne on

17 *Above right* **West Pallant, Chichester,** with the ironwork in front of Pallant House (15) on the right. The cathedral stonework requires repeated attention, hence the scaffolding on the spire.

Overleaf left Sandstone church of St Dunstan at Cranbrook

Overleaf right Weatherboarded houses, Stone Street, Cranbrook

SUSAN DEAN
Purveyors of Gifts
OPEN
Tourism and Craft Information

OPEN

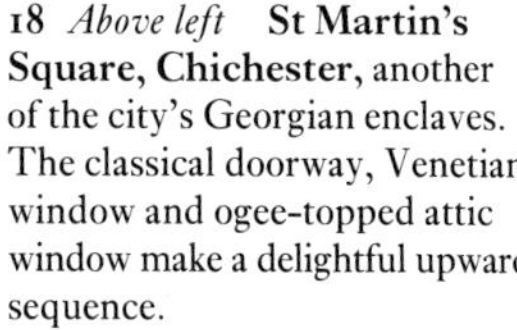

18 *Above left* **St Martin's Square, Chichester,** another of the city's Georgian enclaves. The classical doorway, Venetian window and ogee-topped attic window make a delightful upward sequence.

19 *Above right* **North Street, Chichester,** the only one of the city's four main streets to have a marked curve. On the right the classical Market House by John Nash, 1807, with later upper storey, then St Olave's church with spirelet. Projecting in the distance is the classical Council House of 1733.

the city's outskirts, the remains of which have recently been excavated and displayed. North Street has a series of bow windows, one boldly rounded, another with Gothic-arched sashes, both set over elegant doorways. The street used to end at the North Gate, but all the city gates were pulled down as traffic obstructions in the eighteenth century. Beyond, past gyrating traffic and a huge car park, is the Festival Theatre, the latest of Chichester's remarkable institutions. Built through local initiative and opened in 1962, with a striking hexagonal shape enclosing an open auditorium, it is one of the most likeable of major buildings in the idiom of the fifties and sixties; the architects were Powell and Moya.

There is too much else special in Chichester to describe in a short space – the medieval friary, later the guildhall; the seventeenth-century John Edes House in West Street; the Georgian enclaves of Little London and St John's Street; the post-war Roman Catholic church of St Richard (the local medieval saint) with brilliant glass by Gabriel Loire from Chartres. But something must be said of the city wall. This began as a Roman earthen rampart, faced externally in flint and rough stone – the present facings are the result of centuries of repeated repairs. Most of the circuit remains – the main gaps are to the south-east – and long stretches are accessible for walking, especially to the north-west. The most impressive stretch externally is on the east, facing New Parks Road. But the best impression one gets of Chichester as a walled city is from the south-west, where the land is still open. Till recently rough grazed fields came right up to the wall from this direction; now – following unsuccessful protests in the 1960s, led by the late Ian Nairn, author of the often poetic descriptions of West Sussex in *Buildings of England: Sussex* – the ring road runs across the former fields, the rest of which are converted to sports grounds or car parking. But at least the land is still open, and one sees the cathedral, bishop's palace and other buildings rising beyond the city wall in a way that has few parallels in England.

Cranbrook
Kent

Cranbrook was one of the principal towns of the Weald, and from the fourteenth to the seventeenth century was the chief weaving centre south of London. As elsewhere, the trade was mostly in the hands of clothiers who passed the wool successively to spinners and weavers working in or near their homes. The cloth was trimmed and finished on the clothiers' own premises – usually substantial houses outside the town. Much went to London by packhorse, a lot of it for export. Cranbrook cloth was at first famous for its rich colours, particularly reds, but in the sixteenth century many cloths were exported undyed to Flanders, for finishing there. Unfortunately, an Act of Parliament forbade the export of undyed cloth, and this is said to have caused the decline in the industry, which by the eighteenth century had almost disappeared. Nevertheless, Cranbrook must have prospered modestly as a market town in Georgian times, to judge from its buildings; now it is a seemingly remote place with the status of a village, but the character of a town.

Except for its grand sandstone church (see colour illus. p. 46), rebuilt by stages in the days of prosperity, there is little obvious to suggest the town's former importance. There are plenty of partly fifteenth- to seventeenth-century timber-framed houses, but most are clad, attractively, in Wealden tiles and weatherboarding. The long main street comes in from the west, loosely built at first, then thickens and widens where the markets were held, and turns sharp right where the church is set back. The street southward is largely weatherboarded, and is dominated by the splendid white boarded windmill, built in 1814, on a hillock further south (see colour illus. p. 47). Less easy to find, down an alley, is the Providence Chapel of 1828 with a striking five-sided façade, plastered over but with mock mortar joints as if to imitate stone. Like the smaller, slightly earlier weatherboarded Baptist Chapel nearby, it is a reminder of the strong local Puritan traditions. Many people from this area migrated to America around the 1630s. It is tempting to suggest that they were influential in introducing to New England the tradition of clapboarding, which is similar to Wealden weatherboarding. But most, perhaps all, of the present weatherboarded façades in the town date from the eighteenth century or later, and it would be interesting to know if the tradition had already started at the time of the migrations. Cranbrook School, founded in 1578, has a pleasant School House of 1729, and a more elaborate building of 1884 by Sir Thomas Jackson, in the style, familiar at Oxford, which Sir John Betjeman called 'Anglo-Jackson'.

Crawley
Sussex

Crawley was a small medieval town with a long wide street. Something survives; there are several partly medieval buildings in the High Street, especially one, now a restaurant, with a subdivided central hall, gabled wings, Horsham stone roof, and timbers unfortunately painted black. The church, mainly Victorian restoration, has a fine fifteenth-century arch-braced roof. Crawley was one of the early post-war new towns intended to contain 'overspill' (the word was coined later) from London and so save the rest of what became the Green Belt. It followed the same pattern as the others; people were housed in well-defined neighbourhoods, grouped around a town centre where hardly anybody was expected to live. The latter was developed east from the old High Street, and is centred on a large square. Nobody visiting it on a busy shopping day can doubt that it is commercially successful; the trouble is that almost every building in the town centre, except older ones on the High Street, is a run-of-the-mill piece of architecture (that is too fine a word) of the fifties and sixties. Perhaps some are due for renewal? The best feature of the square is a transplant – a bandstand from the old Gatwick racecourse, displaced by the airport.

But the neighbourhoods are a different matter. Skill, sensitivity and a talent for design seem to have been exercised in most of the early housing – which follows the precepts established by garden-city and garden-suburb architects like Sir Raymond Unwin and also Herbert Collins (page 134) in the early part of this century. Houses are mainly terraced in groups of four or five, set with careful reference to topography and established features such as trees, of which Crawley had and has plenty – fortunately many are oaks, the most resilient of English trees. New trees were planted in plenty, and these are now past adolescence. This type of housing layout – found in other early new towns with less consistent success – was derided in the 1960s by revolutionary architects and planners who wanted more collective and 'urban' types of building, notably high-rise flats, but the controllers of Crawley, to their great credit, stuck to the old formulae, with some experiments in the separation of pedestrians and traffic. There are no high flats in Crawley – or if there are they are very carefully hidden.

Typical early neighbourhoods are Three Bridges, centred on a bulky church of 1954 (St Barnabas) by

Above Farnham, including Town Hall

Opposite Dover Castle

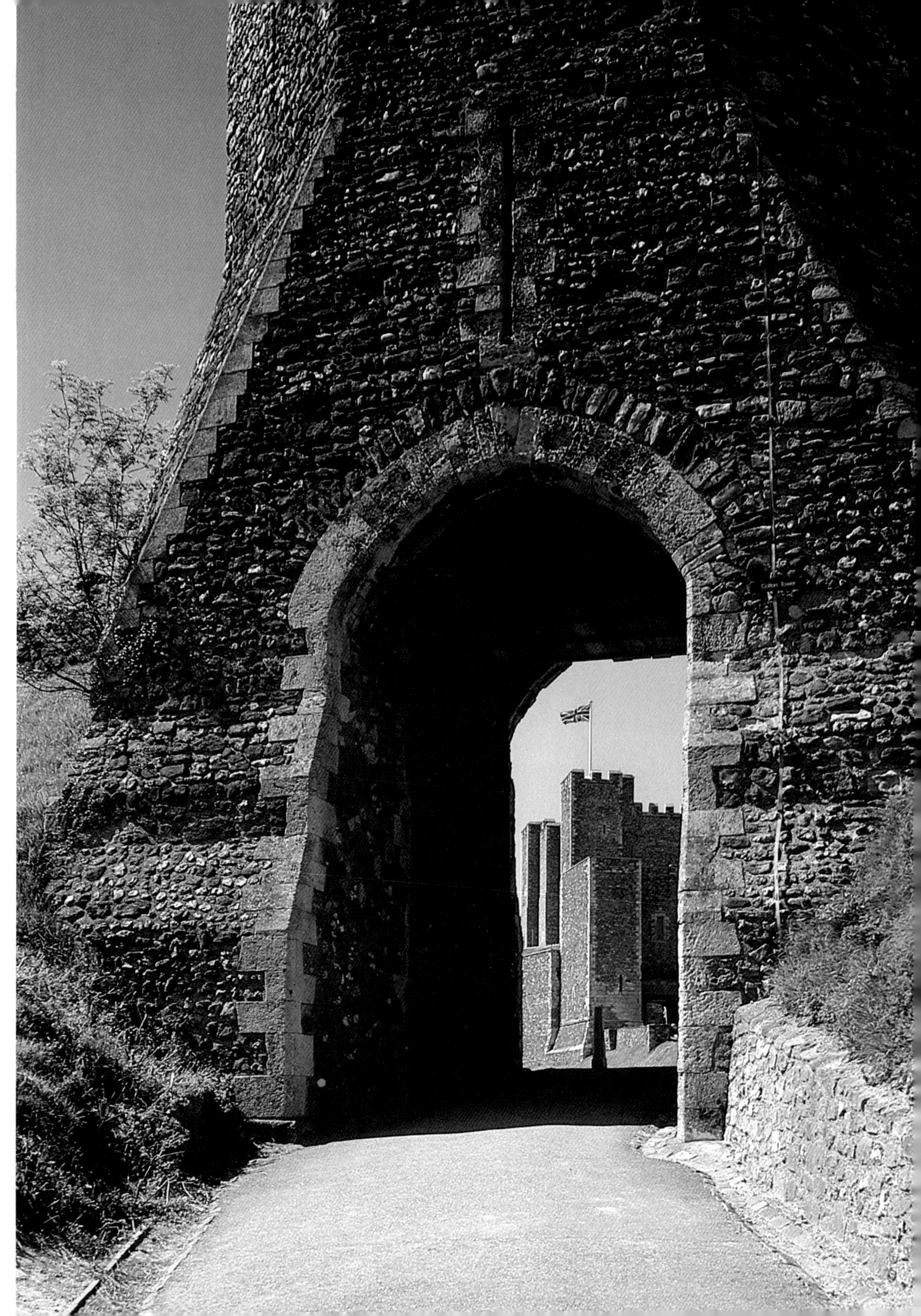
Colton Tower

N. Cachemaille-Day and merging into the Victorian houses of the old railway village, and Pound Hill, climbing the slope to the south-east. Beyond Pound Hill is Worth, with one of the finest Saxon churches in southern England, sadly damaged by fire at the time of writing but certainly repairable. South of Worth, and Crawley generally, is a glorious sweep of country, forest and field, which broad-brush indoor planners of the early seventies indicated as part of a 'corridor of growth' along the line of the London–Brighton railway. Happily the corridor train still has empty carriages. Buried in the western part of Crawley is the Ifield Meeting, a Quaker chapel in a farmhouse-like building of 1676, evocative of the Puritan fervour which was evident in several parts of the Weald, such as Horsham and Cranbrook. It is surrounded by modern garden-suburb housing of the type which owed its inception, to a large degree, to Quaker idealism around the turn of this century.

Croydon

Surrey

Croydon is a suburban city, with more offices than almost anywhere else except central London, and one of the biggest shopping centres in the south. But it has fine buildings, Victorian and ancient, which justify its inclusion in this book. The first syllable of the name is an anglicization of the Latin word *crocus*, which originally applied to the saffron plant, introduced to Britain by the Romans. It must have grown wild here when the Saxons arrived. From the Middle Ages till the eighteenth century the Archbishops of Canterbury had a palace at Croydon, convenient even then for London yet secluded. Parts survive, including the fifteenth-century great hall with its fine roof, and later parts in old dark brick. They were rescued exactly a century ago and restored as a school. Nearby St John's was the biggest medieval church in Surrey until burnt down in 1867. It was rebuilt impressively by Sir Gilbert Scott in the same Perpendicular style – unusually for him, the champion of earlier, 'purer' Gothic styles. The grand tower is medieval; with its tall pinnacles (heightened by Scott) it recalls those at Tenterden and Ashford.

A new traffic road swirls past the church, but pleasant small-scale streets lead to the town centre. The focus of Croydon must have moved to where it is now, on higher ground east of the palace and church, at least by the thirteenth century when the first known market grant is recorded. The market place was a triangle between what are now High and Surrey Streets – a steeply sloping site. By Tudor times the usual encroachments had taken place; up to a hundred years ago there was a dense and largely squalid concentration of buildings, threaded by alleys, in the old market area, leaving the present Surrey Street as the site for the stalls – where they are today, every weekday, selling fruit and vegetables. Nearly all the old buildings in the market area were cleared away in the 1890s and the site redeveloped, with a widened High Street – which, with its continuation North End, had already become a major shopping centre. The rebuilt part of High Street still has a lively and varied Victorian skyline above the shop façades, in contrast to the featureless redevelopment of the 1960s opposite. Down a side street is the ebullient Town Hall and Library of 1892–6, of red brick and stone in a Flemish style, with a tall tower that holds its own. In the very heart of Croydon is Whitgift's Hospital, an almshouse founded, together with a school, by an Elizabethan archbishop, with a dark brick courtyard of 1596–9, entered through a simple doorway from the street. The trustees have repeatedly resisted would-be redevelopers and street-wideners – but they have sold adjoining land, enabling the schools (there are now two) to flourish on different sites. Next to the hospital is the town's largest department store which, with its early twentieth-century façade following the slight twists of the medieval street line, and its recent enlargement, symbolizes the steady, not sudden, evolution of Croydon from a small ancient town to a suburban city. Behind is the Whitgift Centre, on former school land. This, one of the earliest large shopping 'precincts', is still one of the most successful; it is neither brutal nor excessively brash, and it is well related to the older shopping facilities, of which it is an extension, not a replacement. Its most serious fault is that it ends with a mean back entrance in front of Croydon's most under-appreciated building, St Michael's church of 1883, a work of the great J.L. Pearson, architect of Truro Cathedral and many other churches – including All Saints, Hove, St John, Redhill, and also the vaulting of St Leonard, Hythe (pages 32, 104, 82). Its quality is mainly internal; outside the stump of a tower and spire which were never built is all too prominent. Inside it is superb – a lofty soaring space with a complexity of smaller spaces opening off. The church was always in a backwater, but it could have made the climax of the way through the Whitgift Centre. It is rumoured that a benefactor offered money to complete the spire to Pearson's design, but that the church authorities refused, saying that there were other things to spend such money on; if so, they showed unforgivable philistinism. A soaring spire by Pearson would have held its own against, and set off, the office towers that now loom around.

The growth of Croydon as an office centre began in the late 1950s; since then a huge assortment of towers and slabs has risen to the east and south of the older town centre. With imagination as well as enterprise this could have become a miniature English version of parts of Chicago or Toronto, displaying something of the verve those places have. But it has not turned out so. Most of the office blocks are as banal as such buildings can be, impressive only because of their bulk. Almost the only one with compelling visual interest is near East Croydon station, with an odd polygonal shape, effectively seen at a distance along the Victorian street near the Whitgift Hospital. Twentieth-century Croydon is a huge opportunity missed; luckily much of Victorian Croydon, far more impressive, and even something of ancient Croydon survive.

Cuckfield

Sussex

Cuckfield is a small former market town which remains delightfully unspoiled. Its market ceased when a new one was started in 1881 at Haywards Heath, two miles away on the railway. Haywards Heath has grown and Cuckfield has stood still – but today only the rigid maintenance of a green gap between the two towns prevents Cuckfield from being absorbed by its larger and newer neighbour. The main street has many twists and too much traffic, and a greater variety of building materials than usual even in the Weald – sandstone as well as tile-hanging and local brick, and not too much recently exposed timber-framing. One house on the east side of the street, north of the King's Head, has a perforated bargeboard on its gable that is said to date from *c.*1500. The climax of the street, going north, is provided by two short ranges of tall Georgian bow-fronted houses reminiscent of Lewes or the older streets in Brighton – Cuckfield was on the main coaching route from Brighton until a new turnpike road was opened in 1807. The church is well placed with its castellated tower and short spire rising beyond the buildings as one goes south along the street, but lies secluded behind them; it is big and spreading with a spacious interior, which rises to a fine late medieval roof judiciously decorated by the late Victorian artist C.E. Kempe. From the churchyard is a sweeping view, over country which may yet be threatened with what was broadly designated the 'Brighton corridor' of development in the early seventies.

Dartford

Kent

Dartford has a fascinating history, and has been industrial for centuries. It was a medieval market town where the Roman Watling Street crossed the River Darent about two miles above its confluence with the Thames. There was a nunnery north, of the town, which became a royal residence for a short while after the Dissolution. The first important commercial venture was in 1567–8, when the converted nunnery was used for the smelting of an ore-like substance brought back by Martin Frobisher from his extraordinary voyage into the Canadian Arctic; he hoped it contained gold or silver, but it was shown to be worthless. More successful was the venture of Godfrey Box of Liège who, about 1590, set up, again under royal patronage, the first iron-slitting mill in England, on the river just south of the town. Sheet iron, already rolled and heated, was slit by water-powered machinery into bars or wire – a significant early step towards the Industrial Revolution – though further development of this process took place in the Black Country, not Kent. Almost at the same time William Spilman, a German, set up the first successful mill in England for pounding rags into paper, again harnessing the Darent. For a time he had a royal monopoly, but the industry took root and spread – up the Darent valley to rural Eynsford and Shoreham, and also around Maidstone. In 1784 John Hall set up as a blacksmith, and in a few years expanded into engineering, eventually pioneering refrigeration and lifts. The firm occupies the site of the nunnery and the abortive Frobisher venture: parts of the Tudor palace and of the medieval boundary wall remain. An industry of more recent origin is that of pharmaceuticals: the firm of Burroughs Wellcome occupies the site of one of the ancient mills, and its landscaped pond is a prominent feature.

Surprisingly, Dartford still looks like an old market town. The High Street is part of Watling Street, widening to take a market; now it is pedestrianized. Interesting buildings are not many, but prominently placed. The Bull and Royal Victoria Hotel has a Georgian façade, and an archway into one of the best-preserved galleried inn courtyards, unfortunately glass-roofed over. Richard

Trevithick the great engineer died while staying at the inn in 1833; he was working for Hall's. Further on is a Georgian house with flat-fronted bay windows, while opposite is a small group of timber-framed buildings which variously claim connection with Wat Tyler, leader of the 1381 Peasants' Revolt. Most of them are probably later, but old photographs show a much altered building which stood until recently west of the present public house; it looks as if it were a medieval hall house, to which the pub may have been a wing. It could have dated back to Tyler's time, and should never have been demolished.

The church, prominently closing the view at the end of High Street, is an amalgam of various periods with a patchwork texture of flint and two sorts of stone, an effect spruced by the Victorians. The small river, which runs behind the church, is still attractive even in the town; several miles up the valley to the south is the legendary landscape of Samuel Palmer. To the east of Dartford is a weird area pitted by quarries – begun centuries ago to provide chalk for lime burning, and ballast for collier ships to Newcastle, but they expanded hugely in the last hundred years to supply the cement industry, now much diminished. On a site above an old quarry face, not far from the entrance to the Dartford Tunnel, is one of the most beautiful smaller churches in southern England, St Mary's at Stone. Its beauty is internal – there are exquisitely detailed nave arcades and chancel, the latter restored and vaulted by the Victorian architect G.E. Street. Nobody knows why such a superb church was built in what was for centuries a small village.

Deal

Kent

Deal must be unique; for a considerable time it was an important port without any harbour or berthing facilities. Ships, both naval and civilian, anchored on the Downs – the name given to the shallow waters off the Kent coast, not to be confused with the chalk downs inland. They were serviced by boats rowed from Deal beach and back, carrying people, provisions, equipment or cargo. The civilian ships were mostly bound to and from London, for which Deal was a useful outport, while naval vessels frequently used the Downs as a convenient anchorage or rallying point. The practice began on a large scale in the seventeenth century, when the harbour at Sandwich was hopelessly silted, and Dover's capacity was limited. It reached a peak in the Napoleonic wars and ended in the steam age.

Deal was a small inland village (now Upper Deal) before the port trade developed. The first significant buildings on the coast were Henry VIII's castles. The town grew rapidly from the mid-seventeenth century in a way that seems medieval – without any Renaissance

20 **Deal Beach.** Deal was a port without a harbour. Boats, beached like these, serviced ships anchored in the Downs, the shallow waters a short distance offshore.

21 **Middle Street, Deal,** the central street of the dense network behind the beach, where boatmen and traders supplying the ships lived.

22 **Old Houses at Deal.** The house in the background with its Dutch-like curved parapet is one of the oldest in the town, which first developed in the 17th century.

formality. There were simply long streets parallel with the shore – High Street, Middle Street and the road along the seafront – linked by narrow cross-streets. It is a very informal grid; Middle Street is quite twisty. These streets are lined with small and medium-sized houses where the boatmen, traders and craftsmen must have lived. Every one is different; most look Georgian or early Victorian though there are a few that are visibly of the seventeenth century. Nearly all look well-kept, and the total effect is charming.

The two best buildings in the High Street are the Georgian church and town hall – Deal was incorporated in 1699 as a member of the Cinque Port of Sandwich. A curiosity is the Timeball Tower, a tall building with a large black ball which was raised to the top of a mast at a precise time each day, giving an accurate time check for ships on the Downs.

The castle was built about 1540 as one of several along the coast from Kent to Cornwall (Southsea, at Portsmouth, was another), against possible invasion by the French and Spanish. It was built when cannon dominated warfare – with massive masonry, broad and low, three-tiered, everything curving. The highest tier is the broad circular keep, the second has six rounded projections, the lowest is similarly shaped but much broader, overlooking a dry moat, protected by an outer wall. Every direction was covered amply by artillery on the three tiers. On plan it looks like an impossibly regular flower with large rounded outer petals and smaller inner ones. It was one of three on this stretch of coast; the one to the north, Sandown Castle, has been all but eroded away; that to the south, Walmer Castle, was converted in Georgian and Victorian times into the official residence of the Lord Warden of the Cinque Ports – an honorary title given to distinguished people.

Deal was an important military town in the Napoleonic period and later; there are handsome barrack buildings dating from then, and what became the Royal Marines School of Music has a distinctive centrepiece in brown and buff brick, with classical doorcase and cupola. Nearby is Walmer Green – Walmer is the parish south of Deal – with an attractive informal row of houses overlooking a greensward open to the sea. The original village of Walmer is inland, with a Norman church and fragments of a Norman manor house adjoining.

Dorking

Surrey

Dorking is a market town with no spectacular history. It developed along the ancient west-east route under the North Downs, represented by the present A25, where it linked with a route from London into Sussex. It was prosperous in the seventeenth century, less notably so in the eighteenth, and grew only gently in the nineteenth. Today its growth as a commuter town is constrained more strongly than almost anywhere else because of the beautiful, varied and, on the whole, amazingly unspoiled country all round, the greenest part of the Green Belt. The town has a long, pleasantly writhing High Street which at its western, older end has a raised pavement on the south side, and still possesses more distinctive older buildings than nondescript new ones. Some are Victorian, with ebullient skylines; there is a fine double-bowed Georgian shop front in an otherwise late seventeenth-century façade. Elsewhere there are examples of mid-seventeenth-century brickwork with carved cornices and other rustic classical features, as in the narrow North Street, and in West Street – which has a fascinating series of small-scale buildings, late medieval to Victorian, with old brick and tile-hanging still prominent. Alas, like the High Street it is plagued with traffic, since no solution has yet been found to the problem of the steadily increasing west-east traffic going through the town centre. The church, glimpsed occasionally down alleys or over rooftops, is a rebuilding of 1868–77 by Henry Woodyer, in dark flint with light stone dressings and a superb spire – the finest in any town covered by this book except Chichester and Faversham. The other Victorian surprise is Rose Hill, a housing scheme started before 1850, entered through a Gothic archway from South Street. There are varied, romantic, mostly gabled villas ranged irregularly round a rough, sloping tree-shaded pasture field, which is still grazed by horses; the best range is on the west side, where one of the villas is built of near-local white Reigate stone. The spire looms to the north. This delightful piece of early suburban planning – a smaller version of Decimus Burton's Calverley Park at Tunbridge Wells – ought to be kept intact.

Dover

Kent

Dover is a sad and sorry town in a setting that is magnificent, both scenically and historically. It lies in a steep-sided valley within the chalk upland that ends dramatically at the white cliffs. There was an Iron Age hillfort on the castle site. The Romans used the original tidal inlet as a naval base, and built two successive forts in the valley. In Saxon and Norman times Dover was an important port, but, as in so many other places along the south-eastern coast the original habour silted up (its site is under part of the town centre), and shifting shingle banks made berthing very difficult. But, because of its location in relation to the Continent, Dover inevitably continued as a port – presumably only for small vessels until large-scale harbour works were carried out in the nineteenth century. Today it is the busiest port in Britain. Apart from the castle, the best part of the town is the waterfront. It has a splendid stuccoed crescent of the 1830s, belatedly called after Waterloo; a hotel of the 1950s, the Dover Stage, in a lively Festival of Britain style, unfortunately overshadowed by a later looming block; and a long early post-war range of flats which relates rather well to the flank of the castle hill and cliffs. Behind, the town centre is visually a mess.

23 **The Pharos and St Mary-in-the-Castle, Dover.** The Pharos was a Roman lighthouse, with the top part rebuilt in the 15th century; the church was built about AD 1000.

It suffered from bombing and repeated shelling, but reconstruction has been uninspired and disorganized. One stretch of good old street is left – Castle Street, ending dramatically at the foot of the castle hill, but there is no memorable new architecture away from the waterfront. The market place and shopping streets are undistinguished jumbles with occasional conspicuous older buildings. One is the Victorian town hall, by William Burges (though modified in execution after his death), which incorporates part of the Maison Dieu founded about 1220 to accommodate poor travellers and pilgrims as well as permanent infirm residents. The parts that survive, a large restored hall and a low tower, were later additions to the hospital (or hospice) – which must have been very much larger than its counterparts at Portsmouth (page 100) and Southampton, or St Mary's Hospital at Chichester. Its size indicates how busy medieval Dover must have been as a town of transit. Next to it, Maison Dieu House of 1665, now the public library, is a charming example of the 'Artisan' style with small Dutch-style gables and classical motifs carved in brick.

New roads have sliced through some of the old streets; they are bordered by partly cleared spaces which give a bad impression to passing travellers. But archaeological excavations before these roads were built resulted in spectacular discoveries, including remains of both Roman forts and those of a Roman house – this has been preserved as a showpiece called the Painted House.

Dover Castle looks magnificent from any direction – from ships in the Channel, from the town below, and from the motorway to the north-east. The oldest feature is the Pharos, or Roman lighthouse, a weatherworn shell whose top storey was rebuilt in the fifteenth century. Next to it is St Mary-in-the-Castle, built about AD 1000, one of the largest Saxon churches surviving. After being partly ruinous for a time, it was well restored in 1862 under Sir Gilbert Scott, and more dubiously in 1888 by Butterfield. Inside, the chancel has fine thirteenth-century vaulting. The keep, finished in the 1180s, is one of the largest and finest of its kind – and contains two original chapels with exquisite Norman detailing. From the first, the keep was surrounded by the existing inner bailey wall with its projecting square-shaped towers that are among the earliest of their kind in northern Europe – signifying the change of emphasis, in castle building, from keeps to strong encircling walls (see colour illus. p. 51). Within the bailey, facing the keep, were the main medieval domestic buildings, all transformed in the 1740s into military quarters; the effect of the classical façades enveloping the keep is unusual and impressive. This is only the inner part of the castle; outer perimeter walls were built in the twelfth and thirteenth centuries over the rugged terrain, with towers at intervals. The Constable's Tower, which became the main entrance to the castle, makes a wonderful sight with its cluster of rounded towers rising from canted bases over a deep dry moat, with ranges of domestic windows added in the eighteenth century. The whole of the castle was drastically remodelled during the Napoleonic Wars. Rooflines were made even and flat; the towers and keep were strengthened internally to take guns on their roofs; the castle lost much of its former skyline of turrets and battlements. But the present effect is impressive in its own way, with the cubes and curves and horizontal roofs at different levels on the flat-topped but broken-edged site looming over the town and the sea.

Eastbourne

Sussex

Eastbourne developed late as a seaside resort. Before 1850 it was rural; the main village called Eastbourne was nearly two miles inland. Southbourne, a subsidiary hamlet, was nearer the sea; Seahouses, right by the beach, developed as a village-sized resort from about 1780. A branch railway was opened in 1849, and in the 1850s the chief landowner, the Earl of Burlington, who lived for part of the time in nearby Compton Place, started to build ambitiously. The stuccoed Burlington Hotel on the seafront, almost pure Regency in style, dates from then. In 1859 he inherited the title Duke of Devonshire, and thereafter promoted the town even more grandly. At first this continued to be in a conservative, Regency manner; the stuccoed bowed fronts of Cavendish Place, dating from about 1860, might have been built in Brighton forty years before. After that, Eastbourne grew in a more recognizably Victorian way, at first with pretentious terraces, then, following the changing preferences of the middle classes, with solid, mainly Italianate villas. Later in the century architectural fashions changed again, and much that was built around the turn of the century, both central streets and outlying villas, is in brilliant red bricks and tiles from the Weald, set off by ample white window frames, balconies and bargeboards.

At first the town centre developed out of the old hamlet of Southbourne, where the florid town hall dates from 1886, and G.E. Street's St Saviour's church from 1868, with a beautiful spire added a few years later. South Street, linking the two, has the pleasant twist of an old village street; nearby shopping parades of the 1880s and 1890s show an ebullient variety of gabled upper storeys. More recently the large stores and chain shops have developed along Terminus Road, between the station and the front, leaving South Street and nearby Grove Road with something of an Edwardian atmosphere – and a surprising number of bookshops. The station is a striking building of 1886 with a tall turret and walls of pale buff brick enlivened by red – all admirably cleaned and restored by British Rail, who have even left the glass-roofed canopy over the entrance.

In sad contrast to the prosperous resort is the Old Town, formerly a large village on the foothills of the downs. Because it is not on the coast it did not become a pretty place like the old towns of Brighton or Hastings, but simply decayed. A few old buildings survive, but the most prominent feature, next to the church, is a supermarket with a disproportionate roof. The medieval church nearly makes up for the sadness of its setting; it is one of the finest in the area, although, as often in Sussex, this is more apparent inside than out. It had a connection with Chichester Cathedral, which may explain its quality.

East Grinstead

Sussex

The old part of East Grinstead, around the High Street, is, in its layout, and to a large extent its buildings, one of the best examples in southern England of a small medieval to seventeenth-century town. This may seem surprising to those who know it principally from its main shopping street, or by its long-drawn suburban approach from the north. The old town begins at the southern end of the present brash main street. It was already a borough in the thirteenth century, and has a typical medieval plan, with an originally broad street

24 **Cromwell House, East Grinstead,** the latest of a series of timber-framed houses in the old town, with Jacobean oriel windows and brick chimneys. Horsham stone slabs are used on the roof to the left.

25 **Sackville College, East Grinstead,** founded 1617 as an almshouse primarily for employees on the Sackville estates at Buckhurst and Knole; restored in Victorian times, when J.M. Neale the hymn writer was warden.

narrowed in its central part with an island block of buildings which at an early date replaced market stalls. Long narrow house plots (or burgage plots) extend on either side of the original street except where the churchyard is. The buildings on the south side, including those facing the narrow lane behind the island block, make a memorable range. They begin with Stone House, of the local green-brown sandstone, and Clarendon House, timber-framed, both Jacobean with oriel windows. Nos. 36–40, now an outfitters is, in origin, a fourteenth-century hall-house with fifteenth-century gabled wing, the hall having been divided into two storeys and the shop occupying the present ground storey. No one would guess the building was so old looking at it from outside, but the basic timber framework and the roof timbers are original. Behind the island block are more timber-framed buildings, variously altered, some dating from the fifteenth or even the fourteenth centuries; many have passageways leading through to courtyards. At the far end of the High Street, beyond the island, is a splendid range beginning with the eighteenth-century Dorset Arms and Dorset House, and culminating in the early seventeenth-century Cromwell House, tall, jettied, with oriel windows and tall brick chimneys, a splendid specimen from the last years of timber-framing. Many of the houses are roofed with Horsham stone slabs.

Opposite is Sackville College, an almshouse founded by Thomas Sackville, second Earl of Dorset, whose family estates included nearby Buckhurst as well as Knole. It has a collegiate courtyard of sandstone, completed in 1619, and comparable to the slightly earlier Whitgift Hospital in Croydon. Its most famous warden was J.M. Neale, an early Victorian High Church reformer, and author – or, more usually translator – of many resounding hymns, including *Light's abode, celestial Salem*, *O happy band of pilgrims*, and ones with images of heavenly cities, such as *Jerusalem the golden*. His words for the translation of *Good King Wenceslas*, his best-known work, may have been inspired by the plight of the poor cottagers living on the edge of nearby Ashdown Forest, where they had ancient rights to graze and to gather turf and brushwood as fuel.

Surprisingly the parish church, in such a Victorian High Church stronghold, is Georgian. The tower of the original church collapsed in 1683; its successor fell in 1785 and ruined the rest of the church, which James Wyatt was commissioned to rebuild. It is a splendid piece of pre-Victorian Gothic Revival, lofty and spacious, with hollow-sided columns reminiscent of many churches in the Cotswolds. The very tall tower, completed in 1813, is said to have been built so high at the expense of Charles Abbot, Speaker of the House of Commons, in order that he might see it from his nearby estate. When seen from the High Street, the tower rises behind a row of cottage-scale houses, now mostly converted to shops, which shield the churchyard from the street, to good effect – they are probably the result of a Tudor encroachment on what was part of the public highway. The parliamentary connection is appropriate, for East Grinstead was a rotten borough before the 1832 Reform Act. The occupants of each of the original forty-eight burgage plots had the vote. The Sackville family bought sufficient of the plots to control the voting – a common practice where voting went with parcels of land, as also at Haslemere.

Emsworth

Hampshire

Emsworth lies at the head of a long creek of Chichester Harbour. It was a medieval port, but most of its character derives from the Georgian period, when it flourished from coastal trade, boat building, fishing and flour milling. There were several mills, some on streams that flow into the harbour, powered in the normal way, but others were tidal – notably the brick, gabled Quay Mill of about 1770 which, recently converted, stands conspicuously by the waterside. To provide power, an inlet was walled off by a curving causeway, now a promenade. The tidewater entered through a sluice, and the outward flow of the tide was directed to drive the wheel. There were tide mills like this at several places on the creeks and shores of the Hampshire coast, but few other examples survive (the best are Ashlett Mill at Fawley on Southampton Water, and the small Eling Mill, recently restored to working order). Corn came from a wide hinterland, and some may have been brought by boat to be milled. By the beginning of the nineteenth century appreciable quantities of milled flour were sent by coastal vessels from Emsworth and other Hampshire 'mill towns' to London as well as to Portsmouth, where the Navy was a huge customer. Milling survived in Emsworth, at least for animal feeds, till quite recently.

Victorian Emsworth was famous for oysters, not only local 'natives' but also others which were trawled off the French and Portuguese coasts and laid down in the harbour at Emsworth. This needed boats of special design to carry the oysters back alive, and an Emsworth boatbuilder, J.D. Foster, produced vessels for this purpose which were, according to a local historian A.J.C. Reger, 'some of the finest working sailing craft which have ever cleared a British port'. Alas, the oyster trade suddenly ended in 1902 when a typhoid outbreak was traced to Emsworth oysters, and it never recovered. Today Emsworth again flourishes – but from pleasure boating.

The town has a spidery plan, with several streets and lanes leading to different parts of the watersides. South Street, the plainest, goes direct to the quay and former tide mill. Nearby Tower Street is a delight, with three or four of the town's best Georgian houses; it is a cul-de-sac except for a path which continues to the waterside. Queen Street also has good Georgian houses, in local red and grey brick. King Street has varied houses, including one which is (unusually for Hampshire) faced in boarding, with flat bow windows. This was built in 1795 by John King, a shipwright who did contract work for the Navy (it was him, not royalty, after whom the street is named). Emsworth developed after the parish system had been established, and had no church of its own till a small one was built in the eighteenth century, superseded in the nineteenth. For centuries it was in the parish of Warblington two miles away, where the church stands among fields, even today, close to a creek and adjoining a farm with a tall turret – all that remains of a Tudor mansion. The church is a delight, an amalgam of work from vestigial Saxon to high Gothic, and the churchyard contains some superb Georgian headstones with carved cherubs and classical decoration; one shows a ship sinking. There are similarly fine tombstones in other local churchyards, and one wonders if the craftsmen who carved them lived in Emsworth.

Epsom

Surrey

Epsom is a surprising place. It is linked to London by a sea of suburbia, yet it is a town of its own, with a working market place, and real country, including a half-wild common, pressing against its southern fringes. Epsom could argue with Tunbridge Wells that it was the earliest spa town after Bath. The remarkable properties of a spring on the common were noticed in 1619, when cattle refused to drink from it. Visitors came sporadically at first but in larger numbers after the Restoration – wealthy people from the City rather than aristocrats – but the arrangements by the well were rudimentary. Epsom was originally a small village, over a mile from the well, much less important than neighbouring Ewell. In 1685 a charter for a market was obtained and the present High Street developed; a New Tavern was built there in 1690 as assembly rooms. Soon after, a second well, supposedly with similar properties to those of the first, was opened on the edge of the town; the proprietor bought the original well in 1715 and closed it for a time, bringing the water from it in bottles to the new site. Epsom lost its reputation as a spa. But by then it was a favoured residential place. Already by the 1720s City men lived there in the summer and commuted by coach to London. Racing on Banstead Downs (as Epsom Downs were originally called) was an added attraction, especially after properly organized races were established in 1779 (The Oaks) and 1780 (The Derby). By the end of the Georgian period numerous comfortable residences were built in and around the town, and a surprising number survive (though there have been unfortunate losses recently due to demolitions or reconstructions, sometimes following fires). But Epsom grew completely informally. It has the straggling form of a rural market town, edging loosely to the west on to salients of its still partly rough common. The High Street should be visited on market day (Saturday) – Epsom is one of the few places in the south-east where movable stalls are still placed in their traditional locations. The dominant accent is the clock tower of 1854, richly vulgar. The New Tavern of 1690, later Waterloo House, was a very handsome building of which the upper floor survives, typically William and Mary with its ample pediment and decorative cornice, but a shop was first inserted in the ground storey in 1901. Now it is used as offices, and it is a pity that the ground floor elevation could not have been restored. Altogether the western part of High Street just manages to retain the character of a rough-and-tumble country-town street (despite a supermarket with all too typical sweeping roofs), while the eastern part, widened in 1938 and now mellowed, is in genteel neo-Georgian brick. The latest insertion is the Ashley Centre, a large shopping precinct set behind the buildings on the south side – rightly praised as good of its kind. Its visual impact on the High Street is positive – by one entrance is a strange octagonal tower with a conical top, just where such a landmark is valuable.

The Centre takes its name ultimately from Ashley House (in Ashley Road behind) of 1769, one of the best of Epsom's many mansions – Palladian, in buff brick (an early example of this) with a fine porch. Other fine houses are in Church Street, successor to the original village street. As the first part of this street has entirely lost its character, it is best to go from Ashley Road along an insignificant road called The Parade, passing two or three charming weatherboarded cottages – examples of several that appear all over Epsom: reminders of how rustic and informal the old town was. The Parade reaches Church Street at its most interesting stretch – there is a series of mansions, all set back in gardens, including The Cedars, with an appealingly awkward front, Regency Richmond House and the Old Vicarage, a William-and-Mary-type house from Epsom's heyday. The parish church (St Martin's) was rebuilt cheaply in 1824 except for the altered tower, but the inside is surprising. Sir Charles Nicholson – later to enlarge Portsmouth Cathedral – extended the eastern part grandly from 1907 on, and the effect of the gimcrack Gothic nave of 1824 opening into the spacious and complex extension is impressive – although it was originally intended to rebuild the nave as well. Some charmingly sentimental wall monuments of about 1800 are by the sculptor Flaxman.

Other mansions are scattered around Woodcote – a loose-knit area to the south of the town. Two are on the Dorking Road (The Hylands and Hylands House), but the best group lies around the meeting of Chalk Lane and Woodcote Road, where there is a recognizable hamlet centre with weatherboarded cottages. Southward along Chalk Road one of the grandest houses, Woodcote Grove, is set back behind gates, while opposite, Maidstone House, a delightful smaller house, has Venetian windows on either side of its door. Chalk Lane continues past the large Victorian stables and riding school attached to Durdans, bought in 1874 by Lord Rosebery, racehorse breeder, Derby winner and, later, prime minister. The house looks relatively insignificant, but facing the road is a splendid iron screen, partly enveloped in vegetation, which originally came from Canons, the great house in Middlesex; it is probably the finest piece of craftsmanship in Epsom. Beyond is seemingly deep country.

Fareham

Hampshire

Fareham is a fast-growing town between Portsmouth and Southampton, closely related to both. But it is no upstart. There was a Roman settlement near the church, and by the thirteenth century the bishops of Winchester, as overlords, enlarged the original village into a borough and market town, with port trade on the tidal creek, an arm of Portsmouth Harbour. In Georgian times it was well-to-do, because of its trade and because senior naval officers and their dependents settled there, away from the raucousness of Portsmouth itself. There are two original main streets, High Street and West Street, forming an inverted L on the map. For well over a century commerce has been concentrated on West Street, leaving High Street almost unaltered in its Georgian form, apart from tarmac and traffic, and the fact that most of the houses are now offices or institutions. High Street begins beside an island block which separates it from narrow Union Street – representing an early encroachment on what had been part of the market place. Past the block the street opens out, and then climbs majestically to curve out of sight, with remarkable ranges of Georgian and earlier buildings on either side. Four houses on the right form the show-group of the street. First there is Kintyre House, built in 1766 of grey and red brick with a magnificent pillared porch, the finest in an outstanding series of Georgian porches and doorcases along the street. Then there is No. 69, with a segmental porch, and a façade apparently of brownish brick which is in fact mathematical titles, applied over the original red-brick façade in the early nineteenth century when red brick was out of fashion, even in Fareham. Next is a very fine house with two rounded bays, dated 1767, in the local Fareham Red brick, of a strong deep colour, which must have been made in appreciable quantities in the eighteenth century and on a much larger scale in the nineteenth, when it was used for important buildings in London (like the Albert Hall) as well as a great deal in Portsmouth. There is another good doorcase between the bays. The next house was built about 1830 in creamy buff brick, fashionable about then, with a striking elliptical archway and a little iron balcony above. The rest of the street has varied Georgian façades, some concealing timber-framed houses, and an unusually large number of small Georgian or Victorian paned shop fronts – illustrating how a country high street looked before many such streets became overwhelmingly commercial; houses of patrician size and interspersed with smaller properties where shopkeepers lived over their shops. The north end of the street – past an unfortunate gap that reveals the new civic centre – is of a generally smaller scale, and High Street proper ends beside the well-kept churchyard of the parish church with its work of many periods. As a final flourish, the Old Manor House lies a little beyond, with a splendid early Georgian brick front and another very fine porch.

West Street might almost be the main street of any town, but has one or two worthwhile buildings. The former Corn Exchange with a fine columned front, was originally designed in 1835 by the Portsmouth architects Jacob and T.E. Owen and extended in the same style later. Further on is Holy Trinity, the town's second church, built also in 1835 to the design of one of or both the Owens (page 102) with a marvellous interior – iron-framed, with slender piers and flat arches of 'Tudor' shape, a most elegant adaptation of the Gothic style in iron, with a slenderness which would be impossible with stone. This sort of building was anathema to the later, serious Gothic Revivalists. Outside it is of buff brick, with a stone spire. At the opposite end of the town, the railway crosses the creek by a fine viaduct of Fareham bricks – an excellent illustration of their deep red colour.

Farnham

Surrey

Farnham has a fine town centre which is largely Georgian in character, though its layout is medieval, and much of the town's appearance is the result of enlightened improvement over the last eighty years. There was a Saxon village, near which a Norman bishop of Winchester built a castle, overlooking the important route from Winchester to London. The bishops laid out the town as an episcopal borough, partly along the main road – a section of which is still called The Borough – and partly along Castle Street, leading at right-angles to their fortress. In the seventeenth century Farnham's markets prospered, drawing corn from a wide area. Much of the grain was carried on to Guildford, where some of it was milled and shipped down the Wey Navigation (page 72) to London. After about 1720 marketing patterns changed, and Farnham became more famous for hops; and it also had a coaching trade.

The view up the wide Castle Street, with its motley, mainly Georgian frontages framing the castle on its tree-encircled bluff, is one of the finest townscapes in southern England. The castle is unusual: there are remains of a polygonal shell keep (it has twenty-three sides) hidden behind the main range which faces the town. At first sight the castle suggests Georgian domesticity when seen from the street, because of the sash windows, but the tower to the left of the main range is a splendid early example of brick construction, now known to have been built by Bishop Waynflete in 1475. Bishops of Winchester lived in Farnham Castle right up to the 1920s – it lay in the centre of their original diocese which stretched from Hampshire through Surrey to the outskirts of London.

The frontages to Castle Street are not quite so consistently Georgian as they look at first sight. Some are refacings of earlier buildings, like the ironmongers on the west side with an iron balcony, while Lloyds Bank opposite dates from 1930–4. Further down, at the junction with The Borough, is a building with a tall cupola known as the Town Hall (though that was never its function), which dates from 1930–4. Round it is a group of buildings which provide the clues to understanding the present character of the town. Charles Borelli was a jeweller who owned and bought property, and cared deeply for the character of Farnham, which he sought to improve. In 1911 he restored 40 The Borough, which now shows an elaborate half-timbered front, with concave timber patterns as on the Welsh Border (of which there are other examples in the area, as at Godalming). It had been covered with a Georgian cladding of brick or tiles, which Borelli removed to re-expose and restore the timber-framing – a course which is against present-day conservation principles. Soon after, Borelli restored a smaller timber-framed building opposite, on the west corner of Castle Street, more conservatively, leaving the upper floor plastered, but setting the ground floor back to reveal the original jettying and expose the old curved brackets supporting it. These are among Farnham's few pre-Georgian buildings; from then on Borelli concentrated on conserving and improving the largely Georgian character of the town. In this his chief associate was Harold Falkner, a locally-based architect who, like his great contemporary Edwin Lutyens, brought up a few miles away, started by studying the old vernacular buildings of Surrey, and then came to appreciate more and more the Georgian heritage – this was the period when people generally were beginning to admire the long-despised Georgian style. Several Georgian buildings in the town were restored under Borelli's initiative or influence, usually with Falkner as architect – while Falkner also designed some new, convincingly neo-Georgian buildings (see colour illus. p. 50).

Borelli's and Falkner's triumph is the Town Hall, which replaced a Victorian Gothic building which both considered unsuitable. Its style is that of about 1700, with sweeping but not over-prominent roofs, cupola and white-painted sash windows. The way in which it conforms with and yet accentuates the predominant character of Farnham, and provides the main landmark in the heart of the town, makes it a masterpiece when seen in its setting. On the Borough frontage the footway is set within the building, behind arches and a row of columns, and it is a fascinating experience to walk along it, under variedly treated ceilings with views across the street framed by the columns.

Some of the best Georgian houses are along West Street, the continuation of The Borough. Willmer House of 1718, now the museum, has an elaborate brick façade with rich decoration in its cornice, window surrounds and string courses; Nathanael Lloyd in his *History of the English House* called it 'perhaps the most remarkable elevation in cut and moulded brickwork extant'. Sandford House beyond dates from 1757, and the group is continued by Wickham House, whose façade was added in Georgian style to an earlier building by Harold Falkner – very typical. Little streets and paths lead to the church, a composite medieval building with a Victorianized

26 *Top* **Farnham Castle**, built by bishops of Winchester, showing the 15th-century brick tower with decorative machicolation, and the wide Castle Street with a vestige of the market.

27 *Above* **Castle Street, Farnham**, looking down from near the castle. The street was laid out by a Norman bishop to accommodate the market, but the architecture is Georgian and successful Neo-Georgian.

exterior and a rather chilling interior where almost every bit of surface has been whitewashed – a practice now too widespread. The finest feature is the tower, which was left a stump at the end of the Middle Ages but was heightened, very effectively, in 1865.

The best approach to the church is Lower Church Lane, a charming alley still paved with hard small pieces of ironstone – sandstone with an iron content, quarried locally; Georgian brick cottages frame the view of the tower. Southward from the churchyard, a path leads to the pastures which still border the River Wey, providing a foreground to views back to the town, much as at Godalming, and also helping to separate the town proper from its sprawling suburbs to the south. (There is a similar partial definition of the old town on the other side by the castle and its park). Beyond the meadows and river, past a brewery and maltings converted into an arts centre, then across the roaring bypass, is William Cobbett's birthplace, a public house (it was not so in his time) which was for long, and very appropriately, called the Jolly Farmer; it seems inane that it has been renamed the William Cobbett.

Faversham

Kent

Faversham is one of the most attractive small towns in England – well-preserved without being aggressively picturesque. It stands at the head of a creek, in an extremely fertile part of the Kent coastland, just off Watling Street, whose traffic always bypassed it. There was a Saxon royal town, but Faversham became specially important with the foundation of an abbey by King Stephen in 1147. The abbey has vanished, but the layout of the town, with the wide Abbey Street leading to the site of its gate, was influenced by its presence. The market place is the heart of the town – really a stretch of broad street, encroached by the attractive Guildhall of 1814, standing over an open wooden-arched ground storey of 1574. Stalls crowd round on market days – this is one of the relatively few towns in the south-east where they are still set up in the traditional place. Court Street continues north and becomes Abbey Street, broad and very slightly curving, lined with a great variety of modest old houses; a high proportion are timber-framed but Georgianized in front, with plaster, tiling or brick – Faversham was an important brick-making centre almost to the present day. For a long time Abbey Street looked run-down; moves towards its rehabilitation began in 1958 when a study was made of the old houses. Since then most have been repaired and improved, usually with the help of historic buildings grants from the government or an enlightened local council. Now Abbey Street is a model of how a once rather depressed street can be made delightful both to look at and to live in. But it is still a working street. There are *two* breweries, the only two left now in the hop-growing county of Kent. A lane leads past the Victorian buildings of one to the glorious 'flying spire' of the church, added in 1799 by the architect Charles Beazley – it 'flies' from curving buttresses like those on the cathedrals of Edinburgh and Newcastle. The church has an unexpected Doric nave by George Dance, architect of the Mansion House in London, and spacious eastern parts from the fourteenth century. The relative splendour of the parish church compensates in some measure for the loss of the much grander abbey. All that survives above ground is a fragment of the gatehouse incorporated in one of two fine timber-framed houses in Abbey Street, which seem to have been built immediately after the Dissolution. Here lived and was murdered, in 1550, Thomas Arden, mayor of the town and subject of the anonymous Elizabethan play *Arden of Feversham*. Beyond Arden's house, Abbey Street bends towards the quayside. Faversham was for centuries a prosperous coastal port and member of the Cinque Port of Dover; small vessels were built there. There are some old warehouses; one incorporates stone and internal timbers from the abbey buildings. But the best building of this type is on another part of the fore-

28 *Left* **Warehouse, Faversham.** This warehouse, near the quay, is in a mixture of materials; the stone bases of the walls and internal roof timbers came from the now vanished abbey.

29 *Right* **Abbey Street, Faversham.** Houses in this fine street, dating from medieval to Georgian times, have been restored and improved over the last twenty-five years, as part of a conservation scheme.

30 **Guildhall, Faversham.** The open-arched ground storey dates from 1574; the upper part was rebuilt in 1819. Market stalls still surround it, and extend under the arches, on market days.

31 **Church and Brewery, Faversham.** The beautiful 'flying spire' was designed by Samuel Beazley, 1799. The chimney belongs to a brewery, one of two in Faversham, the only ones still operating in Kent.

shore – a fifteenth-century storehouse, now called T.S. Hasarde (a sea training centre), jettied and weatherboarded on one side, not unlike the contemporary Court Hall at Milton Regis.

Almost as interesting as the walk along Abbey Street is that along West Street. This is a narrow gently winding street with a variety of old buildings much like that in Abbey Street, though the general scale is smaller. One is pargetted – a simpler version of the examples at Canterbury (page 40) and Maidstone. The street ends near the head of the creek. Beyond, on a hill, was another monastic establishment, the small nunnery of Davington, of which there survive the restored, austere Norman church and a Gothic house incorporating parts of the conventual buildings. Further on is Oare, where from Elizabethan times till quite recently was one of England's most important gunpowder factories – fortunately at some distance from the town (for there were periodic explosions); part has been restored as a museum. Much of the credit for the present attractive character of Faversham is due to the practical, persuasive and pervasive work of the Faversham Society, founded in 1962, whose Heritage Centre, in an old house in Preston Street, was one of the earliest of its kind. Preston Street ends with a flourish with two fine Georgian houses of local red brick hard by the railway, one given distinction by a window set in an elliptical recess, the other with graceful bow windows.

Folkestone

Kent

Folkestone in its Victorian heyday was a fashionable resort and a flourishing port, wrapped round a small and ancient maritime town. Its known beginnings were in AD 630 when Eanswythe, granddaughter of Ethelbert, the king of Kent who drew Christianity to Canterbury, became abbess of what was reputedly the first nunnery in England. After several rebuildings and resitings, due to cliff erosion and sackings, the church – by then serving monks not nuns – was established on its final site in 1138. It survived the Reformation as the parish church, and now has a fine thirteenth-century chancel, a sturdy fifteenth-century tower, and a Victorian nave. Until bulky buildings rose around it in the nineteenth century, the church was a dominant feature on the bluff above the harbour.

The railway from London reached the obscure town

in 1842. The company bought the small harbour and enlarged it into a Channel terminal. For a few decades Folkestone was the principal port for France, until Dover overtook it again. And it developed further for a different reason. The Earl of Radnor, the principal landowner, promoted a resort on the high land to the west, where an ancient common, called the Leas, bordered the sandstone cliffs. Solid Victorian houses rose from the 1840s onwards, starting near the parish church, and spreading westwards along the edge of the Leas, which gradually turned into an elevated grassy promenade. Development reached a crescendo in the 1860s and 70s, when massive stuccoed terraces were built at right angles to the Leas, separated by wide semi-private gardens on to which the houses backed, an adaptation of the principle of the Georgian London squares, and fairly similar to parts of the contemporary Ladbroke estate in Kensington. Parts of later Folkestone were developed to the same pattern. Two of the terraces face a formal avenue, called Langhorn Gardens, which looks rather like a French boulevard, with a statue of William Harvey, discoverer of the circulation of the blood – born in 1578 to the richest citizen in the town. Beyond, past a crescent of Victorian villas, the splendid clifftop greensward climbs and curves with the coastline, towards two huge former hotels, built in Folkestone's peak period as a fashionable resort. The glitter was tarnished by the first world war, when Folkestone was a transit town, especially for wounded soldiers from the front – and it hardly returned after. The second world war was traumatic too, and the town has never fully got back into its stride since. Nevertheless there was a burst of redevelopment in the 1960s and early 70s, including schemes promoted by the Radnor estate and designed with some flair. There is a street with arched shops ending in a seven-storey block with rounded end facing the sea, in buff brick and concrete, and further along the Leas is a range of houses with receding glass fronts, all by Chamberlin, Powell and Bon, architects of the Barbican in London.

The Old Town is now a sad sight. It was not submerged, but enveloped by the Victorian town, and was mainly the steep narrow Old High Street branching at the top into various other streets and alleys, with an offshoot to the church. Now there are cleared sites in the top part, though the lines of the streets and lanes remain – but Old High Street is still continuous with its low-key Georgian, Victorian and occasionally older buildings and small shops, twisting down to the harbour. The components are, or were, similar to those of the Lanes area of Brighton and the Old Town of Hastings (though both are bigger). With imagination and resources the Old Town of Folkestone could be regenerated into a place of real appeal. The harbour, sadly, is also an anti-climax. But there is an interesting area beyond – the Stade, the traditional fishing quarter. Old illustrations show it was a picturesque jumble. It was cleared and rebuilt in the 1930s by the borough council; the result is a charming and effective row of council cottages fronting the waterside in a contrived picturesque manner – what John Newman called in *The Buildings of England: North and East Kent* 'an instant fishing village'. Beyond, the sandy cliffs begin again, to merge further on into the grander white cliffs.

Godalming

Surrey

Godalming is set in the Surrey sandstone hills, where they are cut through by the winding valley of the River Wey, and by the steep-sided hollows of former tributary streams. The hillsides are still largely wooded even where dotted with houses, and the river is still bordered by fields. In the early Middle Ages it was an important village, the centre of a large manor and parish. It obtained a charter for a market in 1300 through its overlord, the Bishop of Salisbury, and grew mainly along the main route through the valley, later to become the Portsmouth road. Weaving developed by the sixteenth century, as in some neighbouring towns and villages; by the seventeenth Godalming was the chief textile town in Surrey; in the eighteenth stocking-knitting partly superseded weaving. Other industries developed, including paper-making and tanning; today Godalming has a surprising number of industries for a town of its type, some on or near old watermill sites.

The railway to Portsmouth gives a fascinating fleeting impression of Godalming as it crosses the Lammas Lands, described later, with a glimpse of the church. The station of 1859 is built of Bargate stone – a hard brown sandstone quarried in the vicinity, used in old local houses and much favoured by the Victorians. The church is not far away, also of Bargate stone, although the dates of the external parts vary from early Norman (the central tower) to Victorian (the nave aisles); the leaded spire is medieval with a slight twist in its timber framework. Church Street, leading south, is narrow and knowingly picturesque with buildings outwardly in stone, timber or brick, or hung with tiles, which used to give a rich and colourful effect, now much muted through too many of the surfaces being painted white. The climax is the 'Pepperpot' (see colour illus. p. 70), a delightful miniature former town hall of 1814 in the confined space at the meeting of the streets which was

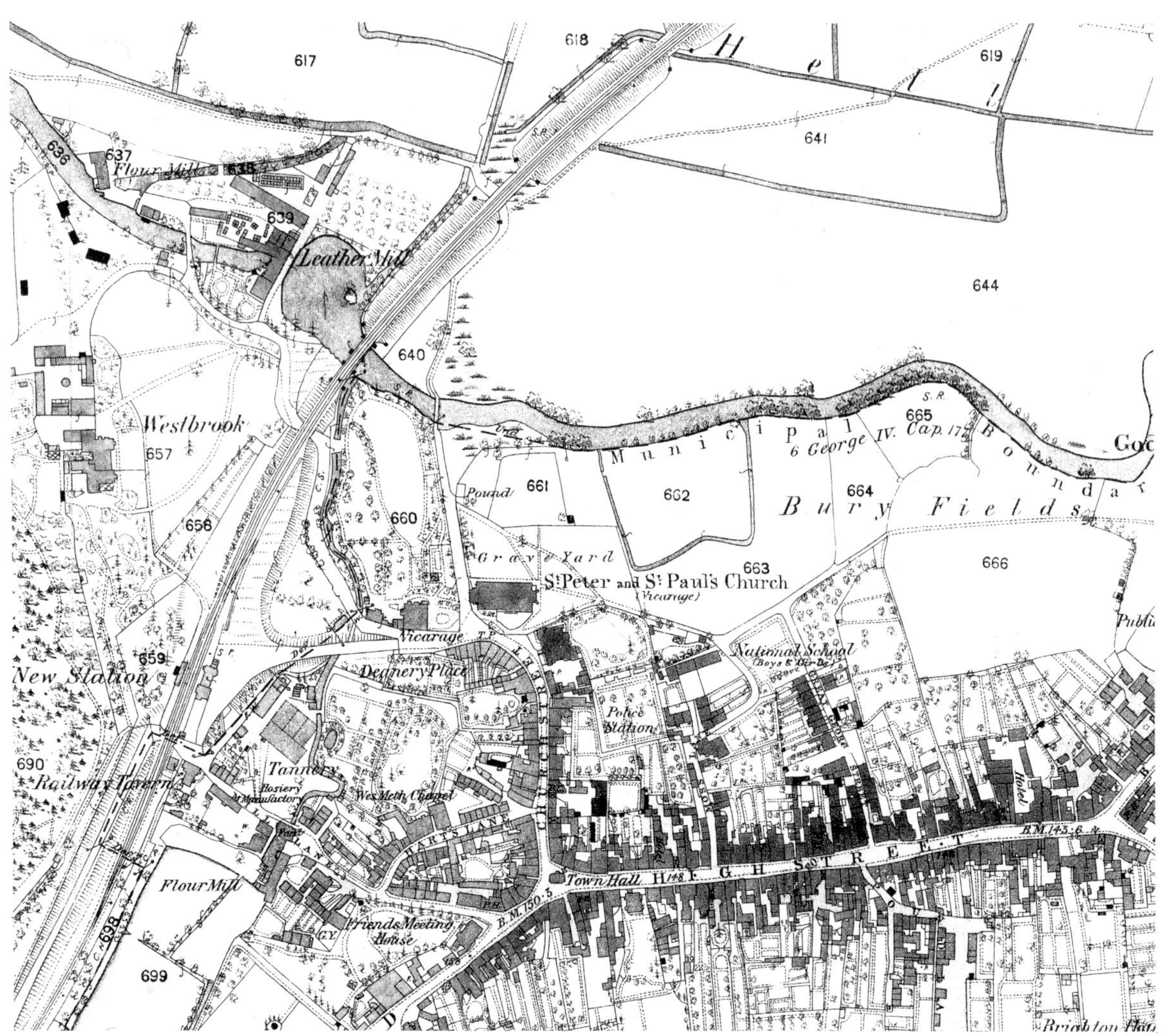

Map IV **Godalming**, when seen from the streets is a tight-knit town. But behind the long house-plots and yards, and beyond the river, is open pasture, giving the old town an immediate rural background just as in the Middle Ages. This map is of 1871, but the effect remains today.

the market place; it now houses the town museum. The open arched space below, marooned in traffic, is a safe place from which to see the High Street. Behind the Pepperpot is a restored timber-framed building with a striking pattern of straight and curved members, reminiscent of the Welsh border country – other houses in this tradition are found in the nearby countryside, and also in Farnham (page 63). A more straightforward, but impressive, timber-framed three-storeyed house, the former White Hart inn, is on the south side of High Street. Further along the street, with its dreadful traffic on busy days, are numerous interesting façades above the modern shops. Two have weird seventeenth-century patterned brickwork; another, handsomely Georgian with rusticated corners (above the shops) was an inn, while the King's Arms, re-fronted in 1753, is still a hotel. A few alleys and courts open into backland areas.

The old town is still compact, though long-drawn. The residential areas, many of them old-established, spread over the plateaux above the steep slopes on either side. On the outskirts to the south is Munstead, an area of former woody heathland, where the great gardener Gertrude Jekyll lived, latterly in Munstead Wood – the house which her friend and admirer the young Lutyens designed for her in 1896–7. It is built in Bargate stone with timber-framing, in the local vernacular manner which so influenced the early works of the great architect – who lived nearby in Thursley as a boy. Her garden has been modified, but the house is still set in thick trees, with the former gardener's house and a guest cottage, both by Lutyens using tiles and timber, visible from the road. The nearby church is that of Busbridge, by Sir Gilbert Scott (1865) in Bargate stone with an elaborate version of a Surrey timber belfry rising from the centre. Inside is an intricate iron screen by Lutyens in the apex of the chancel arch; he also designed the strangely modernistic tombstone of Gertrude Jekyll and other members of her family in the churchyard. On the opposite hill, to the north, is Charterhouse, the seventeenth-century school which moved out of London in 1872. The older buildings form a remarkably impressive group in Gothic with a cluster of spires, making full use of the textural quality of Bargate stone, amply dressed in Bath stone for the detailed work. The chapel, with tall thin windows and soaring interior, was designed as a first world war memorial by Sir Giles Gilbert Scott, and is one of his finest works.

For a final impression of Godalming it is best to go to the foot of the hill on which Charterhouse stands, along Chalk Road, and look across the Lammas Lands. These were part of the original rural economy, parcelled out in summer for the hay harvest for people who had rights, and thrown open at Lammas, in early August, for autumn and winter pasture. They are still grazed, and provide a foreground to a view with the church spire on the right and the huddled roofs of the High Street area seen against the partly wooded background of the hill behind – a scene that can hardly have changed in essence since the Middle Ages.

Overleaf left
'The Pepperpot', Godalming

Overleaf right
Lewes, with a glimpse of the castle

Gosport

Hampshire

Gosport lies across the harbour from Portsmouth, a town of seventeenth-century origin with important naval and military establishments. Bombing and redevelopment have destroyed most of the old town; tall flats, roads and spaces have replaced old close-knit streets. Holding its own is Holy Trinity, originally built in 1695, enlarged in the eighteenth century and restored in the nineteenth, with a tall Italian-type campanile – exotic but very effective – added in 1889. The inside of the church is splendid with its Ionic colonnades; this must be the finest classical interior of any church in the area covered by this book. Behind the church are grass-grown earthen ramparts, parts of the defences of the town that were started in the seventeenth century but not completed at this end until about 1800; they are simpler versions of those at Portsmouth (page 99) and must be the last town defences (enveloping a town like medieval walls) to have been constructed in Britain. Most of the circuit has been flattened; this stretch still looks impressive on its outer side, bending out into a bastion, with the recently tidied moat in front. Backing on to the ramparts by the church is the vicarage, built about 1800 of blue-grey brick, without the usual relief of red-brick dressings – to strange effect. Although intended at the start to be the vicarage it was taken over, when the ramparts were being built, as the residence of the local commander of the Royal Engineers – a post held for a time by Jane Austen's uncle; she is said to have stayed with him there.

32 **Fort Brockhurst, Gosport,** one of the forts built round Portsmouth Harbour *c.*1860 when a French invasion seemed possible. They are the last defensive works in the tradition of castles, with massive walls and vaults of brick, earthen ramparts and moats.

Gosport is a town of scattered interesting buildings, only a few of which can be mentioned. The old railway station, opened in 1842, was built ambitiously because at first it served Portsmouth; now it is a complete ruin, but the long range of Tuscan columns in white Portland stone which formed the entrance remains, looking romantic amid the desolation. Various schemes have been prepared to incorporate this and other remains into new development, none so far achieved. Across an inlet is the Royal Naval Hospital, Haslar, built in 1746–61 when it was the largest hospital in Europe and the biggest brick building in England. The architect was Theodore

ERECTED
BY SUBSCRIPTION
1814.
THOMAS HAINES Esq
WARDEN.

REEVES

Jacobsen, who had previously designed the now vanished Foundling Hospital in Bloomsbury, London. Up to two thousand patients were accommodated here in the early years of the hospital, and the physician in charge from 1758 was Dr Lind, one of the outstanding medical men of the time, who had a great influence on conditions in the Royal Navy. There have been big recent additions, but the magnificent façade, with sculptured figures representing navigation, and the royal coat of arms, is unaltered.

Alverstoke was the original village and parish before Gosport grew. A local entrepreneur tried to promote it as a resort with, as its centrepiece, a splendid Crescent of about 1830, a stuccoed composition as fine as anything of its kind in Brighton, with Doric columns, made of iron but painted, along the ground storey. It is to be found amid quiet suburban roads (Crescent and St Mark's Roads), near Alverstoke church, a Victorian rebuilding by Henry Woodyer (architect also of Dorking church), with a highly individualistic interior – the tower is later, not by him. Finally, towards Fareham is Fort Brockhurst, one of several Victorian forts built across the Gosport peninsula in the 1850s to protect Portsmouth against possible invasion by the French – similar to the slightly later ones along Portsdown Hill (page 99) but, being low-lying, having wet moats, not dry ones. It used to look picturesque with vegetation growing round the moat and elsewhere; now it is an ancient monument, restored to mint condition, displaying some of the most massive brick construction ever achieved. A bomb partly destroyed a vaulted chamber and revealed eight courses of brickwork supporting several feet of earth, on which were mounted heavy guns.

Guildford

Surrey

Guildford is entangled by traffic routes and dominated by crude commercial development. Or so it might seem to people approaching from many directions, especially from the station. But behind the swathe of crude mid-twentieth-century rebuilding there is still a historic town of rare and concentrated interest. It is best to get, by whatever means, into the High Street, with its dramatic views up and down. It was part of an ancient route which crossed the River Wey where it flows through a steep-sided gap in the chalk hills. Guildford was already a town in the tenth century when it had a mint; the High Street with its long, narrow-fronted house plots may have been laid out then or, at the latest, in the Norman period when the castle was built. By Tudor times the town flourished through weaving; in the seventeenth century, especially after the opening of navigation along the canalized River Wey in 1653, it became a distribution centre for the area. In Georgian times, the growth of Portsmouth dockyard made it an important transit town on the way there. Like many ancient streets where each plot has its own building history, the High Street has a great variety of architecture over several centuries. There are two medieval stone undercrofts, unseen from the street, one in the Angel Hotel; several gabled overhung timber-framed houses, their upper storeys plastered over (the ground storeys are all shops); many Georgian façades and ebullient Victorian compositions; the worst recent intrusions are at either extremity. But the three most striking buildings in the street are from the town's architectural heyday, the seventeenth century. First there is Abbot's Hospital, an almshouse founded in 1619 by Archbishop George Abbot, of humble Guildford origin. It has a great brick entrance tower with corner turrets, a late example of the Tudor gatehouse tradition, leading to a courtyard like that of an Oxford or Cambridge college. Second, and very different, is Guildford House (as it is now called), further down High Street, built, or remodelled, in 1660. It is extremely interesting as a small but elaborate town house of the period, possibly like many built in London just before the Great Fire. It is in a mercantile Renaissance style, with large transomed

33 **Abbot's Hospital, Guildford,** founded in 1619 by a local man who became archbishop.

windows of small leaded panes and later, Georgian, shop windows; inside are a fine staircase and ceilings. Finally there is the Guildhall, an older building to which the façade was added in 1683, with mullioned leaded windows on the upper floor (bigger than those on Guildford House), an iron balcony for proclamations, and a cupola. 'The effect is more like the poop of a seventeenth-century ship than anything else' wrote Ian Nairn in *The Buildings of England: Surrey*. What makes the Guildhall specially memorable is the clock, projecting from a beam over the pavement, *the* landmark of the street, since it is on the brow. The view down is memorable also for the green slope of downland, crested by a strip of woodland, which is still the closing feature, meticulously conserved by councillors and their planning advisers through ensuring that undesirable buildings were kept just out of sight to left or right.

Narrow streets and alleys lead off the High Street; the best by far is Quarry Street, passing St Mary's, the only one of three churches of ancient foundation not rebuilt since the Middle Ages. It has a beautiful interior, predominantly transitional from Norman to Gothic, with a vaulted eastern part; built internally of chalky stone which may have come from the old quarry to which the street led. The small flinty tower is late Saxon, the oldest structure in the town. Quarry Street leads on past Georgian houses to the Castle Arch, adjoining a house in the Surrey vernacular style which is now the local museum. Through the arch is the still impressive castle keep, built about 1170 on earlier earthworks, mainly of dark sandstone from the hills to the south. On the other side of Quarry Street, a steep path called Rosemary Alley descends between houses, revealing their colourful brick and tiled backs, to a busy road, across which is the Yvonne Arnaud Theatre. The theatre was one of the fruits of Guildford's prodigious period in the 1960s, which saw the completion of the cathedral and the foundation of the university, as well as the erection of many ugly buildings. It is a pleasant informal modern building set among trees by the River Wey, grouping with an almost monumental former mill in Georgian and Victorian brick.

It is possible to walk from here, near the river, through a semblance of country which fairly soon broadens into real country – Guildford has been restrained from growing too far to the south. Across the river is a still attractive, very informal area with old villagy houses and Victorian villas, some in sandstone or tile-hung, overshadowed by two appallingly inept lumps of multi-storey offices – they may be out of sight from the High Street, but nearer at hand they disjoint their surroundings. Buildings like this, bad in themselves and disastrously placed, stand in perpetual condemnation of the developers who promoted them, the architects who designed them, the councillors who permitted them, and possibly the planners who advised the councillors (unless the last advised otherwise and were overruled, as sometimes happens). Luckily these are not the only prominent buildings of the twentieth century in Guildford. It was a very brave decision to build a cathedral when a new diocese was formed between the wars, rather than tinker with an unsuitable parish church, as happened at Portsmouth. A hilltop site was chosen on the edge of the town – sadly difficult to reach from the centre of the town but topographically superb. The architect, Sir Edward Maufe, produced one of the last triumphs of the Gothic Revival, started in 1936, finished thirty years later. If Gothic is primarily a style of external massing and internal enclosure of space, then Guildford is a splendid example. Outside it is stark and soaring, in local pale red brick, culminating in a tower which is just right in relation to the rest. Inside there is a majestic main space, with narrow aisles and other side spaces to provide a variety of vistas. But the details and fittings are sparse and, on the whole, not of great merit. The University of Surrey was formed from an older college which moved out of London in 1968 to a site on the slope north-east of the cathedral. The buildings, by the Building Design Partnership, are in one of the more acceptable manners of the sixties, amenable rather than aggressive, placed with contrived irregularity on the slope with patches of lush landscape in between, and gaps for occasional glimpses of the cathedral. Pale brick predominates; no harsh concrete. So Guildford gained more in the sixties and seventies than traffic gyratory systems, shopping 'precincts' that might be anywhere, and intrusive office blocks. The preservation of at least part of the High Street is a major triumph. So is the fact that it is still not too difficult to walk from the town into fine country in some directions.

Haslemere

Surrey

Haslemere was a remote town in the hills, which probably first developed in the thirteenth century when the bishop of Salisbury, lord of the huge manor of Godalming of which it was on the edge, gained a grant for a market. In 1596, for no very clear reason, Queen Elizabeth gave it the right to send two members to Parliament. Voters were the freeholders of the burgage plots, and this gave rise to a great deal of abuse. From the 1780s, the Lowther family, Cumberland landowners, tried to control the voting by buying burgage plots and granting temporary freeholds to miners and other employees, whom they brought south and installed as residents at the right times for the elections. (Probably Haslemere was the first place where coal miners were able to vote.) Between 1832, when rotten boroughs were abolished, and 1859, when the railway to Portsmouth was opened, Haslemere relapsed into obscurity. After that, literary and artistic people, as well as simple life idealists, were attracted to the locality. Tennyson settled at Aldworth in the hills to the south. A group of artists formed what eventually became the Haslemere Society of Artists; the best known was Birket Foster, who actually lived in nearby Witley. Helen Allingham came to Witley with her husband in 1875 and became associated with the society; she, like the others, were attracted by the landscape and vernacular buildings. She painted local cottages with their weathered textures of timber, brick and stone, patchy colourwashing, tile-hanging, and irregular roofs in tiles or Horsham slabs, always with authentic cottage gardens and posed figures in rustic dress. Her paintings are enchanting, and show idealistically but not unrealistically what the south Surrey countryside was like before the stockbrokers arrived. It was the same world which captivated the young Edwin Lutyens and Gertrude Jekyll.

Haslemere also became a place for crafts. Enthusiasts set up workshops for weaving and other activities, and these flourished up to the first world war. At the end of the war, Arnold Dolmetsch settled in the town; he opened workshops for making musical instruments and instituted the local music festival; both flourish. Another local institution is the museum. This originated with Sir James Hutchinson, a surgeon who was a Quaker and a friend of Tennyson; he came to the area in the 1860s, formed a private museum and encouraged local interest in the history of mankind. His collection moved to its present location in a Victorian house in 1926. In its final form it attempts to portray the evolution of the world and the history of humanity. From Hutchinson's time it set out to encourage parties of children to come and learn, and in this it was a pioneer. It still seems remarkable for the breadth of its vision.

Haslemere has few notable buildings but much charm. The old town centre is, on the whole, unsullied, with a widening main street descending to a simple market hall of 1814 – scene of the last corrupt elections – and narrower streets leading off. There are still vernacular buildings with something of an Allingham quality, though without cottage gardens, and there are self-consciously picturesque rebuildings from the arts-and-crafts era, as well as two or three urbane Georgian fronts. Appropriately the Museum building with its pillared porch is the chief accent in the northern part of the High Street where it narrows and climbs. Haslemere has grown significantly in only one direction – westwards past the station. In other directions there is glorious country – the sandy Surrey hills, the bolder Sussex hills towards Midhurst, the Weald to the east. The writer, when at boarding school a few miles away, used to prefer cycling round this countryside to playing cricket.

Hastings

Sussex

Hastings is a complex town of three distinct parts: the Old Town, hemmed in a valley between two ridges, with the castle at the seaward end of one ridge; St Leonards, further west, founded as a fashionable resort in the 1820s; and the Victorian and modern central area in between. Its origins are also very complicated. When William made his fateful landing not far away in 1066 the coastline was very different. The ridge where the castle was built extended over what is now the shoreline, and there was a harbour to the west, where the lower parts of the town centre are now. The original town spread round this harbour. In the twelfth century the harbour silted, the original town was depopulated, and what is now called the Old Town started to develop. Erosion followed; much of the Norman castle was destroyed by landslips in the thirteenth century. The town was left with no natural harbour; for centuries boats have been hauled on to the beach. Hastings was one of the original Cinque Ports – the confederation which obtained privileges from the king in early medieval times in exchange for supplying quotas of ships for national defence. The Ports also had the right to use the North Sea fishing grounds – and this the Hastings fishermen exercised up to the eighteenth century. Their boats, with those of Rye (a later member of the

34 **St Clement, Hastings,** one of two medieval churches in the old town, probably rebuilt after the French raid of 1377 in a patchwork of materials; the tower may have been intended to be taller.

federation) and, by Tudor times, Brighton (never a Cinque Port), sailed in the autumn off Great Yarmouth for herring, selling most of their catches there, though some were brought back dried. Earlier in the year they fished off Scarborough for cod, and at other times the boats were used for fishing in the Channel or for general cargo. Even today there is an active fishing fleet, hauled on shore by power-driven capstans. Seaside visitors started to come about 1770, and the town expanded a little in the Regency period, but not with the same élan as Brighton. St Leonards, consciously separate, kept its distance for a while. Hastings as a large resort is essentially a creation of the Victorian period.

A good place from which to get the feel of Hastings is West Hill, reached by cliff lift or winding paths. This is the ridge which ends with the castle ruins – which look romantically jagged from below, but are rather disappointing within; they represent only part of the big early fortress which has largely been lost through erosion. From the nearby grassy slopes there are views westward over the modern town centre in the hollow where the original harbour was and, in the opposite direction, over the crowded, infinitely gabled roofs of the Old Town in its valley, backed by the partly bush-grown East Hill ridge, ending at a clifftop. Fishing boats and seaside paraphernalia are seen on the shingle beach. Inland, the tall tower of All Saints church is set against the further green slope, and on the skylines northward are charming informal groups of Georgian and early Victorian houses set for the

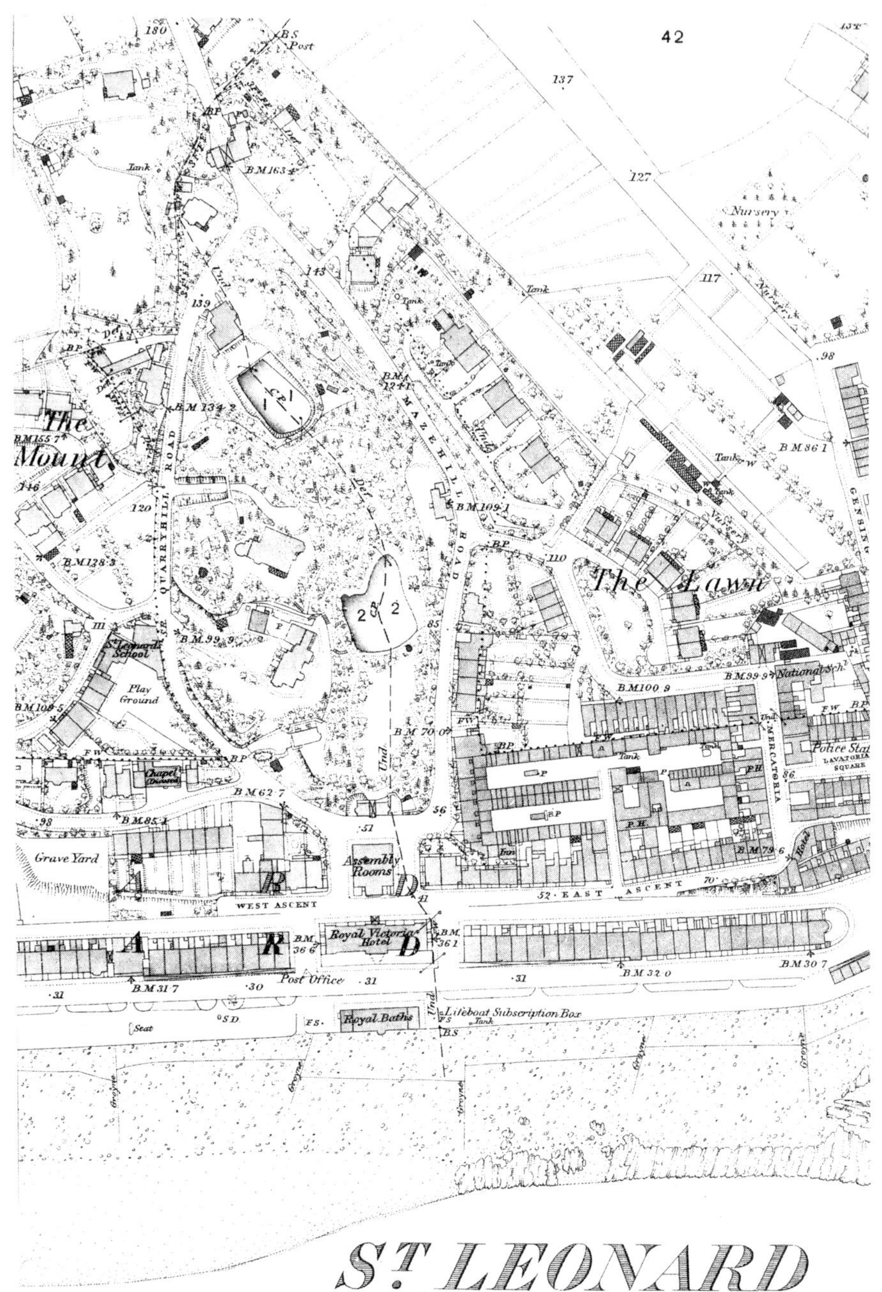

Map V **St Leonards,** the western part of present-day Hastings, was started as a new resort by James Burton in the 1820s. On this map of 1873, grand terraces and a hotel face the sea (37) while behind, in contrast, are the informally landscaped public gardens, surrounded irregularly by villas.

reverse views. The ridges define the Old Town, which is a historic entity of rare charm. Several alternative footways tumble down into it from West Hill; the best is Coburg Place, reached by a passageway under a Georgian house (Harpsichord House) which bridges it; it descends round sharp bends to emerge near St Clement's, one of the two remaining medieval churches of the town. This was rebuilt after a destructive French raid in 1377; the broad tower of many materials looks as if it may have been intended to be taller.

The church stands at the meeting of narrow streets with altered timber-framed houses and taller Georgian ones. It is best to go first up Hill Street and then into Croft Road; on the curve between the two is a delicious series of bow-windowed houses, their interplay of curves accentuated by iron balconies. The Croft itself is a side road running under the slope, overlooked by a delightful range of tall late Georgian houses, mostly bow-windowed, stuccoed in front, some showing side elevations in red tile-hanging. Back by alleys to High Street, a long street which is almost wholly unspoilt, the worst things being merely nondescript. The frontages show a wonderful variety. Many are two-storied timber-framed houses that were plastered over – in some cases the plaster has been recently stripped. Others are Georgian, usually three-storied and stuccoed, though sometimes of brick, with a repertory of bow windows in the early seaside manner. The street runs along the lower slope of the hill, so that the west side is higher, emphasized by a raised pavement. The Catholic church of St Mary Star of the Sea has an inventive Gothic interior by Basil Champneys, architect of Newnham College, Cambridge. At its far end the street opens disconcertingly on to a wide traffic road – cut in the 1950s along the floor of the valley between High and All Saints Streets, where there were previously yards, workshops and cottages. Something was undoubtedly lost by the building of this road, but the gain – taking traffic off High Street – was so enormous that the losses were probably worthwhile (the alternative of taking a main traffic road over West Hill would be unthinkable). Overlooking the traffic intersection is All Saints church, fifteenth-century seasoned by Butterfield; its most interesting feature is a medieval wall painting of the Doom – heaven and hell – over the chancel arch. All Saints Street, the counterpart of High Street across the valley, is the show street of the town, more manicured than

35 **High Street, Hastings,** almost totally unspoilt, is a nice mixture of older timber-framed houses and taller Georgian ones dating from the earlier years of the resort.

36 *Above left* **Net shops, Hastings.** Built for drying fishing nets and storing equipment, these are of uncertain date and cluster under the cliff at the east end of the town.

37 *Above right* **Marina, St Leonards,** adjoining Hastings. The remains of James and Decimus Burton's classical seafront of *c.*1830, its unity confused by accretions, and its scale overwhelmed by the 1930s block of flats at the end.

High Street but with rather less character. It has several basically genuine timber-framed houses and some Georgian ones, but rather too many which were weirdly reconstructed in the 1950s – perhaps these will be appreciated in fifty years' time. Like High Street, it has a raised pavement which gives it much of its charm. Alleys climb up the steep hill to the east at intervals, including Ebenezer Road with boarded Georgian houses and a chapel of that name set at the end against a green slope. Other alleys were cleared of old fishermen's cottages before and after the second world war, but some of the tight-knit new housing on their sites is fairly attractive. It is worth climbing to Tackleway, which runs along the edge of the open East Hill, if only to get the view back, over the Old Town, to West Hill, with the striking Georgian houses in The Croft and elsewhere set just below the brow. A steep pathway, Tamarisk Steps, descends to the fishing quarter.

The beach front to Old Hastings is a mixture of popular seaside and serious fishing, the latter predominating towards the east. By far the most striking features are the tall, thin, weatherboarded, gable-roofed net shops where the fishermen store their tackle and hang their nets. There are over forty now; at the beginning of the century there were over a hundred. They may have originated in Tudor times, though it is not certain whether any of the existing structures are more than about a hundred and fifty years old – but they seem timeless. Most are still used; a few in bad condition have been, or will be, restored as part of a conservation programme. Around and between them are booths where fish is sold. Further on the cliffs close in, but it is better to walk along their tops – there is a cliff lift – for miles if one wants.

Of the Regency extensions to Old Hastings the most impressive is Pelham Crescent, facing the sea in front of the formerly crumbly (now safe) cliff under the castle. It has a rhythm of elliptical verandahs at first-floor level, and miniature balconies above, culminating in the temple-like portico of the church of St Mary-in-the-Castle (now disused, its future in question). The whole is placed on a podium; there were always, as now, shops at ground level with the forecourt of the houses and church above them. This ought to be a splendid piece of townscape set against romantic landscape, but the buildings on either side are bad companions. Further west, round a corner, is Wellington Square, smarter looking than it was a few years ago, with swelling balconies on its western side. Alas, there is little to say now about the town centre, which is losing its once strong Victorian character. There used to be a likable clock tower where five streets meet. Now it has gone, and the focal point is now a jumble of signs and traffic. True, there are a few lively buildings left, like the Brassey Institute of 1878, now the public library, and S.S. Teulon's nearby Holy Trinity church, both ebulliently Gothic.

St Leonards is well to the west. It was an ancient parish which became almost uninhabited – even its church disappeared by Tudor times. In 1828 James Burton, a successful London developer who built much of Bloomsbury, started a new, exclusive seaside town; he was joined in its later stages by his better-known son Decimus. Early ambitious plans were modified, and what was built contrasted grandeur with contrived informality – grandeur on the seafront, informality behind. Along the front, called Marina, is a series of monumental stuccoed terraces, centred on the main hotel, much in the manner of Nash in London, or of Wilds and Busby in Brighton. Much survives, but it is sadly disjointed by twentieth-century developments. Particularly sad is an early postwar block of wrong proportions built on a bomb gap at the west end of the terraces, separating them from the charming house now called Crown House with its façade set back behind Ionic columns. It was built as James Burton's seaside home, and occupied by the Duchess of Kent and her daughter, Princess Victoria in 1834/5 – they supplied the royal patronage thought essential for a successful resort. But this post-war intrusion is nothing to Marina Court, one of the largest blocks of flats in England when it was built in 1937/8, with thirteen storeys (Burton's houses have four), which are contrived to create a grandiose end-on view when seen westward along the front from Hastings proper; the suggestive resemblance to a great liner's stern is not accidental. Fortunately there is more to see of the work of James Burton, carried on by Decimus. Behind the hotel, and hidden from the front, is the Doric Masonic Hall, built as the Assembly Rooms. Behind this, and higher, is the equally impressive double entrance lodge to St Leonards Gardens. This was the entrance to a different world. St Leonards Gardens – originally called the Subscription Gardens, since they were accessible only to subscribers – were in their small way a masterpiece of picturesque landscape design, offsetting the classical grandeur of the seafront. They were fashioned out of a valley which had been made irregular by quarrying. Houses were built among the trees on either side; the most striking has a pinnacled tower, the dominant landmark when one looks down from the top of the gardens towards the sea. The way out of the gardens on the landward side is through a romantic castellated gateway, a counterpart to the Doric one at the other end. St Leonards has two remarkable churches, both rebuildings of ones destroyed in the second world war. One, St John's, beyond the gateway, has some of its original Victorian fabric outside, but the interior is a wonderful reconstruction by the architect H.S.

Goodhart-Rendel in a very original version of Gothic. The other, St Leonard's church near the seafront, a replacement of James Burton's church which was totally destroyed, is an almost equally individual work by Adrian Gilbert Scott, son of the architect of Liverpool cathedral, and great-grandson of the original Sir Gilbert; it has striking parabolic arches on the façade and inside.

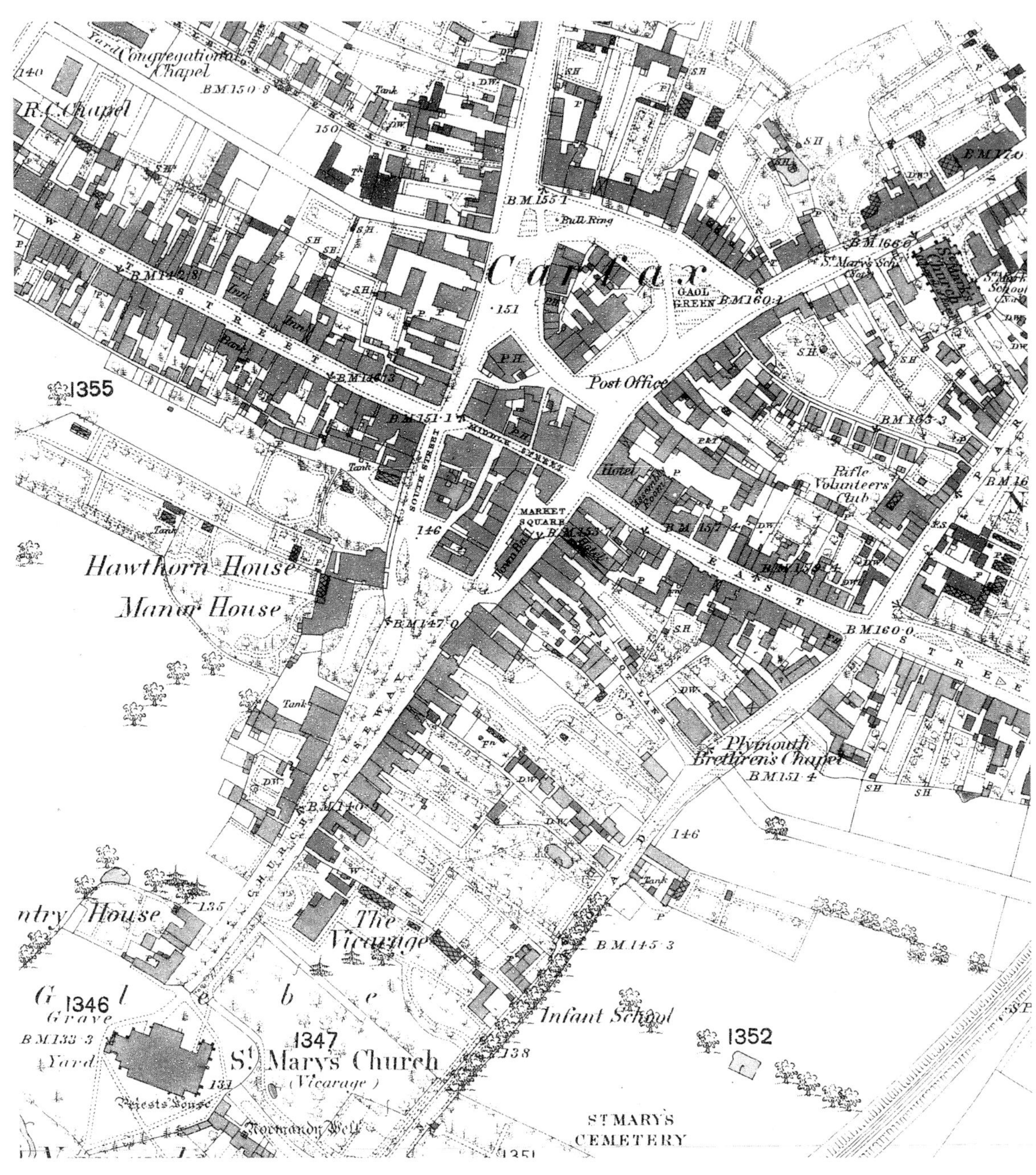

Horsham

Sussex

Horsham is a fascinating town, confusing to the extreme on first acquaintance, but making sense topographically when one understands how it grew. Originally there was a huge wedge-shaped green, pointing south – perhaps related to the pastureland at Horsham recorded in 947 and 963 (the name, spelt then exactly as now, means 'horse pasture'). By the thirteenth century it was a borough and market town, and sent members to Parliament almost continuously from the first one of 1295, though with scant regard for democracy, until the Reform Acts of the nineteenth century. Markets and fairs took place on the green but, as elsewhere, stalls eventually became permanent, so that the triangular space was fragmented. Carfax, the irregular area which occupies the northern end of the original green wedge, and the Causeway, at its southern pointed end, remain open. In between there is a network of alleys, lanes and small spaces where the main marketing area was – an expanse towards the east is still called the Market Place, containing the stone-built town hall, a replacement of the older hall where both the Assizes and the Quarter Sessions for Sussex were often held. Buildings round the Carfax are oddly mixed, ranging from small older ones, much altered, to prominent Victorian ones – like the stuccoed terrace of *c.*1840 with pillared porches, the ebullient bank of 1897 with interesting roofline (it is by the same architect, F. Wheeler, who designed the fine bank at Petworth), and a nice bandstand of 1892 which is almost the town's focal feature. The only seriously intrusive building on Carfax is the entrance to a shopping precinct at its corner, with excessively sweeping roofs. But it is the Causeway that makes Horsham special – the tapering end of the original wedge, reached casually from the streets to the north. It has trees down its length and a delightful succession of medium-sized houses in varied local materials – sandstone, tile-hanging, Horsham stone roofs; some have timber-framing exposed (which were probably tile-hung till recently). One, a fine stuccoed mainly seventeenth-century house, is now the museum. At the far end of the Causeway, making the perfect climax, is the massive shingled spire of the parish church. The church is a great surprise, a grand building of the thirteenth century; Victorian restorations altered or added details, but the main structure is original, in local sandstone and, of course, with roofs of the famous Horsham stone slabs which were in fact quarried widely in this part of the Weald; they are seen on old roofs as far afield as East Grinstead and Steyning. The churchyard is attractive, with its tombs still *in situ.*

Horsham has many loose ends beyond its central core. On Worthing Road are two evocative and very simple chapels: a late Georgian Quaker meeting house, and a Unitarian (originally Baptist) church which was built in 1721 and looks like a cottage, with its mottled brick walls and Horsham roof. Leading north-east from Carfax, North Street passes the striking stone spire of St Mark's (1870), then Park House, a country house built about 1720 and now council offices, and finally, on the corner opposite the station, a surprising group of small cottages in large gardens, built in a mixture of local materials, called by Ian Nairn in his *Buildings of England: Sussex* 'an extraordinary enclave like a sixteenth-century garden suburb which ought to be kept if possible'.

38 **The Causeway, Horsham,** a quiet tapering street, with timber-framed and Georgian houses roofed in local stone slabs.

Map VI *Opposite* **Horsham** began as a village round a huge wedge-shaped green, with the church at its southern point. By the thirteenth century there was a market, and irregular groups of buildings encroached on the green, leaving a succession of twisty spaces, narrow alleys and, to the south, the still open Causeway, ending at the church. The map is of 1876.

Hythe

Kent

A former port left high and dry, Hythe has as complicated a history of sea-change as any of its fellow Cinque Ports. Originally a river flowed east over the northern part of the present Romney Marsh, reaching the Channel near where Hythe now is. By Saxon times the river turned south to a harbour near Romney itself (page 113), but part of the old estuary remained further east, usable for a time as a harbour. Hythe developed alongside this, first at West Hythe (now a hamlet), then gradually eastward as the estuary silted, to form what became a very long-drawn town. There was flourishing trade till the thirteenth century, but in the fourteenth the harbour finally dried up and the town shrank – a process hastened by a great fire in 1400. By Georgian times Hythe had settled as a market-village half a mile from the shingle-beached Channel coast. Changes began again in the Napoleonic wars, when the Royal Military Canal was dug, roughly along the line of the original estuary, purely as a moat against a feared French invasion. Military establishments were set up in the vicinity, some of which remained till recently. In Victorian times the marooned town spread to the shore as a small resort.

What is now the old part of Hythe occupies only a section of the site of the town in its heyday. The still busy High Street runs below the foot of the steep coastal ridge; the old quays must have been immediately to the south. Parallel streets are terraced along the slopes above, linked by steep lanes and alleys, providing the explorer with an intricacy of routes. Even now these hillside streets and alleys are not all close-built. Long stretches are lined with old garden walls in rough local ragstone, often overtopped by trees. Church Hill, which is stepped, and Oak Hill Passage are among the most attractive alleys; the latter curves between stone walls to a weatherboarded house at the bottom corner. Near the top of the network is Hythe's chief glory, the church. It was one of four which existed before the town's decline, but may have been the most important. The chancel is a magnificent piece of Early English architecture of cathedral quality – perhaps partly explained by Hythe's being on the archbishop's estates; one of their fortified residences was the still romantic Saltwood Castle a mile to the north. But the church was never finished in the Middle Ages to its intended form; completion came under the inspired direction of J.L. Pearson, who designed the present vaulting in 1886. The High Street is modestly pleasant, with a gentle curve, an important tree and a town hall of 1794 with open, columned ground storey. From across the canal to the south – the scene of a long-established biennial 'Venetian' festival – there is a pleasant view of the old houses tiered to the church, with trees above.

Kingston

Surrey

Kingston upon Thames is memorable for its market place. There was a market in the thirteenth century, but the town was important long before that. The claim that six Saxon kings were crowned there between 902 and 958 is authentic – but why? Possibly because it was a river crossing linking the ancient kingdom of Wessex with what had been Mercia. When a bridge replaced the ford over the Thames is not known – certainly by 1193: for centuries it was the first one upriver from London Bridge. From being a small but busy market town, Kingston has grown into a huge suburban shopping centre. Yet amazingly the market is still the essence of the place. It is an irregular triangle,

Map VII **Medieval Kingston** is very apparent on this map of 1868, and much of the layout survives today round the Market Place – which must originally have included the smaller Apple Market to the east, until encroaching blocks of buildings separated the latter from the main market area. Clattern Bridge, over a tributary of the Thames to the south-west, still has medieval arches under the modern roadway.

with an islanded former town hall, Italianate of 1838, for some reason painted blue-grey (it is really of stock brick). The Georgian tower of the church (which has a fine medieval interior) rises behind the buildings on the north side. The buildings are a market-town miscellany – the best are Edwardian on the north-west corner. One built by Boots (they are no longer there) is a splendid neo-Tudor confection with statues illustrating Kingston's history; the other, to the left, over a modern shop and now brightly painted, was a fashionable restaurant built in 1901. In between, on the corner, is a building genuinely of *c.*1590 with wooden classical pilasters. The apex of the market place is presided over by the big rounded Guildhall of 1935 with a massive tower, complementing the church at the other end. In its forecourt, what is supposed to be the Saxon coronation stone is protected by fearsome Victorian railings which are more interesting to look at. Much more impressive is the small adjoining Clattern Bridge crossing the Hogsmill River, a tributary of the Thames; seen from the opposite side are the two original late twelfth-century stone arches, slightly pointed – it has been widened on the Guildhall side. Is this the oldest bridge in England? A little further to the east is the small, delightful Apple Market, a widening of a lane, linked by an alley to the market place. Undoubtedly the main market place originally extended to the Apple Market and the buildings between are an encroachment. A medieval vaulted undercroft has recently been discovered near the approach to Kingston Bridge.

Lewes

Sussex

Lewes is one of the most dramatic hill-towns in England. Its very name means hills. It developed where the River Ouse flows through a gap in the South Downs, making a fairly easy crossing for an ancient west-east track which may have followed the line of the High Street – to the south the river was wider and to the north was the Wealden forest. Its known history begins with King Alfred's establishment of a fortified *burh* in his campaign against the Danes. In the tenth century it was a money-making centre – King Athelstan allowed London eight mints, Canterbury seven, Winchester six, Rochester three, Lewes two and Hastings and Chichester one each; this gives an indication of Lewes' relative importance. After the Conquest Lewes came into the hands of William of Warenne, earl of Surrey and Sussex, who had estates at Reigate and elsewhere but made his chief stronghold here. He built the castle, of which the original keep – ruined but still impressive – survives, one of the first in England to be built of masonry (see colour illus. p. 71). With his wife Gundrada, reputedly a daughter of William the Conqueror, he founded a priory on the southern side of the town, a dependency of the great abbey of Cluny in Burgundy. The priory, one of the most magnificent in the south of England, was Henry III's headquarters on the eve of the Battle of Lewes, fought outside the town in 1264. At the Dissolution the priory came into the personal possession of Henry VIII's agent, Thomas Cromwell, who employed Italian engineers to destroy the church, and converted part of the domestic buildings into a house for his son. Lewes developed a strongly Protestant tradition, and was the scene of the burning of twelve martyrs from all over Sussex in Queen Mary's reign. In Stuart and early Georgian times the town thrived as the main market and social centre of eastern Sussex, with a maritime link down the Ouse to Newhaven – which was created as a port in the sixteenth century, after the harbour in the older town of Seaford had silted up. Georgian Lewes was the scene of lively political activity, following two very different tendencies. The Duke of Newcastle, a member of the Sussex-based Pelham family, made his town house in High Street into a political club, where Whig sympathisers met – the family controlled the election of M.P.s in five rotten boroughs – Lewes, Seaford,

39 *Above left* **House in High Street, Lewes,** by Amon Wilds, who built a great deal of Brighton; the 'ammonite' capital, based on fossilized shells, was his hallmark (page 31).

40 *Above right* **St Ann's Hill, Lewes,** at the top of High Street, showing flintwork treated in different ways.

Hastings, Rye and Winchelsea. Across the street, the White Hart was used for meetings by Thomas Paine, radical author of *The Rights of Man*, who lived in Lewes from 1768 until he went to America in support of the revolutionaries there.

In many ways Lewes was influential in the development of Brighton. Dr Russell publicized the fishing town as a place for bathing when he was in practice in Lewes. Thomas Kemp, developer of Kemp Town, was for long M.P. for Lewes, and owned the castle. The elder Amon Wilds, who built much of Brighton, began as a builder in Lewes. Lewes's building traditions, especially that of shallow bay windows rising through two or three storeys, and the use of black, often shiny, bricks and tiles, were related to those of Brighton. Conversely, Brighton had an effect on the way Lewes developed. By overshadowing it as the dominant commercial centre in the area, Brighton indirectly saved the centre of the old county town from large-scale development. Despite its prominence as a railway junction, Lewes grew little in or after Victorian times. Till recently it suffered from steadily increasing road traffic, but even that burden has been lightened since the by-pass was built.

Lewes High Street is one of the longest, least spoiled and variedly interesting of any small town in England. It descends, sometimes steeply, sometimes gradually, with gentle changes of direction and degrees of width, to the ancient crossing of the River Ouse. Coming from the west, it begins at St Anne's church, the best of six remaining from over twice that number which once existed. It descends, passing on the left a series of flint-faced houses where the flint is treated in several different ways – left rough, split or squared. Then, after a double twist, it reaches where the West Gate stood – Lewes, like many walled towns, grew very early outside its walls. Before the site of the gate there is a series of Georgian plastered fronts and then a timber-framed one, next to which Keere Street, a brick-paved lane, drops dramatically down to the right. Keere Street runs outside the line of the former town wall, which was behind the houses on the east; the wall seems to have been partly a flint facing on an earthern bank. Its line can be followed by going along Pope's Entry, a tiny alley leading off the other side of High Street, which becomes a footpath running along the worn-down bank, giving an exciting view of the castle. Back to High Street, there begins a particularly interesting series of buildings on both sides. On the right is one of the typical Lewes Georgian façades, with shallow bow windows, faced in red mathematical tiles imitating brick – those rounding the bows below the windows themselves could not possibly be of real brick. Beyond is a gabled timber-framed house, partly fifteenth- and sixteenth-century, where Thomas Paine lodged – he married the landlord's daughter. Many Lewes houses probably looked like this before they were replaced or refronted in Georgian times. Opposite is the fine-coursed flint-faced Georgian façade of St Michael's church, spoiled by intruding Victorian Gothic windows (inside, the church is partly medieval, and there is a round tower, roughcast over). Next to the church is a stuccoed house built in 1810 by Amon Wilds before he moved to Brighton, a forerunner of many he built there, showing the 'ammonite' capitals. The castle is reached by a side lane, alongside Barbican House, with a Georgian brick front, now the County Museum – where the father of T.R. Kemp, of Kemp Town, lived and which Kemp himself inherited. Next to it is the Barbican itself, the best preserved part of the castle, a splendid fourteenth-century gateway of flint, dressed in greenish sandstone. The romantically ruined keep rises to the left; the Georgian 'Gothick' windows in the walling between the keep and Barbican were inserted by the Kemps, who helped to preserve the castle from total disintegration.

The High Street frontages continue the splendid mixture of Georgian brick, stucco, tile-cladding and occasionally exposed timber-framing. Little lanes lead off to the south, plunging downhill and revealing chinks of countryside. The most remarkable is St Martin's Lane, passing between two buildings which have bland fronts to High Street but which reveal on their sides that they are jettied timber-framed buildings, that on the west preserving an original wood-framed Gothic window, against which the plausible date 1330 has been painted. Nearly opposite are three gabled merchants' houses hung with tiles in the Wealden tradition. Further on, in contrast, is Newcastle House, rebuilt by the county authorities in 1928, supposedly as a copy externally of the Duke of Newcastle's local house, but in Portland stone, matching the law courts of 1812 next door. It keeps its original staircase and other features inside. Opposite, Thomas Paine's White Hart now has a stuccoed front, added a little after his time. Here is the climax of the town. Looking up, High Street climbs and bends romantically out of sight; looking down, there is a steeper continuation called School Hill, with a piece of partly wooded, boldly rounded, downland closing the view in the background. In School Hill are several impressive Georgian houses, and a series of winding, partly flint-bound alleys lead off to the right beside some of them. Where the street flattens out – at the site of the East Gate – is a striking Gothic building of 1862, built to the design of Sir Gilbert Scott as a very early public library in memory of a local M.P. Here the street becomes

41 *Above left* **St Martin's Lane, Lewes,** on the corner with High Street, showing a genuine 14th-century Gothic window in wood; the Georgian house in the background has a front of mathematical tiles.

42 *Above right* **View of Lewes** over Southover Grange showing the castle keep, and the houses tumbling down the hillside.

busier commercially, and the shops continue across the Ouse bridge – with its glimpses of riverside warehouses and a towered Victorian brewery – into Cliffe High Street, the main street of what was a suburban village, with a pleasant variety of upper floors above the shops. Some are slate-hung – the slates must have been brought by ship from Devon to Newhaven. The townscape ends abruptly at the foot of the well-named Cliffe Hill.

Of comparable interest to the High Street proper, but on a smaller scale, is Southover High Street, in the low-lying land to the south. It can be reached past the station of 1889, with its multi-coloured façade and intricate roof, or, more romantically, down Keere Street and past Southover Grange, a house of 1572, much enlarged, the older parts built of creamy Caen stone taken from what was left of the priory. It is owned by the council, and from the far end of the well-maintained garden there is a view up to the backs of the houses on High Street, with the castle keep rearing behind. In Southover itself are Priory Crescent of 1835, the only formal urban composition in Lewes, and also Anne of Cleves House (her association was very tenuous), an attractive amalgam of Wealden-type building from the fifteenth to the seventeenth centuries, now an excellent museum. The chief landmark in Southover High Street is St John's church, with an old brick tower and partly Norman nave, which was converted from the early hospice at the gateway of the priory. In a Victorian side chapel is the carved black marble tombstone of Gundrada, Lady Warenne, co-founder of the priory; it was dug up on the priory site last century. Alas, the priory is reduced to a few flint walls and foundations; the most impressive standing wall is that of the reredorter or monks' lavatory (as we understand the word) – the holes in the wall were made to receive beams when the building was converted into a malthouse, and were not part of the drainage system.

Lymington

Hampshire

Lymington is traditionally the market town for the New Forest, but in origin it was a port, as it still is today – for the crossing to the Isle of Wight. But the present pier for the Island ships is on the other side of the harbour from the town, and thousands pass Lymington without seeing more of it than a view across the harbour – which is the tidal estuary of a small river flowing from the Forest. As a town it dates from around 1190–1200 when William de Redvers founded a new borough. The Redvers were earls of Devon and lords of the Isle of Wight; they were also overlords of Christchurch. They founded new boroughs on either side of the shortest crossing to the Island – at Yarmouth as well as Lymington – and William's predecessor, Richard de Redvers, founded Newport near his castle at Carisbrooke (page 91). Medieval Lymington developed wider trade; it imported wine and exported cloth from Salisbury, but in this respect it was insignificant compared with Southampton. But the area was very important for salt production from the Middle Ages until the early nineteenth century; sea water was impounded near the coast, allowed to evaporate partially in the sun, and then, as brine, boiled in metal-lined containers fuelled with wood or, later, coal brought coastwise. Shipbuilding was an old-established industry, and specifically yacht-building began in the early nineteenth century; now Lymington is a major centre for pleasure boating. It was already a favourite place of residence for the retired, or those of private means, in the eighteenth century, which partly explains the number of fine Georgian houses.

Apart from the harbourside, old Lymington is nearly all one long street. From the open quay a narrow street leads to the lowest part of the main street, Quay Hill, self-consciously pretty with cobbles, and some fine bow windows. The High Street was almost certainly laid out at the foundation of the town. It is a classic example of a medieval market street – broad to accommodate the stalls, and with a pattern of deep house plots, still very evident (though they vary in width) on either side. It climbs steadily at first, then levels off. The gradient has been lowered towards the top of the slope, leaving pavements on either side following the original levels, to very good effect. Until 1855 a market hall stood in the street just at the brow; now the wide street continues uninterrupted to the church, which comes into view as one reaches the flatter stretch. Lymington should be seen on Saturday – market day. The stalls are still disposed along the street as they have been since the thirteenth century, though they are now only one deep – possibly there were more rows in the past. Architecturally the street is a pleasant medley in style and scale. Nothing obvious survives from before the late seventeenth century, though there may be older structures behind façades. As in most streets of medieval origin, every plot has its own particular building history, and in Lymington it is specially rewarding to follow the sequences on either side of the street. Many of the buildings are two-storeyed and modest, but some of the Georgian ones are grander, of three storeys or even more. They nearly all have shops in the ground floors – some are fairly intrusive, but a few are attractive, notably No. 41/2 with its Victorian ironwork. The Angel hotel has a first-floor iron balcony, and so has a bank. Many upper storeys have Georgian bow windows; in Lymington flat-fronted ones with canted sides are more common than rounded ones. The finest range of Georgian fronts, mostly in deep red brick but with one, the tallest, in yellow bricks from Beaulieu, is on the north side towards the church, which closes the view along the street splendidly. It began as a chapel-of-ease to the nearby church at Boldre, and some medieval work survives in the eastern parts. The plain tower of white Purbeck stone, with a later cupola, was built in 1670 and resembles that of Portsmouth Cathedral. The nave interior is surprising, with classical columns and galleries, looking something like a theatre – the result of successive alterations in the Georgian period. Amazingly, there was a pre-war plan to Gothicize it all. The street swings south of the church past a late seventeenth-century house called Monmouth House (there was much local support here for the rebel Duke, who is said to have been proclaimed

43 **High Street, Lymington** on market day – the wide street was laid out about 1200 to accommodate markets like this.

king by the local people, in his absence, in the High Street). Looking back along the street, the descending view is closed by an obelisk rising among the trees across the estuary. This was erected in 1840 to commemorate Admiral Burrard Neale, M.P. for the borough, which had sent members since 1584, when the right was conferred by Queen Elizabeth, as at Haslemere. The Burrards, who lived in Walhampton House, usually controlled the voting up to the time of the first Reform Act.

Maidstone

Kent

Maidstone became the county town of Kent because of its focal position: it is much more central than the ancient capital, Canterbury. But it took a long time to become important. In Norman times it was a village, and does not seem to have gained a market until 1261. From then it grew prosperous, due to its position at the effective head of navigation on the River Medway. All sorts of products from the surrounding area were dispatched by water from here, or from quays a little downstream. There was ragstone, quarried extensively south of the town and shipped to London for building. Agricultural produce including fruit and later hops, together with timber from the Weald, were similarly sent down the Medway and then up the Thames. The presence of deposits of fuller's earth, used in the last process of clothmaking, stimulated a weaving industry: cloths were treated in numerous fulling mills along the Loose and Len streams, tributaries of the Medway. Refugees from Flanders and Wallonia after 1560 stimulated the cloth industry, but later the town came to specialize in the making of linen thread, using locally grown flax. Paper mills were opened from the seventeenth century onwards, using the waters of the Len and Loose for both processing and power. Other industries developed in the nineteenth and twentieth centuries which, together with modern county administration and a major shopping centre, continue to make Maidstone a busy place. Traffic is a terrible problem; the motorway bypass has not taken off the traffic in other directions, which continues to thread through the town. But, despite roaring roads and some crude redevelopment, Maidstone has not yet lost the feeling of being an important historic town.

Maidstone was a manor of the Archbishops of Canterbury one of whom, William Courtenay, refounded the parish church as a collegiate church, served by priests who lived in a college to the south. The church was rebuilt grandly, though plainly, from 1395, and next to it Courtenay extended the old manor house into a palace for periodic occupation. This survives, as altered by lay owners after the Reformation and restored in the present century (see colour illus. p.106), overlooking the Medway and making an impressive picture with the church; both are built in creamy grey ragstone. Parts of the college buildings remain to the south, put to various uses. Nearby, but separated by a hideously busy road, is the finest building of the group, the archbishops' former stables, shaped like a great stone-walled barn but with a timber-framed storey over the entrance porch. Inside it is two-storeyed, with the fine original roof timbers visible on the upper floor, where forage and stores would have been kept. It now houses, quite suitably, a splendid collection of historic carriages; both building and contents deserve to be better known. The centre of Maidstone is the High Street, originally a broad thoroughfare leading up from the river, probably laid out in the thirteenth century when the town started to develop. In course of time an island block encroached on the middle part, separating the narrow Bank Street from High Street proper. Bank Street has a fascinating series of altered timber-framed buildings, including No. 78 with pargetting (plasterwork in relief) on the first floor – a practice usually associated with East Anglia but found also at Canterbury (page 40). The date 1611 appears on the plasterwork, and this could go also with the broad window with its arched central part, typical of merchants' houses of the period. The upper storeys were

44 **Bank Street, Maidstone,** the narrow street separated from the main High Street by an island block of buildings on the left. The tall building with Georgianized upper storeys has 17th-century pargetting – or plasterwork in relief – on the first floor. The high-rise building in the background depresses the scale of this range of variously altered timber-framed houses.

re-formed in Georgian times, with plain plastering and sashes.

The wide top of High Street, above where Bank Street merges with it, is in effect a town square. The pleasant brick and stone town hall of 1763, a larger version of Reigate's, ends the island block, and on the north side are an elaborate bank of 1909, and the handsome stone classical façade of an insurance office built in 1827. The architect of the latter was the locally based John Whichcord. His son, who had a national practice, designed the Grand Hotel at Brighton (page 30) and also the extraordinary building of 1855 on the opposite side of the street, which has iron framing on the first floor, with a frilly ironwork frieze and green decorative tiling. Alas, the effect of what was an interesting little square has been shattered by a crude multi-storey block which was allowed to close the view up High Street in the 1960s. A footway leads north from High Street, past a group of Victorian former market buildings, with ground-floor arcades, attractively brought out in strong colours, and past a little red-brick Unitarian chapel of 1736, into Earl Street, another wide street with a typical Maidstone mixture of buildings of all periods, attractive or otherwise. There is a similar mixture in the much narrower Gabriel's Hill and its continuation Stone Street, leading south from the top of High Street. There is a great deal else in Maidstone – the museum, the spreading county buildings, the lively market (held on open ground across the river). With its mixture of the mellowed and the brash the town can be stimulating, but very often it is exasperating.

Midhurst

Sussex

Midhurst is a fascinating town (provided one keeps to the right parts), set in a hummocky vale between the sandstone hills to the north and the chalk downs to the south – although in its buildings it belongs to the sand and clay country rather than the chalk. 'Few towns are more deceptive', wrote Ian Nairn in his part of Pevsner's *Sussex*: 'few towns withhold themselves so firmly until the traveller gets out of his car and on to his feet'. Midhurst was an offshoot, a chapelry, of adjoining Easebourne, but became a market town in the early thirteenth century, when its overlord built a small castle on a hillock ('hurst' usually means wooded hill), now called St Ann's Hill, east of the church. This is a good place, in fine weather, to begin a walk of the town; although there are no evident traces of the castle there is a view through the trees to the ruin of its magnificent Tudor successor, Cowdray – described at the end of this section. A lane leads down from the hill to the complicated centre of the town. Originally there was a roughly square market place south of the church, but encroachments and infillings have turned it into an intricate pattern of small spaces and connecting lanes. Looking from the churchyard south there is a substantial early Georgian house, in red brick with pale brick pilasters; on its right is the engaging former market hall, two-gabled, timber-framed, brick-filled; its ground floor was once open. Now it is an annexe to the adjoining Spread Eagle Hotel. To the left is the plain Georgian-fronted old town hall (its core is earlier), where the county quarter sessions were sometimes held, and the members for the parliamentary borough (which Midhurst was till 1832) were elected by the few qualified voters; one of the members was the Whig Charles James Fox. Behind this are several Georgian houses in various shades of brick, facing lanes or little spaces. The church is picturesque outside, partly due to a restoration of 1882 when the pencil-point top was added to the tower. Church Hill to the west is a pleasant wide street, funnelling northward, but has far too much traffic, moving and parked. It narrows, then turns left into Knockhundred Row; the buildings by the bend have the essence of Midhurst – especially the former row of cottages now the public library, with sinuous roof, tile-hung upper storey, brick, timbered and sandstone lower storey (alas partly whitened), and an odd assortment of windows. Even more engaging is Wool Lane, one of a network of alleys further west, with a range of jettied timber-framed cottages where the upper floors are in succession plastered, exposed with timbers blackened (not of course a tradition here), and tile-hung (very much a local tradition). But it is distressing to find, round the corner in West Street, that the tile-hanging on a pub has actually been painted white.

The long wide North Street, which many think is the main part of the town, is not specially interesting, but is worth walking down. At the bottom is the former Grammar School, which was founded in 1672, reached a peak (or plateau) in the early nineteenth century, was closed for a time, then re-opened; H.G. Wells, while his mother was at neighbouring Uppark, became an assistant teacher through the benevolence of the headmaster. Its best building is set back in a yard, a severe classical schoolhouse, in yellow brick, of 1821. Opposite, behind a car park, is the entrance to Cowdray. The mansion was first built by Sir David Owen, supposedly a son of Owen Glendower, and completed by Sir William

45 **Timber-framed buildings at Midhurst.** The near building, the former market hall, has brick nogging, partly diagonal; the middle one has a plastered jettied front; the distant gabled building has had its frontage painted, untraditionally, in black and white.

46 **Wool Lane, Midhurst,** one of the town's many unexpected lanes; the scaled tile-hanging of the jettied frontage is typical of the Wealden area.

FitzWilliam who bought it in 1529. He became Earl of Southampton in 1537 – but should not be confused with the unrelated and slightly later Earl of Southampton, of Titchfield Abbey (page 135). Later it passed to the Brownes, Viscounts Montagu, appropriators of Battle Abbey (page 17) till the last of their line was drowned in Germany in 1793 – a short time after the house was destroyed by fire – the two events legendarily fulfilling a curse made by the last abbot of Battle that his family and inheritance would perish by fire and water. But the legend may have arisen after the events. Cowdray is now a splendid ruin – enough of the shell is left to make it fine architecture, and it is ruined enough to be romantic. Ian Nairn, again, has the right words: 'an . . . epitome of Tudor architecture at its plainest and most sober, very English in its understatement, its dignity and concern for volumes and solidity'. (*Buildings of England: Sussex*).

Milton Regis

Kent

Milton Regis is now one town with Sittingbourne, which is dominant. But Milton was formerly more important – it was a royal possession when Kent was a separate kingdom, and, like Faversham, was a coastal port at the head of a creek. Sittingbourne, a medieval village on Watling Street, grew into a town in the coaching era, and expanded in Victorian times through brick-making – many of the buff stock bricks of which so much of London was built came from round about. Now the chief industry is paper-making. The very industrialized area between the centres of the two towns does not prepare one for the uncannily well-preserved Milton Regis High Street. This twists and rises to the brow of a broad hillock, lined largely with fifteenth- to seventeenth-century timber-framed houses, concealed to varying degrees with plaster, weatherboarding or Georgian brick façades. The most striking are a pair including the post office and High House with restored, though basically original, timber-framing to a geometrical pattern reminiscent of the Welsh border (as at Godalming and elsewhere, page 68). Further on is the recently restored late fifteenth-century Court House, a good example of a type of building of which few other examples survive in the south-east; the market halls of Titchfield, now in the Weald and Downland Museum (page 136) and Faversham are related, but have open-sided ground storeys; that at Milton was always enclosed. Beyond, housing estates extend to the distant parish church which marks the site, no doubt, of the original settlement which is recorded as having been sacked by the Vikings about 890 and by the rebel Earl Godwin in 1052. Quite probably the town was resited where the High Street is after the latter event. The church is mainly thirteenth and fourteenth centuries with a massive tower, but the north wall is basically Saxon, suggesting that there was a sizeable church here before Godwin's sack.

The town centre of Sittingbourne, despite battering, still has Georgian gems. There are striking red-brick façades over modern shop fronts, some of them once belonging to inns. Two impressive houses, both bow-fronted, retain their façades intact: one, Brenchley House, is dark-tiled, the other, No. 92, has its bow windows nearly continuously glazed with threefold sashes, under elliptical hoods, making a charming interplay of curves. This must once have been a handsome street.

Newport

Isle of Wight

Newport, the chief town on the Isle of Wight, was founded about 1180 by Richard de Redvers, a member of the powerful family who were also earls of Devon, and became lords of the Isle in 1100. Their stronghold was Carisbrooke Castle, an originally Norman castle on the site of a Roman fort. Carisbrooke, now a village on the outskirts of Newport, was the original chief place of the Island, but had the disadvantage of being nearly a mile from the head of the estuary of the River Medina where was the nearest quay – a specially important facility on an island. Newport was focused on that quay, with a complicated street pattern which largely survives. There is a rough grid of streets, including High Street running east-west, together with a diagonal street, Quay Street, leading north-eastwards to the quay. There were two market places, St Thomas' Square, originally rectangular, and St James' Square, which was a widening of one of the north-south streets. Although preserving its medieval layout, Newport has no medieval buildings, and very few from before the eighteenth century. Almost all that matter are Georgian and Victorian. They are nearly all classical – there are no Gothic fancies except the church – but immensely varied in detail and colouring. A few are of Island stone, some are stuccoed, but most are of brick. There

Map VIII **Newport**, the chief town of the Isle of Wight, was founded in about 1180 by the lord of nearby Carisbrooke Castle. It has a loose grid of streets, with one leading diagonally to the quay on the River Medina, and two market places, the larger containing the church. The map is of 1863.

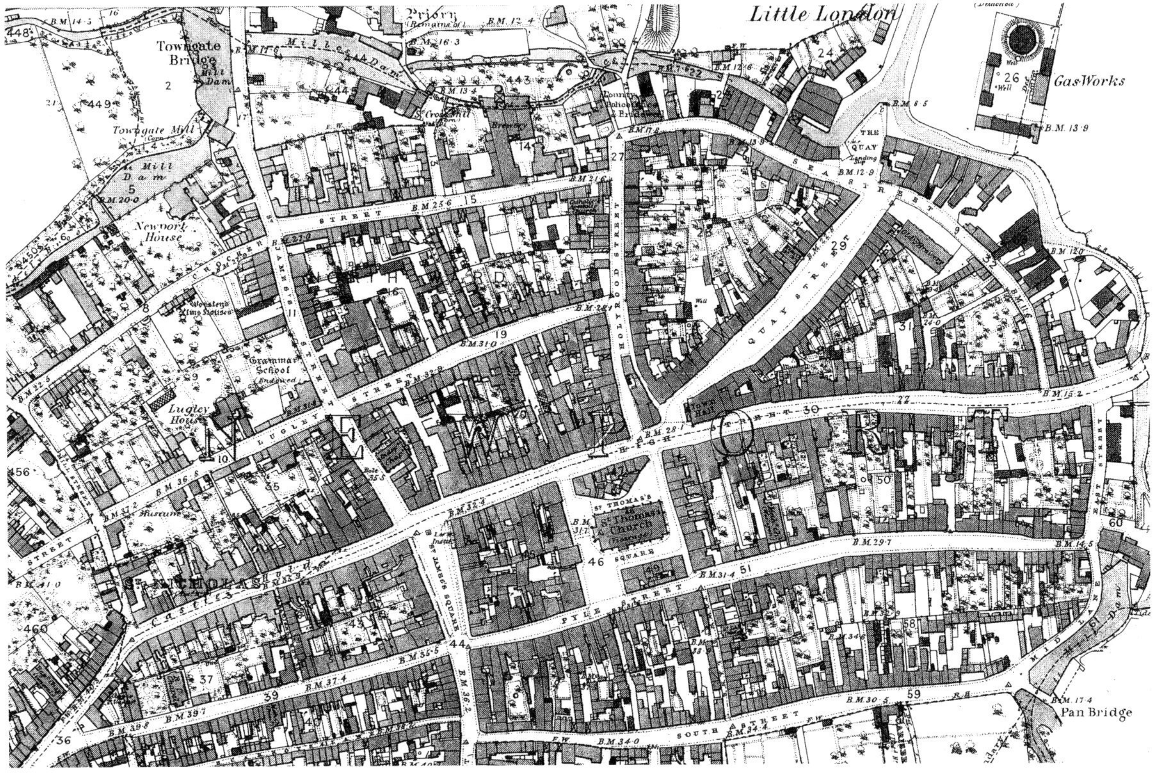

is a great variety of clays suitable for brick-making on the Island, and this is reflected in Newport's buildings. Many are of dark red bricks; a large number are of rich purplish-greys, with red-brick dressings; some are built of bricks which are individually mottled; many are of buffs and browns fashionable in the early nineteenth century. There is a fair number of bay windows; some are rounded, more are flat-fronted and canted, and a few are of a special local type with flat fronts and curved ends. Because of the shops along the main streets, a large proportion of the old façades survive on the upper storeys only.

A good place to start is St James' Square, a broadening street, focused on a florid memorial to Queen Victoria, lady of the Island. The dominating building is the County Club, built as the Literary Institute in 1810, to the design of John Nash – he, like the Queen later, had his retreat on the Island, at Cowes. It is one of Nash's most sober buildings, of white stone, with a pedimented upper storey projecting over the pavement on open arches. Round the corner is a long vista along High Street, with just enough minute changes on its medieval frontage to make it notably more interesting than an absolutely straight street would be. Its landmark, part of the way along, is the Guildhall, also by Nash, this time of stucco, its columns standing free in front of an open gallery, with another arched passage below. To it the loyal islanders added a Diamond Jubilee Tower in 1897, upsetting the balance of the building but providing a marvellous landmark in High Street. The Guildhall is at a complicated meeting of streets; Quay Street leads diagonally off, and opposite there is an opening into St Thomas' Square. What was originally a rectangular market place was encroached first by the original church (a chapelry of Carisbrooke), dedicated to the newly martyred St Thomas, then by islanded blocks of buildings replacing market stalls. This has resulted in a small but subtle central space with lanes and passages leading off, dominated by the present St Thomas' – an assertive rebuilding of 1855 by the architect Samuel Daukes, of rough stone with finer dressings and a tall and very successful tower which culminates in a corner pinnacle. Enough of the buildings around are pleasantly small and simply classical to provide excellent foils to the church, as well as define the spaces effectively; the most distinctive is God's Providence House of 1701, with a later Georgian shop front and a shell-hooded doorway on a side lane. Quay Street is impressive but battered; it widens as it goes down to the quay, beside varied classical façades, many in purply brick. It used to end with warehouses, but now there is an open view to the estuary. A few years ago this was a marvellous area with a series of warehouses, individually gabled, in various bricks and stones, abutting on to small inlets formed by tributary streams. Most have gone; those that remain are distinctive, with round-headed windows containing iron grills. There is – or was – a great deal more in other streets; despite erosion in the 1960s and 70s, Newport is still a town of great character, even if not appreciated enough.

Newtown

Isle of Wight

Newtown is a town that came to nothing, except as an attractive hamlet. It was founded on a creek off the north coast of the Isle of Wight in 1255 by a Bishop of Winchester – one of the see's many ventures in town-building on their lands. Because of its potential strategic importance, Edward I took it over as a royal borough in 1284. The French sacked it in 1377, and it never recovered; Newport proved a better site as the *entrepôt* for the Island. Traces of the layout survive – there were two long, slightly curving parallel streets, and two wider cross streets which contained the markets. Only parts of these are preserved as thoroughfares in the present scattered hamlet of partly stone-built houses; some of the others are represented by rough lanes. A small church with plaster-vaulted interior, by Augustus Livesay who designed Andover church (page 15), was built in 1835 on the site of the medieval church, which had fallen to ruin. More poignant is the little Georgian town hall of brick and stone, standing in a green space which had been one of the market places. The town had already nearly vanished when it was built – it was simply the base for the spectral borough corporation, and the place where the very few qualified voters cast their votes in this supremely rotten borough until the Reform Act of 1832.

Odiham

Hampshire

Odiham is an old market town which the railway missed, and which failed to grow in Victorian times. Only very recently have pressures for large-scale development started to build up in what is now a vulnerable corner of Hampshire. It has a long main street of varying width – broadening, narrowing, climbing, flattening – and the predominant material is, or was, Georgian brick of a warm rich red, but, unfortunately, too many of the brick façades have been painted over. Many of the buildings are, as usual, older behind the façades, and it seems that brick nogging (brick infilling within timber framework) began early here, as in some other parts of Hampshire. Narrower streets lead south towards an irregular space, The Bury, beside the church, which is a big medieval building altered in the seventeenth century, when the top of the tower with its decorative brickwork was built. Two stained glass windows by the artist Patrick Reyntiens, who lived in the town, are in deep vivid colours, and the one representing the Tree of Jesse, with its blues and yellows, is haunting. Behind the church are simple seventeenth-century almshouses, with an impressive range of brick chimneys. Two odd minor features on the southern outskirts of the town are the cemetery chapels, one for Anglicans, one for Nonconformists, built about 1860, with striking conical roofs, supported inside by intricate timbering.

Petersfield

Hampshire

Petersfield is a market town *par excellence* – one of the few in the region with a rectangular market place which has not been infilled by permanent buildings, and where open markets are still held twice a week. The town seems to have been founded around the middle of the twelfth century by one of the powerful earls of Gloucester, whose estates were mainly in the west but who controlled the local manor – to a street plan still recognizable as regular, though subtle. The church stands to the south of the market place, with a fairly tame exterior that belies the magnificence of part of the interior. Its early history is a great puzzle; at first it was a mere dependency, or chapelry, to the parish church of nearby Buriton. Yet it was started very ambitiously, in about 1120, with a central crossing space which would have been comparable in style to, though smaller in scale than, that of Winchester Cathedral. The church was never finished to the first grand design; the rest of the building, where not restored, is more modest, though still impressive, later twelfth-century work. There is no documentary – only architectural – evidence for the origin of the church, but it may have been started by Robert Earl of Gloucester, bastard son of Henry I, and finished under his son William who inherited the estates in 1147 and is usually thought to have founded the town. But if so, why start a church so ambitiously before there was a proper town?

Map IX **Petersfield** developed in the 12th century. It has an interesting plan, seen on this map of 1870, with a diagonal street linking two squares, one still the market place, the other (The Spain) now a pleasant green.

In the middle of the square there is a splendid statue of William III, commissioned in 1757 (long after his death) by a local Whig resident whose family controlled the voting in what was then a rotten borough. Otherwise the interest of the square is accentuated at the corners, where streets lead off. At the north-west corner the outgoing road bends past a fine Georgian house with a stone doorcase, now a bank, and a timber-framed house with, unusually, flint 'nogging', or infilling in the timber framework. To the south-west is a recent group of buildings, including the public library, with a bizarre skyline, taking the corner with Sheep Street, which leads, past timber-framed houses, into The Spain. This was originally a second market place, rectangular in shape, which long since reverted to grass and now looks like a charming village green, intersected by roads, and surrounded by a variety of buildings, Georgian and earlier, some urbane, some rustic. There is an attractive view back along Sheep Street, which links the two squares diagonally. In the remaining old streets of Petersfield, which form a rough grid, the many interesting buildings tend to be dispersed, not concentrated in groups, as in Dragon Street and its northward continuation College Street which still (until a bypass is built)

take the main traffic from Portsmouth to London, as they have since coaching days. The Red Lion is an old coaching inn, with broad bow windows, which lighted an assembly room on the upper floor. An antique shop in Dragon Street has a fine Georgian shop front in a stuccoed façade incised to resemble stonework, and Dragon House opposite has a typical southern Hampshire façade of blue-grey brick, with red brick round the window openings. The Old College is a splendid brick-fronted house of 1729 which housed Churcher's College, founded by an East India merchant, before it moved to Victorian buildings further north. These are only a few of the attractive buildings dispersed along Petersfield's streets. There is a visual climax where two churches adjoin, in striking stylistic as well as sectarian contrast; the Methodist one has a commanding Gothic steeple of 1903 in dark flint profusely interspersed with red brick; the Catholic one of 1891 has a copper-clad dome. Both are seen briefly together, as an improbable exotic group, from trains on their way to Portsmouth. The street south from here, Chapel Street, leads to the part of Petersfield which developed after the railway opened in 1859, with a charming row of Victorian gables over the shop fronts.

Petworth

Sussex

Petworth is a town in compression. It is pressed against the forbidding wall of its great house; it occupies no more space than a fair-sized village, but with the narrowness of its streets, and the density of its buildings, it seems what Ian Nairn called a 'miniature city'. The manor came to the Percys, already famous in the north, in the thirteenth century. The Percy heiress married the overbearing Duke of Somerset in 1684. He built the present House, turning its back on the town; he pulled down town houses and diverted streets west of the church, and erected the present boundary wall, with its many right angles, which shuts off the town from the House. A later owner, the third Earl of Egremont, who died in 1837, was by contrast supremely outgoing. He patronized the arts, building up the existing sculpture collection, and commissioned Turner to paint the park, by then remodelled by Capability Brown; he was a benefactor to the town. The National Trust has owned the house since 1947.

The best place to start a necessarily intricate walk in the town is the church, a much more rewarding building than is often said: thirteenth and fourteenth centuries, remodelled for the Earl of Egremont in 1827 by Barry who added a fine spire – which was demolished in 1947 as unsafe; the present termination of the still tall tower is ugly but assertive. Inside, the church was redecorated after 1900; the effect is pleasantly colourful, in contrast to the puritan whitening which has smothered so many other church interiors lately. Of the monuments, the most striking is to Sir John Dawtrey who died in 1542 – he was the customs collector at Southampton who remodelled Tudor House there (page 130). In the little space south of the church, shapefully irregular, but bedevilled by traffic, is a convoluted lamp standard of thin writhing ironwork, designed by Barry. Down the narrow, cobbled, picture-book Lombard Street we turn, quite casually, into the confined Market Square. This is dominated by a vigorous baroque bank of 1901, but centred on the blander town hall of 1793. A narrow street leads down to Golden Square (which in fact was the meat market), where a patrician Georgian house faces a perky Victorian Congregational chapel. From here the narrow High Street leads eastward into Grove Street, with Middle Street turning north. All these are fronted with the closely woven ribbons of building which form much of the fabric of Petworth – mainly modest, often of golden-brown sandstone, with timber showing in some of the older examples, and a good deal of tile; there is a particularly picturesque tile-hung group on the curved corner of Grove Street and Middle Street. Here and there are grander, often Georgian, houses – especially in East Street, where Daintrey House is almost a country house in town, set behind a lovely fence of thin ironwork with intersecting wavy lines. Traffic conditions should not deter a walk along North Street where a single, long and varied line of houses faces, across the appalling traffic, the wall of the park (the Duke of Somerset pulled down the whole of the opposite side of the street when he enlarged the park). The gems of North Street are Somerset Hospital and Somerset Lodge, both mid-seventeenth century (and hence preceding the Duke). The first is of brick and stone; the second is a lovely thing, built of large, roughly coursed, stone blocks, with mullioned windows and curving gables, looking like a prosperous weaver's house of the period in the Yorkshire Pennines. It was derelict for a time, and saved only after long public protest. Nearly opposite is a devious public access, through a service yard, into the park, whose expansive eighteenth-century landscape is in wonderful contrast with the intricacy of the town.

Portsmouth
Hampshire

Portsmouth has its roots in the Middle Ages, though it did not become really important till Georgian times. Even in its natural state the harbour was ideal for anchorage. At first the main settlement was Portchester on the northern shore, where the Roman fort was turned into a Norman castle. About 1180 a small town was founded at the mouth of the harbour by John de Gisors, also lord of the manor of Titchfield. He rebelled against Richard I, who took over the youthful town and re-founded it as a royal borough in 1194. For a time the town did not fulfil its first promise and was overshadowed by Southampton. But the harbour was used from time to time for the assembly of ships against the French – who retaliated by sacking the town several times. The original town – the present Old Portsmouth – stands at one corner of Portsea Island, which is about four miles from north to south and is separated from the mainland at its northern end by a narrow creek.

Henry VII built a dry dock on the edge of the harbour, near where HMS *Victory* now is. Henry VIII built Southsea Castle on the coast outside the town, and nearby the *Mary Rose* sank in a skirmish with the French and Spanish in 1545. But for some time Portsmouth was less important as a naval base than the dockyards nearer to London – first Deptford, then Chatham. It started to develop significantly under Charles I, and still more after the Restoration. The dockyard expanded steadily through the eighteenth century and became, with those at Chatham and Devonport, one of the largest centres of employment in Britain, until overtaken by some of the great factories of the early nineteenth century. In the Napoleonic Wars Portsmouth really came into its own, and it is fitting that the city's historic centrepiece should be HMS *Victory*, berthed in a dock built three years before the battle of Trafalgar, and adjoining naval buildings of slightly earlier date. After the defeat of Napoleon there was a local lull, but in the 1840s the Dockyard expanded again, to provide for the age of steam. There was further expansion in the 1870s, culminating in the Edwardian era when huge battleships were built there. Meanwhile Portsmouth expanded from a town into a large city.

As the Dockyard is the reason for the city's being, it is described first, followed by the military defences and then the more interesting parts of the city, under these headings: *The Dockyard, The Defences, Old Portsmouth, The City Centre, Southsea.*

The Dockyard

The Dockyard has always been apart from the old and the modern centres of Portsmouth. It lay to the north of the old town from which it was separated, until the nineteenth century, by an inlet. Not until Georgian times did the area immediately adjoining the Dockyard become densely developed with streets – forming the district called Portsea. Nothing is left of Henry VII's dry dock, and the Great Stone Dock of 1691–8, the first of the recognizably modern docks, was completely altered in the 1760s and later, as No. 5 Dock. The earliest buildings, of which none survive, were of timber. From the 1760s there was continuous new building and replacement, at first using deep red local brick, then (after 1800) usually yellow brick. After 1840 there was a reversion to red brick, and buildings were erected on an even grander scale.

Visitors to HMS *Victory* and the associated museum pass three great

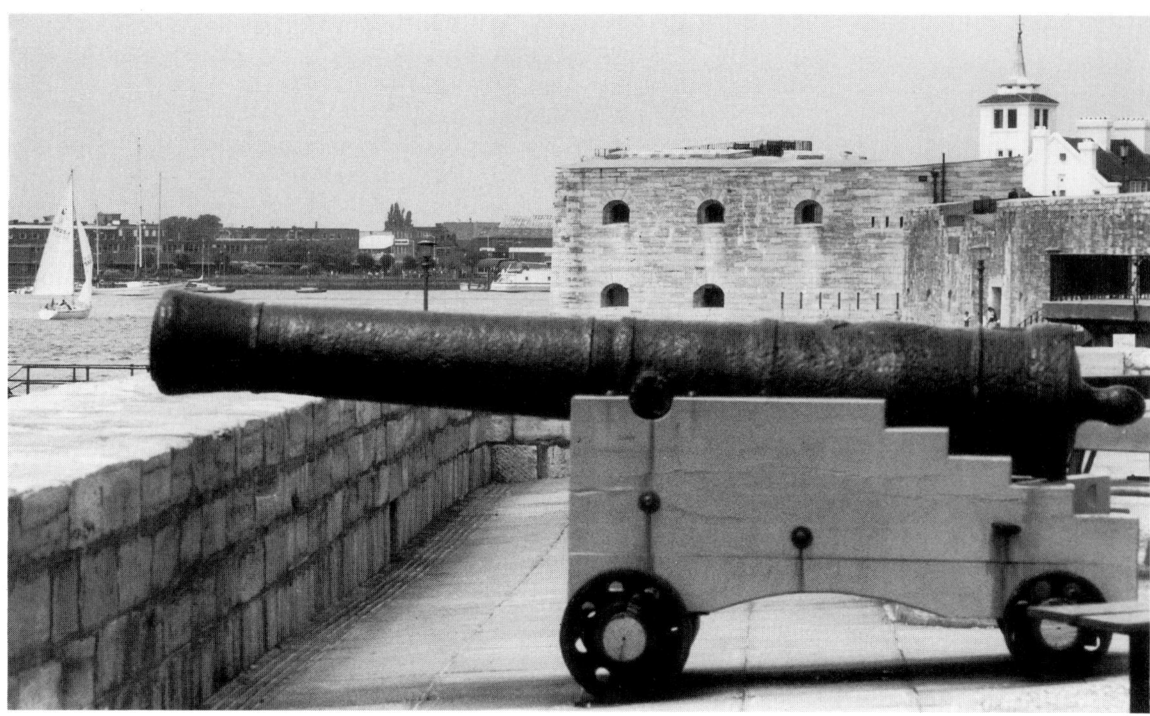

47 Eighteen Gun Battery, Portsmouth, part of the old town's defences, remodelled in the mid-19th century from the 17th-century originals.

former storehouses, dating from 1782, 1776 and 1763 (going from south to north), to handsome classical designs, almost as if they were austere country houses; the inset passageways are part of the recent conservation scheme. Opposite the middle store is the end of the very long former Rope House, built in 1770 and burnt out six years later by Jack the Painter – a saboteur who sympathized with the rebelling American colonists, who had set fire to buildings elsewhere, and who was eventually hanged from the tallest mast available, in the Dockyard. Ropes ceased to be made there in 1868, and it was further adapted after the second world war. There are many other fine Georgian buildings out of sight of the usual visitors' route to the right, including what was originally the Royal Naval Academy, built in 1732 (the oldest building in the Dockyard), St Ann's church of 1786, and Admiralty House by Samuel Wyatt, the residence of the commander-in-chief. But the centrepiece is HMS *Victory*. She was built at Chatham in 1759–65, altered in 1800–3, and restored recently to the state in which she fought at Trafalgar. She is berthed in a stone-lined dock dating from 1801, one of a series then being built (incorporating the older Great Stone Dock) under the engineer Sir Samuel Bentham, brother of the political philosopher Jeremy Bentham, who had previously served in Catherine the Great's Russia and designed a new dockyard there. There is something particularly poignant about the great ship, built in timber following traditions of construction which did not change in essentials since the late Middle Ages, being berthed in a dock which was an early product of the age of technology. (Some will find it even more poignant that the remains of the *Mary Rose* are placed in an adjoining, similar, dock.) Bentham also built, in 1800, the Block Mills, unremarkable as a building but the scene of very important developments in technological history. Marc Isambard Brunel, originally a French naval officer who fled from the French Revolution and worked in New York for several years, came to England in 1801 – primarily, it is said, to marry Sophia Kingdom whom he met while still in France; it was a propitious marriage, for their son was the great Isambard Kingdom Brunel, born in Portsmouth in 1806 (in a house which no longer survives). Brunel worked under Bentham, in collaboration with another engineer, Henry Maudslay, in designing machinery, first installed in the Block Mills in 1802, for the making of pulley blocks. These, which took the strain of ropes in rigging, were of immense importance to the Navy and had previously been hand-made by an outside contractor. Brunel's machinery was steam-driven, and is said to have been the first in the world to mass-produce small components such as these. Some of the machinery is in the Science Museum in London; some is still *in situ*, but the Block Mills are not normally open to the public.

Despite this advance in the making of components, the Navy was at first very reluctant to adapt to steam propulsion or iron construction in the building of ships; there were, admittedly, technical difficulties in using coal-fired engines in long-distance vessels, which applied equally to civilian shipping. It was not until after 1860 that the Navy turned entirely to steam-driven, metal-built ships. But the Dockyard was greatly enlarged from the 1840s with buildings on a grand scale. The most magnificent is the one now called No. 2 Ship Shop, of 1848, designed by a Royal Engineer called Captain Sir William Denison. Outwardly it is one of the finest industrial buildings ever erected, with its round-arched openings and frieze of white Portland stone contrasting with the deep red brick of the walls. Unfortunately this, and other smaller but impressive Victorian buildings in similar style are in the part of the Dockyard seldom accessible to visitors.

Little is left of the Georgian dockyard workers' district of Portsea outside the gate – a scatter of bow-windowed houses, a pleasant church of 1754 (St George's), and an interesting early charitable school building of 1784, the former Beneficial School in King Street. Facing the Hard, near where the ferries to the Isle of Wight and Gosport depart, is a lively row of Victorian and Edwardian buildings in a variety of styles, many of them pubs.

Defences

In Portsmouth and Southampton together we can cover almost the whole history of defensive building up to the age of air attack – Southampton for its medieval walls (page 129), the Portsmouth area with Roman and medieval Portchester, the seventeenth- and eighteenth-century town defences, and the great Victorian forts. Portchester Castle, now within Portsmouth's suburban fringes, began as one of the Roman forts built in defence against Saxons and other barbarians, as at Pevensey, Richborough near Sandwich, Dover (page 56) and Lympne, west of Hythe. The outside walls of the fort survive almost entire, the highest Roman walls remaining above ground in northern Europe. Into one corner were built a Norman keep, also well-preserved, and a small inner bailey with the remains of royal apartments, used on occasions when there were rallyings of ships in the harbour. Also, just outside the fortress, the mainly Georgian village street of Portchester remains remarkably unspoiled at its southern end.

Southsea Castle was one of several coastal forts built by Henry VIII from Kent to Cornwall; it was less elaborate than the slightly later one at Deal (page 55), and its low central keep looks remarkably like medieval precursors. It was reconstructed in the seventeenth and, more thoroughly, the early nineteenth centuries, and is now a museum illustrating Portsmouth's defensive history. Nearby is the new purpose-built D-Day Museum.

The town of (Old) Portsmouth was defended only rudimentarily in the Middle Ages; it had nothing like the walls of Southampton. Medieval stone walls generally became obsolete with the development of cannon, and by the sixteenth century new forms of town defence were developed, including low, broad earthworks with projections, or bastions, at intervals, and moats. Both Berwick-on-Tweed and Portsmouth were fortified under Queen Elizabeth I in this way, and became the only towns in England, except possibly Plymouth, to be so defended. Because Britain, as an island, was free from continental-scale wars, the medieval walls of most other towns were not then kept in good repair, let alone improved (though some were hastily strengthened in the Civil War). This was in great contrast to the Continent with its almost endemic warfare, where most towns of any importance had to be elaborately fortified, following the new principles which were developed further by military engineers, of whom the most famous was the Frenchman, Vauban. Portsmouth, however, was of great strategic importance, and from 1665 its town defences were entirely remodelled, in the manner of Vauban, under the king's engineer-in-chief, Sir Bernard de Gomme. As modified in the eighteenth century they survived till 1870. They consisted of broad grassed ramparts with arrow-headed bastions at intervals, and a moat which contained further defensive works; beyond that was a series of outworks (called a glacis) which from the outside appeared as grassy banks. These at first surrounded only Old Portsmouth. In the 1770s they were extended northwards to provide continuous landward defence to the Dockyard and the adjoining district of Portsea. Almost all the ramparts were swept away in 1870–5, leaving only a short stretch, called the Long Curtain, near the sea in Old Portsmouth. This is a grassed embankment, ending in an arrow-headed bastion, with old guns reinstated; in front is a moat. It can give only a limited impression of what

48 Long Curtain, Portsmouth, the only surviving stretch of the old earthen ramparts.

the rest of the ramparts were like since, as it adjoined the open sea, it always lacked the elaborate outer works which existed elsewhere. (It must be added that Gosport was also fortified, more simply, to similar principles, and that parts of the earthworks survive there, page 69). North of the Long Curtain more conventional stone defences face the open sea, incorporating the original medieval Square and Round Towers (both drastically altered), and a remarkable range of gun emplacements called the Eighteen Gun Battery, built in the seventeenth century and enlarged in the nineteenth – including a two-tiered section projecting into the water. All these remaining defences have been transformed by the council into a complicated series of spaces and walkways open to the public, giving splendid views over the Solent. This is not entirely new, as it seems that the old earthen ramparts were often accessible to townspeople, even if unofficially, and provided a marvellous green amenity which it was tragic to lose.

Access to the fortified town was through a series of gates. To reach the Landport Gate, the principal entrance to Old Portsmouth, one had to pierce the outer defences and cross the moat twice before reaching the actual gate, a handsome classical structure rebuilt in 1760 with a strange octagonal turret. It survived the flattening of the ramparts on either side, the filling of the moat and the transformation of all else around, and now forms the impressive but forlorn entrance to the naval sports ground in St George's Road. Other gates survive re-sited, including the very fine classical Unicorn Gate, originally one of the entrances to Portsea, which is now an entrance to the Dockyard.

The earthen ramparts were built in response to the threat from simple cannon. A much later development was that of rifled artillery, firing explosive shells, which was introduced about 1860 – immediately trebling, or quadrupling, the range of guns from either land or sea. So a range of forts was built to defend the harbour from landward attack – it was seriously thought that the French might try and land on the Solent coast and attack Portsmouth from the side or rear. One line of forts was built across the Gosport peninsula, Fort Brockhurst among them (**32**) (page 72), and another line on Portsdown Hill, the long chalk ridge north of the harbour. Of these, Forts Widley and Nelson are now public showpieces. In some ways they were updated versions of medieval castles like Portchester on the plain below, with their massive outer ramparts of earth and brick, their 'defensible barracks' which in principle and appearance are remarkably like keeps, and their external moats which on Portsdown Hill have to be dry. They are among the most massive constructions ever to have been built of brick; some of the brick-vaulted chambers and tunnels look wonderfully impressive inside. There was much derision about these expensive and, as it turned out, unnecessary structures – and still more about the four forts on artificial islands which were built in the Solent – and they were given the name 'Palmerston's Follies' after the Prime Minister who advocated them.

Old Portsmouth

Although its ramparts were nearly all flattened in the 1870s, the old town of Portsmouth remains an entity, especially as much of the site of the ramparts

49 Lombard Street, Old Portsmouth, one of the most attractive corners in the old town. The façades with the 'Dutch' gables were added to timber-framed houses in the 17th century, and have been altered many times since.

is occupied by sports grounds. It was the main part of Portsmouth until well into the nineteenth century, when the present city centre developed and the old town became a backwater. It was heavily bombed; the gaps were filled by new private housing which at least respects the old street pattern, and the old town became a residential suburb. Most of the older houses that survived are now well looked after. John de Gisors, founder of the town, started the first church in the 1180s; the western parts were rebuilt after damage in the Civil War, and enlargement started after the church became the cathedral for a new diocese in 1927. But some of the earliest work survives at the east end, and very remarkable it is, unmistakably Gothic – among the earliest work in this style in the country. Pairs of arches are contained in wider arches – an arrangement unique in England except at Boxgrove Priory, east of Chichester. The additions after it became a cathedral, suspended in the second world war and never resumed, have resulted in an awkward building, but there are now proposals to round off the unfinished part. Nearby is the Royal Garrison Church, founded in the early thirteenth century as a hospital for poor travellers and the infirm, with the aisled nave as the ward and the structural chancel as the chapel – much as in St Mary's Hospital, Chichester (page 45). It was restored by G.E. Street; the nave roof was lost by bombing, but the chancel is intact, with exquisite thirteenth-century vaulting.

There is little else of pre-Georgian date in the rough grid of streets which forms Old Portsmouth. Buckingham House, in High Street has a stuccoed Georgian front, but behind is the timber-framed house where the Duke of Buckingham, favourite of Charles I and inept minister of state, was murdered in 1628. He had arranged an unsuccessful expedition from Portsmouth to relieve the Huguenots at La Rochelle, and was preparing another. The house's owner was Captain John Mason, who had a distinguished record in promoting colonies, and was one of the founders of New Hampshire. Behind the cathedral, in Lombard Street, is a picturesque group with seventeenth-century Dutch-style gables. Otherwise there is a scatter of Georgian houses, often with the characteristic Portsmouth bow windows which have graceful shallow curves, each composed of three sash windows under a delicately detailed cornice. They contrast with the much more boldly rounded bows characteristic of Southampton.

The furthest part of Old Portsmouth is called Point, originally a shingle spit, behind and beyond the shoreside stone defences. It was notorious as the place where sailors came for comfort and excitement, especially when rowed ashore from ships anchored at Spithead. But it had other activities. Bathing took place off the shingly beach, and in 1754 a weatherboarded bath house was built, its lower level containing baths which were replenished by the tides. It is now called Quebec House (because it was later attached to the Quebec Hotel which accommodated passengers bound for North America) and is probably the oldest surviving structure in Britain built in association with sea bathing. Tower House nearby, north of the Tudor-to-Victorian Round Tower, was the home of W.L. Wyllie, painter of sea scenes, and one of the many artists of around the turn of the century whose work is probably due for reappraisal. Otherwise what is left of old Point is picturesque and well cared-for, with three pubs on the end of the spit which are familiar features from ships leaving the harbour. Finally, on the landward side of Old Portsmouth, are two remarkable buildings formerly barracks. Portsmouth had, till quite recently, a substantial garrison – the Army in readiness to defend the Navy. What is now Portsmouth Grammar School was built in the 1850s as a barracks, in a style characteristic of thirty years before, suggesting how conservative the army was on the eve of the Crimean War. Round the corner is another barrack block, now the City Museum, wildly different in its style, reminiscent of anything from a Scottish baronial hall to a Bavarian schloss. It is the only survivor of several barrack blocks which were built on part of the land freed by the removal of the ramparts.

The City Centre

By 1800 building spilled outside the ramparts of Old Portsmouth and the dockyard town of Portsea, especially along the winding road – later Commercial Road – which led from the Landport Gate of Old Portsmouth to the only bridge out of Portsea Island on to the mainland, about three miles to the north. This development soon consolidated, forming the district called Landport. The railway entered Portsmouth in 1847, terminating at first on the site of the present main station in the middle of the area – it was extended later, across Commercial Road to Portsmouth Harbour station. The presence of the railway encouraged the development of a shopping centre, which was well placed to serve the new housing areas which spread rapidly over the central parts of Portsea Island as the Dockyard expanded. By the end of the century it was the main shopping centre of greater Portsmouth, superseding the High Street of the old town (from which shops have since almost disappeared) – though there was rival shopping in Southsea. The status of the area as the main centre of Portsmouth was confirmed in 1886, when work started on the Guildhall, replacing a much more modest building in Old Portsmouth. It is the most imposing town or city hall south of London apart from the later Civic Centre in Southampton, and rivals the great town halls of the north, such as that at Leeds. The architect, William Hill, indeed came from Leeds, and designed the Guildhall on the same lines as an earlier one of his at Bolton, with a great portico and a tall turret. It was burnt out in the bombing, and when reconstructed within the shell lost some of its original skyline of subsidiary turrets.

Bombing devastated much of the city centre. The main shopping area north of the railway was unimaginatively rebuilt, although partial pedestrianization has resulted in improvement. South of the railway, where there were always fewer shops, more Victorian buildings survived. The Theatre Royal, with a lovely interior of 1900 by Frank Matcham, the leading theatre architect of the day, was nearly lost after the war but was saved through the persistence of local conservationists, who hope to bring it back into full use. It has a strange two-tiered frontispiece projecting over the pavement with an open-arched ground storey and a bar, recently re-opened, above. Next is a florid half-timbered pub of the type characteristic of Portsmouth around 1900, and on the other side a very impressive building designed by Alfred Waterhouse for the Prudential Assurance, in his characteristic style, rising with subtle elaboration to a fretted skyline, and faced with deep red brick and terracotta. Further south, a larger building of 1899 with turrets and florid gables, now called Charter House, was first built for the Pearl Assurance, and helps give scale and character to this part of the city.

For long the immediate surroundings of the Guildhall were in a dejected state. Plans were prepared in the 1960s by Lord Esher for a new civic square; they were partly carried out in the '70s by his successors, Teggin and Taylor. It is one of the more successful examples of civic design from the period. The square is just the right size to set off the Guildhall with its huge external staircase, and in the middle, at a carefully considered change in level, a statue of the aged Queen Victoria by Alfred Dury has been re-placed. On two sides are municipal buildings with glazed fronts, and at one corner is the very different, chunkier public library. The whole is an exercise in contrast and co-ordination. Originally there was to have been further re-development to the south (though retaining the Theatre Royal), but this part of the scheme has been modified. Behind the Guildhall is a very distinguished building of 1903–8, by the local architect G.E. Smith, built to house the Municipal College and the public library. It is exuberantly 'free baroque', with a decorative dome, and an undulating façade where the library was. Now it is all used by Portsmouth Polytechnic, into which the Municipal College has evolved. The Polytechnic has expanded over much of central Portsmouth, including some of the former military area; some – by no means all – of its recent buildings are impressive, notably the library designed by Ahrends, Burton and Koralek.

Southsea

Southsea is Portsmouth's seaside quarter, which began as a residential suburb rather than a resort. Its development started with a series of terraces, including Landport, Hampshire and King's Terraces, built in 1800–15 facing what were then the grassy outer earthworks of the ramparts. Mostly they were developed piecemeal, and they have been patchily altered since, but a few Georgian fronts survive, notably one in Landport Terrace with a two-tiered verandah. Behind were humbler streets, many of them damaged by bombing and redeveloped, but some are still colourful and attractive, notably Great Southsea Street and the winding Castle Road, dominated by a weird half-timbered clock tower of about 1900. In total contrast to these tight-knit streets is the early Victorian sylvan suburb further east, developed by Thomas Ellis Owen – a thrusting entrepreneur who was both speculative builder, trained architect and local politician. He was the son of a civilian engineer, Jacob Owen, who worked for the Army but also had a private architectural practice – his is the internally iron-framed Holy Trinity at Fareham (page 62). The younger Owen developed, with great flair, a large tract of what is now central Southsea. He catered for naval and military officers and their dependents, as well as for prosperous tradesmen and professional men who might previously have lived over, or near, their premises or practice in Old Portsmouth or Portsea. The movement of such people from old town centres to new residential districts was taking place all over the country at the time. Hitherto, such people would usually have moved into Georgian terraces, but from about the 1830s they increasingly sought detached (or semi-detached) houses in large gardens, as secluded as possible from each other and from the crowded and polluted inner districts, while remaining within carriage driving distance from the latter. This was the beginning of what were later called 'garden suburbs', such as were developing at the time round London, Birmingham and other big cities. Owen catered for this new demand, but for a time he also built terraces of the more traditional sort. 'Owen's Southsea' – this is the official title of a Conservation Area – has suffered from sporadic rebuildings, alterations and changes of use, but much of its sylvan, secluded character survives. His earliest houses are terraces of 1837–40 on the corner of Kent and Sussex Roads, set back behind well-planted gardens. The later Sussex Terrace, reached by a deliberately double-twisted road, has strange Moorish-like porches. All around are, or were (some have been replaced) stuccoed villas in versions of Gothic or Italian themes. St Jude's church with its striking spire was built by Owen as a centrepiece for the area. To the south, Portland Terrace of 1846, recently refurbished, was a last grand design by Owen in the late Regency tradition. The most attractive piece of Owen's suburban scenery, The Vale, lies to the east of what is now the busy Palmerston Road shopping centre; it is a narrow twisting lane laid out in about 1850, from which gabled villas are glimpsed amid well-grown greenery, above brick and stone garden walls. Owen died in 1862, and later builders in Southsea did not have the same flair.

Ramsgate

Kent

Thanet was originally an island. In Roman and early medieval times ships sailed the Wantsum channel, now drained and dry, which separated it from the mainland. By the fifteenth century the Cinque Port of Sandwich was silting too, and the still small village of Ramsgate became its official limb in 1483. A wooden pier built in Tudor times provided some protection for ships, and from the seventeenth century coastal trade developed with London and Newcastle (for coal), as well as connections with the Baltic and with Iceland (for fish). The rudimentary shelter which Ramsgate provided was much sought by ships when storms blew, so a new stone harbour was started under an Act of Parliament of 1749. Squabbles and changes of plan made building very slow, and there was further reconstruction between 1790 and 1821, when an obelisk was built to commemorate the departure of George IV in a ship for Hanover. Old photographs show the harbour full of sailing ships; now it is filled with pleasure craft and has a Continental atmosphere (which is not sustained in the streets leading off). Ships for the Continent now depart from a new terminal to the south. Visitors started to come to Ramsgate early in Georgian times, but the town did not grow much until after 1810. From then till about 1850 terraces, crescents and a few squares were built in buff stock brick. The grandest is Wellington Crescent on the east cliff, which has an almost endless colonnade with balconies above. More characteristic of the town are some of the streets further on, especially Augusta Road, which has very elaborate balconies of cast iron stretched across bay windows. There are more houses of this type at the other end of the town, in and near the attractive Spencer Square. Liverpool Lawn, named after Lord Liverpool the prime minister, is a charming backwater round a triangular green, with two-storeyed stuccoed houses and taller brick ones, some with oddly bowed frontages. Vale Square and Guildford Lawn are other enclaves worth seeking out, the latter with bow-fronted houses enveloping an attractive public library of 1904 by S.D. Adshead.

But the climax of Ramsgate, architecturally, is Augustus Pugin's masterpiece, the Roman Catholic St Augustine's which the fanatical medievalist founded, together with an adjoining monastery, in 1845. The church has an internal grandeur quite unexpected in a building of only moderate size. Outwardly it is austere, with walls of dark flint in the local tradition. Next to it Pugin built his own house, more raggedly romantic, and altered. It overlooks what is now a cliff-top promenade. At the opposite, inland, end of the town, past a few flinty old houses, is the pre-Pugin St George's with a two-tier tower ending in a thin octagonal turret with flying buttresses, like a shortened version of Boston Stump but in buff brick, with dressings of stone. Further again, near the station, is the old village of St Lawrence in whose parish Ramsgate grew, with a flint-built square-towered medieval church.

Reigate

Surrey

Reigate is not memorable for buildings or townscapes, but is pleasant none the less. It is built on hummocky sandstone hills, under the much bolder slope of the chalk downs, whence came its famous stone. Open spaces, both within and around the town, are among its most distinctive features. One is the site of the castle, built by the militant-pious Warenne dynasty, who first obtained the overlordship, like that of Lewes, after the Conquest. Nothing solid is left of the castle, save a charming 'Gothick' arch built out of salvaged stonework in 1777, but the grounds are a pleasing warren of municipal planting. The castle hill is about as high as the rooftops of High Street below, down to which a steep path descends. The street has a pleasant shape, gently curving and widening at both ends, with just enough interesting buildings: a few of them are Georgian or earlier, but some of the most prominent, as so often in Surrey, are Victorian with busy and prominent skylines; the dead hand of redevelopment has so far blighted High Street only a little. The heart of the town is the delightful Old Town Hall of 1729, in Georgian red brick, with a rounded end, islanded in the wide eastern end of High Street. North of it is the town's most surprising feature, a road tunnel, under the castle hill, built in 1824 to ease the route for coaches from London to Brighton, but now closed to traffic. At the other end of High Street several streets meet at a confusing junction, with some pleasant buildings but no visual coherence. But it is worth going along West Street even though, like High Street, it is plagued with traffic – Reigate has not yet sorted out the problem of its through traffic. Towards its far end a house of 1786 stands on a wedge-shaped site, with two public fronts, a pleasant prologue or epilogue to the centre of the town.

Reigate's two finest buildings are away from the town centre. The Priory, on the site of a monastery founded by the Warennes, was the home of Lord Howard of Effingham, commander at the time of the Armada. Now it has a demure stuccoed Georgian main front, facing what is now a public park; inside there are a superb Tudor fireplace and an early Georgian staircase. The church is well to the east of the centre, indicating that the medieval castle-town developed away from the site of the original village, where the church remained. It is a big regular building, much restored, but distinctive outside for its walls of white stone – the chalky stone quarried from the neighbouring hills which was much used in London in the Middle Ages; Westminster Abbey was largely built of it. Unfortunately it does not usually weather well (which is why Westminster Abbey has had to be entirely refaced externally in different stones), but lends itself to fine carving and can last indefinitely internally – as the Abbey interior shows. But in Reigate church much of the internal stonework has been renewed, including the very fine late twelfth-century arcades – which were carefully and accurately reconstructed by the second George Gilbert Scott in 1877–81. The undulations to the south-east of the town are covered by well-to-do houses, Victorian and early twentieth-century. They rise to Redhill Common, a surprisingly half-wild tract which extends into the more open Earlswood Common on high ground overlooking the Weald. Here is the parish church of St John, Redhill, originally early nineteenth century but reconstructed by the great J.L. Pearson in 1889–95; his is the beautiful slender spire, soaring above the grassy slopes, the finest of its kind in the region except those of Chichester Cathedral, Dorking church and the 'flying spire' of Faversham. Redhill, though joined municipally to Reigate, has its own town centre which developed round the station on the Brighton line, originally opened in 1841. For long the town was determinedly Victorian, but a shopping precinct called Warwick Quadrant now catches the eye, with round-framed glazed roofs in romantic reminiscence of buildings like the Crystal Palace, following a current architectural fashion.

Rochester

Kent

Rochester, Chatham and Gillingham together form the biggest urban area in south-east England outside London, except those on the south coast. Rochester was Roman and medieval; Chatham developed after the dockyard was founded in the sixteenth century; Gillingham, although an ancient village, was essentially an eastward extension of Chatham. Strood, across the

50 **Rochester Cathedral**, the second oldest foundation in England. The Norman west front with its turrets and later window is the finest external feature.

river, is another member of the group. For hundreds of years Rochester was of vital strategic importance as the place where the road from London to Canterbury and the Channel ports crossed the River Medway. *Durobrivae* was a small Roman town by the crossing; its second syllable, *-ro*, became the first in the town's modern name. In 604 Justus, who had come over from Rome with St Augustine, became the first bishop of Rochester – the second cathedral see to be established in England. He was succeeded by St Paulinus, who had been the first bishop of York. The next great bishop of Rochester was Gundulf (from 1077) – who organized the building of the Tower of London; in Rochester he built the first castle, enlarged the cathedral and founded the associated priory. Only a little of Gundulf's work survives in the cathedral; the nave, with its splendid west front, is later Norman, and the retrochoir, with the crypt underneath, is outstanding Early English (internally; it is plain outside). Other parts are of various dates, and the not very effective tower is the last result of a succession of rebuildings. Gundulf's castle was partly succeeded by the present tremendous keep after 1127; its shell survives as originally built except where repaired at its south-west corner – which had collapsed after being undermined during a siege by King John's forces against rebel barons in 1215. The corner was rebuilt soon afterwards to a curve instead of a right-angle, following the then latest ideas in military engineering, since a curved corner was more difficult to

Above The Archbishop's Palace, Maidstone

Opposite Landgate, Rye

andgate Pictures

51 *Above* **Rochester Castle;** the keep built *c.*1130 of Kentish ragstone.

mine than a sharp angle. The keep is built of brownish-grey ragstone, shipped down the river; it overshadows the cathedral from almost any viewpoint. Little else of the castle survives except parts of the outer wall.

Rochester must have been perpetually busy as a highway town. Pilgrims to Canterbury and travellers to the Channel ports passed through and, later, coaches stopped at the inns. More recently Rochester became overshadowed as a trading centre by Chatham as the latter developed in conjunction with the dockyard. This explains why the main part of Rochester High Street has changed strangely little over the last hundred years or more; the shops are still small, and the dominant character is Georgian, though there are striking earlier buildings. Since all but servicing traffic was taken off High Street a few years ago, it has become a pleasure to walk along it – something which was difficult before. Few streets, even in south-east England, have so much interest and charm along or just off them. (These remarks apply to the main part of Rochester High Street; the name also applies to a continuation, of different character, towards Chatham.) A good place to start is what is now the Charles Dickens Centre – in Eastgate House, built in 1581 for Sir Peter Buck, paymaster of the newly established Chatham Dockyard – partly of dark Tudor brick, partly timber-framed, and much restored when it first became a museum in 1897. Nearly opposite is a fine trio of timber-framed houses of slightly later date, gabled and jettied, with typical Jacobean oriel windows. A little further on, recent demolition has revealed a stretch of fine fourteenth-century city wall on the right, and on the left an inconspicuous passage leads to another stretch, in part Roman. Past the site of the city's

52 *Opposite bottom* **Rochester Castle,** showing the corner turret rebuilt in rounded form, after its predecessor, squared like the others, had been destroyed through undermining in 1215.

53 *Above left* **Houses in Rochester High Street,** early 17th-century, with typical oriel windows.

54 *Above right* **Rochester High Street,** showing older jettied houses clad in weatherboarding in the 18th century, and a Georgian front with garland pattern in plaster.

Overleaf top left Upper Strand Street, Sandwich

Overleaf bottom left The Barbican, Sandwich

Overleaf right Tenterden

Eastgate (the houses already described were outside the wall and gate) is a Tudor-style building, strangely in fine white stone, called Watts' Charity; the charity was founded by another Elizabethan dockyard official for the benefit of poor travellers, who were entitled to stay for only a single night. Next to it the gas showroom (of all things) is in a remarkably handsome neo-Renaissance building of the 1930s. The Gordon Hotel, just beyond, has a fine early eighteenth-century front of red and grey brick chequerwork. Here and elsewhere the street has been paved in brick, with stone kerbs, part of the council's commendable improvement scheme. Less commendable was the demolition (several years ago) of a stretch of frontage to reveal the side of the cathedral – which was hitherto hidden from the High Street by buildings, and reached from there along alleys, or through the medieval College Gate further on. The architectural saga continues with the Dutch-looking classical brick façade of the former Corn Exchange built, with its projecting clock (reminiscent of that at Guildford), in 1705 by Sir Cloudesley Shovell, a distinguished admiral and M.P. The original exchange has disappeared, and only the front part survives, but that is better than preserving nothing. Less conspicuous, because set back, is the Guildhall, a splendid building of 1687 in a somewhat similar style, with a columned ground storey which once sheltered market stalls. It is now an excellent local museum. Across the street is a fascinating group, including a building of 1778 with a draped ribbon and garlands in plaster on the façade. Next to it is a pair of boldly jettied timber-framed buildings entirely clad in weatherboarding –

LEW S & HYLAND
BATEMAN

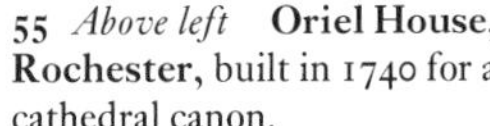

55 *Above left* **Oriel House, Rochester,** built in 1740 for a cathedral canon.

56 *Above right* **Restoration House, Rochester,** with a 17th-century 'Artisan' frontage to an older building, portrayed by Dickens as Miss Havisham's house in *Great Expectations.*

probably added to the older buildings in the eighteenth century; this was very much a tradition of the Thames and Medway estuaries, where the deal for the boarding was imported from the Baltic. These have been well restored, and a charming alley leads past one of the houses to reveal a sudden view of the castle. Here and elsewhere one has the impression that Rochester's historic buildings are, on the whole, well cared-for.

The cathedral close is small and informal, but intricate to explore. Not much is left of the monastic buildings south of the cathedral. The site of the cloister is a pleasant garden, with ruinous remains of the once splendidly sculptured entrance to the chapter house. Narrow roads wind past Georgian canons' houses like those in Minor Canon Row, a terrace dating from 1736 beside the medieval ragstone Prior's Gate, and Oriel House of 1740. The latter lies at the entrance to the Vines, once, no doubt, the monastic vineyard but now a park. At the far end is Restoration House, with a façade in the strange 'Artisan' style of the mid-seventeenth century including carved brickwork (parts of the buildings are older); it is so called because Charles II reputedly stayed there on return from exile. But Dickens called it 'Satis House' (a name he transposed from another house, near the castle), and made it the home of Miss Havisham in *Great Expectations* which, like other Dickens novels, is partly set in the area. Dickens was a boy in Chatham, and loved to explore the neighbouring cathedral city; in later life he lived at Gadshill to the north. The city council successfully exploits the novelist's local associations; this has helped to justify the considerable efforts the council has made towards conserving the old parts of the city. There is one other fascinating street in Rochester – St Margaret's Street, which climbs irregularly south from the cathedral, past ragstone walls and varied buildings, some weatherboarded, one boldly bowed, to the hilltop church of St Margaret, late Georgian with a medieval tower, from which there is a fine view over the river to the hills beyond.

Romney

Kent

The town of New Romney – Old Romney is a much smaller village – was probably founded as a port in about AD 1000, on a piece of relatively dry land adjoining what may have been a wide estuary. Geographers are still uncertain about the early topography of the area, but much of what is now Romney Marsh was certainly once tidal water. In 1287 there was a catastrophic tidal flood which, as it retreated, left a transformed coastline and ruined port facilities. Winchelsea suffered in the same flood. Unlike the original Winchelsea, Romney survived as a town, and perhaps struggled as a port for a little longer, but by the fifteenth century it was, as now, surrounded by farmland, with the sea over a mile away. It had modest prosperity as a market town in Georgian times, but today its main fame may be as the terminus of a narrow-gauge steam railway. Nevertheless it retains, with Hastings, Hythe, Dover and Sandwich, its status as one of the original Cinque Ports.

The street pattern is probably that of the Saxon and Norman town, with a long main street wide enough for markets, and parallel or cross streets forming a not completely regular grid. At first sight the dominant style is Georgian – exemplified by the dun brick building at the central crossroads, and the pleasant small Assembly Rooms towards the church, the latter indicating a local social life at the time. But something survives from the Middle Ages. Behind the Assembly Rooms is evidence of a thirteenth-century stone house, and in West Street a former hall house of the same date is still recognizable. This and several other houses, particularly in High Street, have floor levels a few feet below the present streets. It has been plausibly suggested that these may represent the ground level before the 1287 flood, which covered the town with several feet of deposit. The finest building by far is the church, similarly below present ground level internally, with a massive and magnificent Norman tower, arcades of the same date, and major extensions in the fourteenth century, suggesting still continuing prosperity fairly shortly after the flood. It was one of four original parish churches.

Romsey

Hampshire

Romsey has always been dominated by its abbey – as a nunnery before the Reformation, and as a very large parish church since. The nunnery was founded by 907 at the latest. It has its own saint, Ethelfleda, an abbess; another abbess was sister of St Margaret, queen of Scotland, and the latter's daughter Matilda, later queen of Henry I, was educated there. The church was rebuilt on a grand scale from about 1120 and survives almost intact – probably the finest Norman building in England apart from Durham Cathedral. Its Romanesque qualities are brought out superbly by the creamy grey stone – from Binstead in the Isle of Wight, of which the main parts of Winchester Cathedral are built – although the later parts to the west, where the Gothic style begins to take over, are of the more greeny Chilmark stone from Wiltshire, of which Salisbury Cathedral is built. In the Middle Ages the townspeople worshipped in a small outer aisle, since demolished, and in part of the north transept, but at the Dissolution they bought the whole church at its 'scrap value' of £100 (the estimated resale price of the materials), to their eternal credit. Romsey has grown recently and its eastern approach has always been scrappy, but the intricate town centre has kept its historic character well, apart from one bad patch, thanks, largely, to the vigilance and the practical action of local conservationists. The centre is the roughly triangular Market Place, itself part of an originally larger triangle which has, as so often, been reduced in size by early encroachments – represented today by an island block containing the Victorian former Corn Exchange and a later Victorian bank with an impressive curved façade. The dominant material is Georgian brick, in deep red or buff, often concealing older timber-framing – which is still seen to considerable effect in the gabled house called the Manor House in Palmerston Street. This is early Tudor in date and has what is probably an early example of brick nogging – the insertion of bricks in the panels of the timber framework. Church Street is the one old street that has been messed about, but off it is the so-called King John's House, a supremely interesting small stone-built house of the early thirteenth century, recently well restored. Further along Church Street and its sinuous continuation Cherville Street the Romsey and District Buildings Preservation Trust has been doing excellent work, buying and saving old houses threatened with demolition, and building new ones to restore broken street frontages.

The abbey has a definite precinct, though not so called. It is entered from the Market Place through a flint-faced Gothic gateway, built improbably in conjuction with the adjoining Congregational Church in 1888. A row of pleasant Georgian-looking houses occupies the site of, and incorporates parts of, the conventual buildings. A path continues west, increasingly rural, over successive branches and sidestreams of the River Test, to pass an old mill and eventually reach a Georgian

bridge at the eastern end of the town. Southwards is Broadlands, the mainly Georgian house which was the home of Lord Palmerston (commemorated by a statue in the Market Place), and more recently of Lord Mountbatten.

57 **Market Place, Romsey,** with the Abbey rising behind; the statue is to Lord Palmerston, who lived in neighbouring Broadlands.

Ryde

Isle of Wight

Ryde, one of the two biggest towns on the Isle of Wight, is a creation of the nineteenth century; two previous hamlets were insignificant. The first pier was opened in 1814, to half the length of the present one, and a regular service of steamboats from Portsmouth started in 1825; from then development was rapid. The seafront is not specially notable; the interesting parts of Ryde are along the streets on the steadily rising slope to the south. The finest building is the Royal Victoria Arcade of 1835–6, designed by William Westmacott and named after Victoria as Princess; she stayed at about that time in Norris Castle near Cowes. The entrance front on Union Street is altered, but the classical interior is superb, though small, with its panelled-ceilinged passageway leading to a circular domed space. It must be the best pre-Victorian (though only just) arcade in England outside London. Behind is Brigstocke Terrace, the only one of its kind in Ryde, a monumental composition of 1833 by John Sanderson, with a rhythmically projecting and receding front; for long in a bad state, it was rehabilitated a few years ago. Not far away is the Town Hall, also by Sanderson, with a stucco and yellow brick exterior, built in 1834 – indicating how rapidly Ryde had acquired town status, even though it did not yet have a council. The tall thin clock tower was added in 1864. As often in early town halls the ground floor was intended for marketing, as was the colonnaded building to the east. Houses were built individually or in small groups, and there are still many stuccoed examples of about 1815 to 1840, some with bold bows, in the streets east and west of the town centre. From the 1840s the villas followed Victorian stylistic fashions, and many were built in the varied local stones. Ryde has two notable churches; All Saints (1868–72) is an ambitious work of Sir Gilbert Scott with a spire said to have been modelled on that of St Mary's at Oxford; it is a landmark from and across the Solent. St Michael's at Swanmore (1861–3), a remote suburb to the south-west, has a fantastic interior in High Victorian Gothic, with polychrome brickwork in buff, red and black.

Ryde's western suburb, Binstead, is interesting not

for itself but because it was the site of famous limestone quarries. Stone from here was used by the Romans – for instance in the walls of their fort at Portchester near Portsmouth. Bishop Walkelin used the finest variety to build the Norman Winchester Cathedral, as did William of Wykeham for his remodelling three hundred years later. Quarr Abbey nearby, named from the quarries, was founded in 1131. The stone was found in several varieties, called variously, and not very consistently, Binstead stone, Quarr stone or, for no obvious reason, Bembridge stone. The best is hard and creamy, as used at Winchester and in Romsey Abbey; other layers produced rough stone often with a brownish mottled texture, seen in the Southampton city walls and in numerous parish churches on the mainland. The best deposits were exhausted centuries ago, and some of the early quarry sites are now covered in woods.

Rye

Sussex

Rye is a historic town *par excellence*. It is very well preserved – over-restored in places – but fundamentally nearly all 'genuine'; there is no need for historical faking in Rye. It has been a tourist attraction for a long time – Henry James complained of sightseers when he lived there – and has matured as a self-consciously pretty place. But it remains very much a town of its own right, the market and servicing centre for a wide and still deeply rural area extending from Romney Marsh into the Weald. Rye was founded as a town at about the time of the Norman Conquest by the abbey of Fécamp, which already possessed the site before the Conquest. The site is a bluff, between the tidal River Rother and its tributary the Tillingham, two or three miles from the sea. Originally, it seems, it adjoined a large inlet, on the other side of which was the first town of Winchelsea. The tremendous storm of 1287 which drowned old Winchelsea and damaged the town of Romney (pages 144, 113) altered the coastline and affected the courses of the rivers. This was not to Rye's disadvantage, since the redirected River Tillingham

58 **West Street, Rye,** showing a typical mixture of frontage treatment, including weatherboarding, painting in black and white, and the splendid effect of a plastered rounded corner. This view is taken from the house where Henry James lived.

tion between three parts of the town – the old parishes of St Peter, St Mary and St Clement, each centred on its church. The original part is St Peter's parish, the central third of the present town, representing the first Saxon settlement, which was originally approached by land only from the south. Coming from this direction today the streets branch and fork like a river delta – High Street, St Peter's Street, and also King Street, from which there is a turning into Market Street, the hub of the town. Near the last is St Peter's church, with a Dutch-looking tower of the 1660s, but otherwise medieval. It has long since ceased to be used for regular services and is maintained by the Redundant Churches Fund; the lofty interior is very impressive with no furnishings to fill the space. From the far end of Market Street, Potter Street curves past plastered timber houses, into Strand Street with the most dramatic range of historic buildings in Sandwich. Strand Street stands entirely on reclaimed land. Until the fourteenth century its site was all open water; reclamation brought forward the original shoreline up to the site of the existing carriageway of Strand Street, where a quay was formed. Houses were built on the reclaimed land facing that quay, resulting after a time in the present impressive range of buildings on the southern side of Strand Street. Later, further land was reclaimed, and buildings were erected between Strand Street and the new waterfront, determining eventually the existing north side of the street. The interest of Strand Street, as one would expect, is concentrated on the older, southern side. There is an almost continuous range, only occasionally broken by later buildings, of fifteenth- and sixteenth-century timber-framed houses, of two or three storeys, usually overhung. Until recently all their frontages were plastered over, and most still are – but the plaster has been stripped off some of the façades, leading some recent writers to suggest, quite erroneously, that these buildings are 'fakes', because their timber-framing, previously hidden, has been revealed. Whether the timbering of framed buildings should be revealed is often problematical, but it is likely that all or most of those in Strand Street are old enough for the timbers to have been originally exposed. Only after about 1600 did it become the wide practice in the east and south-east, partly to follow fashion and partly to provide protection, to cover timber-framing with plaster or – later – tiles or weatherboarding.

An old alley, Three Kings Yard, leads under an archway from Strand Street and takes us back in history. In the yard is the shell of a thirteenth-century flint and stone building, originally a house. This abutted on to the first shoreline, before any of the site of Strand Street was reclaimed. Earlier merchants' houses in Sandwich were built of stone and flint like this, before timber-framing became general; the remains of others can be seen elsewhere, either embedded in later buildings or surviving as fragmentary ruins. One of the latter is on the corner of Harnet Street and Guildcount Street, where what looks like a much-patched boundary wall of stone, flint and brick is part of the shell of an early medieval house – which may have been burnt in the French raid of 1457 and never restored. This part of Sandwich, on the western side of the town, has a more regular pattern than the central part; the streets are narrow but usually meet at right angles. It is the old parish of St Mary, which, like the corresponding parish of St Clement on the eastern side, is

60 *Above right* **Three Kings Yard, Sandwich.** The shell of a 13th-century stone-built house, partly rebuilt in brick. It stands on the original shoreline; the houses on the right face Strand Street, on the land reclaimed in the 14th century (**59**).

61 *Right* **King's Arms, Sandwich,** on the corner of Strand Street and Church Street, St Mary's; a 17th-century building 'Gothicized' in Georgian times.

thought to have been laid out either just before or just after the Norman conquest as an extension to the Saxon town. The most attractive street in this locality is probably Church Street, St Mary's, with the usual Sandwich mixture of timbered houses, variously altered, some with their timbering recently re-exposed, some with Georgian fronts in the local buff brick, too often painted over. St Mary's church itself was damaged when the tower collapsed in 1668, and oddly patched afterwards; like St Peter's it is not now used for regular services. The one living parish church in Sandwich, St Clement's, is on the eastern side of the town; its main feature is the splendid Norman tower. From its churchyard one can look at The Salutation, a house by Lutyens in early eighteenth-century style, in a large walled garden originally designed with Gertrude Jekyll. One of its most fascinating features is the entrance lodge in Knightrider Street, with sash windows set on either side of a flat-topped arch

62 *Above* **King's Arms, Sandwich,** showing the carved 17th-century brackets.

63 *Right* **Quay Lane, Sandwich,** looking to Fishergate, the only surviving true town gate; its upper storey is in Elizabethan brickwork, with diagonal pattern.

64 *Opposite* **Potter Street, Sandwich,** a typical medieval lane with overhanging timber-framed houses, plastered or refronted in the Georgian period.

Overleaf St Mildred, Tenterden, rising behind the High Street

in a way only Lutyens could contrive. This is near the one stretch of open quayside in Sandwich, facing the tidal River Stour whose winding course provides the only memory of the original harbour. The odd and picturesque structure called the Barbican (see colour illus. p. 110), by the riverside, is one of the most familiar features of Sandwich. It was, as its name implies, an outer defensive work, but it was adapted in fairly recent times as a toll house for the adjoining bridge. It was not therefore a proper town gateway, as many people imagine. Sandwich was never surrounded by stone walls; on the landward side it had broad earthen ramparts, which survive, softened and landscaped, as a pleasant promenade. There were, however, stone gates of which the only survivor is Fishergate, opening on to the quayside from the narrow and cobbled Quay Lane. The main part is of flint, but the domestic-looking gabled upper storey of 1571 is of the peculiar local buff-red brick, embellished with darker diagonal patterns.

(continues on p. 124)

POTTER ST.

Tenterden Fireplace Centre
BRENDA'S
Hair & Beauty
Centre
SAUNA SUNBED
L'OREAL GOLDWELL
SAM LEISURE WEAR

One can wander almost indefinitely about the labyrinth of lanes, alleys and occasional wider streets within the ramparts of Sandwich, so abundant are the medieval, seventeenth-century and Georgian buildings of the town – or, more often, those of composite date which are more complex and older in origin than they look at first sight. Probably the most confusing part of the town is that around the Guildhall, which retains its court room of 1579 with early fittings. In Georgian times the exterior was encased in brick, in typical Sandwich fashion. But this was not considered striking enough for a Cinque Port, and in 1910–12 the building was enlarged and the old part re-fronted again in make-believe Tudor style with heavy half-timbering. It is almost the only building in Sandwich to be extensively 'faked'. Recent extensions in a different style, linking it with neighbouring buildings (it used to be free-standing) have not improved its setting. But the authentic Sandwich lies all around.

Sevenoaks

Kent

Sevenoaks grew casually as a highway town, probably in the thirteenth century when a market is first recorded. The older centre of importance was Otford, down in the Darent valley, but this was bypassed by the route from London to certain Channel ports (Rye, Winchelsea, Hastings), and the town grew up at the fork, on the northern slope of the sandstone ridge, where it met another road from Dartford. The form of the town is still basically a 'Y', related to these routes – which today carry far too much traffic, despite a bypass. The archbishops of Canterbury had an ancient manor house at Otford, but this lay low. In 1456 Archbishop Bourchier bought Knole, already a fairly substantial house in an enviable position, and enlarged it as a palace. It came after the Reformation to the Sackvilles and is now owned by the National Trust. But Sevenoaks was largely independent of Knole. There was much traffic from the coast until the seventeenth century, including fish from Rye and Hastings, carried by packhorse, and from then on there were fashionable travellers to and from Tunbridge Wells. After the railways came in 1862 (a branch) and 1868 (the main line), wealthy Londoners moved out in increasing numbers. Fortunately, green-belt restrictions precluded more extensive development in the nick of time, and most of the surrounding countryside is still gloriously unspoiled, except where scarred by motorways.

The best part of Sevenoaks is the southern, highest end of the High Street, the sinuous stem of the 'Y'. There are timber-framed houses variedly altered, sometimes oddly, the medieval church with its tall ragstone tower, and a striking series of classical buildings. One is the Red House of 1684, so-called from its brick, the *beau ideal* of a country-town house of the time – though the sash windows must be early alterations. Further south are Sevenoaks School and associated almshouses, both founded (like Tonbridge School later) by a local man who became Lord Mayor of London – in 1419, just before Dick Whittington's last term. But what we see are classical buildings of about 1720, with the main school block set back, and almshouses in two long ranges on either side. The original design was by Lord Burlington, no less, but obviously altered and much simplified in execution. The almshouse blocks look dignified, but the main school building, originally of three storeys with two-storey wings, is visually wrecked by an extra storey having been added to one wing, not the other. Perhaps some benefactor could see this put right. The combination of provision for young and old was typical of many early charities. Nearby there is a way into the deer park of Knole – a transition from town to country which is seldom so sudden today. The busy part of Sevenoaks is further north. The original market must have been held within the angle of the 'Y', and from an early date the market place must have been encroached on by permanent buildings, producing a miniature network of alleys called the Shambles. There was once a delightful octagonal market hall, supported on open-arched pillars and surmounted by a conical roof, possibly built by one of the archbishops; it was sketched before demolition in 1843. (It is illustrated in *The Pleasant Town of Sevenoaks*, by John Dunlop.) Its successor is pleasant enough – a classical building with a rich frieze and a round-arched ground-storey, once open, now offices. There are a few more interesting features along both arms of the 'Y'. Off the London road is Lime Tree Walk, a row of cottages artfully designed and built by the late Victorian architect Sir Thomas Jackson who lived locally; he felt that while so many houses were being built for wealthy people from outside, more should be done for the local poorer people; he also provided a coffee house, since closed. Down the Dartford road is Sevenoaks Vine, where cricket was probably played before the ground was given to the town by the Sackvilles in 1773; it is one of the oldest regularly used grounds in the country.

Shoreham

Sussex

Shoreham is one of the many southern ports whose fortunes were ruined by the vagaries of the sea – although unlike most of the others it has recovered in modern times. The River Adur originally had a long estuary reaching from Steyning (page 126) and entering the sea directly. For a time Old Shoreham, a mile inland, was a port, but in about 1100 William de Braose, lord of the area and builder of Bramber Castle, founded the town of New Shoreham at the river mouth. It flourished till the fourteenth century, when action of the sea caused

65 Marlipins, Shoreham, now a museum was probably built as a warehouse in the early 12th century, and refronted with chequered stone and flint in the 13th; it has a Horsham stone roof.

Map X **Shoreham** was an important medieval port. Originally the River Adur entered the sea where the oyster beds are marked. Gradually the river was pushed eastwards with the building-up of a shingle bank to the south of the map. The river then eroded part of the town, which used to extend further south of High Street. Even the great parish church, symbol of past prosperity, was reduced in size – the outline of the lost nave can be seen on this map of 1873. Today Shoreham is part of the developed area west of Brighton.

the build-up of a shingle spit, deflecting the river, which then eroded the southern part of the town, and entered the sea further east. Shoreham languished, though it never quite lost its maritime and boat-building trade. Then the growth of Brighton stimulated improvement, and in 1818 a new mouth to the estuary was cut through the shingle bank at Kingston, east of the town. Shoreham is now a prosperous small port, but the quays and wharves are well to the east of the town proper. Two buildings remain from the town's heyday. The church of St Mary de Haura, New Shoreham, built from about 1100 to 1220, is the finest purely parochial church (it was never monastic) on the south coast, even though most of the nave has disappeared. The tall tower is Romanesque of a very French sort, but the beautiful chancel, with its aisles, is early Gothic, with varied rich detailing, suggesting it was built piecemeal over a period; it is of Caen stone with flint walling outside. The other early building is Marlipins, now the museum, probably built as an official storehouse at the inception of the town and altered as it is now, with a front of chequered stone and flint, in the thirteenth century. Shoreham used to have an irregular grid of streets north and south of the High Street, but on the south only their stumps survive, the rest having been eroded by the deflection of the river, which now flows immediately south of High Street, crossed by a footbridge leading to the sea-side area on the shingle spit. High Street itself was once irregular in width, but was evenly widened in 1938 to ease traffic flow. A few old houses survive in the narrow, originally medieval streets north of High Street; the best by far is Church Street, with attractive fronts in rounded flints or pebbles. On the edges of the town are two other outstanding churches; St Nicholas at Old Shoreham, Saxon and Norman; and St Julian at Kingston-by-Sea, humble outside but, as often in Sussex, much finer within, with a beautiful thirteenth-century vault under the central tower. These and a few others, including Steyning, make the area one of the most remarkable for churches in the south.

Steyning

Sussex

Steyning was one of the chief places in Saxon Sussex. It was at the head of the Adur estuary, then navigable, and was often called St Cuthman's Port after a local saint. William de Braose, a Norman magnate, built a castle at neighbouring Bramber (fragments survive), which for a time was the administrative centre of the area. But by that time the estuary was silting, and a port developed at Shoreham at its mouth. Steyning from then was a small market town, and Bramber no more than a village, though both were boroughs and, like Shoreham as well, sent two members to Parliament until 1832. Steyning has a long and colourful High Street, more like that of a large village than a town. The lesser Church Street is more dramatic, dominated by the long timber-framed Old Grammar School, originally built in the fifteenth century for a guild, and converted when the school was founded in 1614; the tower-like entrance bay of brick was built then. Till recently the whole of the overhanging upper storey, on either side of the entrance, was tile-hung, to bizarre effect, as no windows were visible on the top storey except dormers. Now the tiling has been stripped, and the revealed timber-framing painted black, with white infilling – which, to say yet again, is not typical of the region. But its Horsham stone roof relates it very much to the area. Nearby is a typical Wealden house, with inset central part. The climax of Steyning is the church, which provides an extreme example of the Sussex characteristic of a homely exterior belying a fine interior. The interior is in fact stunning – a Norman nave with cylindrical piers, a tall clerestory, a wonderful wealth of carved detail, and a superb overall proportion. This is only part of a larger monastic church, which was a dependency of Fécamp in Normandy; the choir and central tower were lost after the Reformation and the present massive but earthy tower dates from the seventeenth century.

Southampton

Hampshire

Southampton first became a major port around 700–850 when, as *Hamwic* or *Hamtun* it had a thriving trade with northern Europe from the Seine to the Rhine. Archaeologists have revealed a pattern of regular streets, indicating that it was one of the largest English settlements at a period when few other places were recognizable as towns. *Hamtunscir* (Hampshire) was recorded in 757 – the first known reference to a county named after a town. This early town lay near the present St Mary's church (on the site of the first Saxon church) adjoining the Itchen estuary. It declined after about 850, when the activities of the Vikings affected the whole pattern of trade on which it

66 *Above* **Bugle Street, Southampton,** the city's best old street; in the background are the many-gabled Tudor House with a restored front of *c.*1500 and the 1963 flats on the site of the castle keep.

67 *Above right* **High Street, Southampton**; the appalling post-war buildings on the left contrast with those on the right, including the Dolphin of 1775 with, reputedly, the largest bow windows in England; in the background is the restored south front of the Bargate.

depended. At about that time development started on a site to the west, adjoining the River Test, from which the modern city grew. The re-sited town, already called *Suthamtun* (to distinguish it from *Northamtun*), was important at the time of the Norman Conquest. A castle was built by the Test shore, and colonists from Normandy settled in the area around St Michael's and French Street. When Winchester was the royal residence, and Normandy politically linked with England, Southampton was a vital place of transit, and it developed trade further along the European coasts. By the end of the twelfth century rich merchants built stone houses, parts of which survive, along and near the waterfront. After the breaking of English ties with Normandy, trade continued with western France, as well as Flanders and Spain. Wine was imported, together with dyestuffs, vegetable oil and fruits; wool and cloth were exported. Southampton was deeply involved with the French wars. Edward III's forces embarked there for the campaign which culminated at Crécy, as did Henry V's before Agincourt. But the French devastated the town in 1338, and it took decades to recover. After that, strong walls were built along the waterfront, and were effective in repelling another French attack in 1377, at a time when Portsmouth, Hastings, Rye and other south coast towns were sacked.

Southampton reached another of its peaks of prosperity in the fifteenth century. Traders from Venice and Genoa made it one of their chief ports of call in northern Europe, bringing spices, silks, dyestuffs and other expensive cargoes in exchange for wool and woven cloth. The imported goods were mostly carried overland to London; the wool and cloth came from a wide hinterland including Wiltshire and even the Cotswolds; Salisbury merchants traded through the port. But in the sixteenth century there was a decline. The Italian ships ceased to call. More overseas trade, including that in West Country cloth, became concentrated on London. Southampton was reduced to a modest Channel port competing with places like Weymouth and Poole, though the connection with Portugal remained. There were inflows of Walloon

(French-speaking) refugees from the Low Countries in the 1560s, and of Huguenots a century later.

Southampton became a Georgian resort. A spring with medicinal qualities was exploited, and the Prince of Wales visited the town in 1750. Baths, replenished with sea water, and assembly rooms were built by the shore. But Southampton never seriously rivalled Brighton. Rather it became a favoured place for residence and retirement. Jane Austen lived in the town from 1806 to 1809 (her house no longer exists); she described the balls held in the assembly room at the Dolphin inn.

Southampton's trade braced up a little in the early nineteenth century – it became again a place of military assembly during the wars. But the modern city really dates from 1840, when the railway from London was opened – the first long-distance line out of London except that to Birmingham. Two years later the first dock was opened. From then Southampton grew into a world port – Peninsular and Oriental, Royal Mail and what became Union Castle were some of the shipping lines making it their base in Victorian times. The London and South-Western railway company bought the docks in 1892 and developed them with flair. In 1907 the White Star Line made Southampton, instead of Liverpool, the main port for its transatlantic liners (including the *Titanic*); the Cunard company followed suit in 1919. The main reason for preferring Southampton was that it had open quays which – because of the Solent's double tides – were accessible to the biggest ships most of the time. Southampton's peak as a passenger port was reached in the 1930s. The railway company – then the Southern – constructed enormous new docks on reclaimed land, and the town responded by building what was probably the most ambitious inter-war group of civic buildings.

In the two world wars Southampton was of crucial importance – in both as a place of embarkation, and in the second because it had become the centre of an inventive aircraft industry, which included among its products the Spitfire fighter plane. Bombing devastated the shopping centre, and much of the riverside areas, including the Spitfire factory (but not before production had been transferred elsewhere). Rebuilding in the 1950s was sadly uninspiring; in the 1960s planners followed fashionable trends with tall blocks and ring roads. The university, rooted in a pre-1914 college, expanded to interesting overall effect. Present-day Southampton is a strangely mixed city – bland and featureless in the shopping centre; dramatically historic in the long battered but now sympathetically conserved old town; leafy in its ancient open spaces converted into parks (in the city centre) or kept half-wild (the Common); delightful in the inter-war suburbs designed by Herbert Collins. But, despite all the subsequent development, it is still the remains of the medieval town that impress most.

The best place to start an exploration of Southampton is the Bargate. This was the north gate of the town; now it is at the southern end of the main shopping centre. Right up to the 1930s buildings hemmed it in and vehicles went through; since then it has stood in a traffic circus. The core – an arch embedded in the gateway – is late Norman. Two large half-round towers were added on the north side in the thirteenth century. The south façade was thoroughly restored in 1864, but the splendid north façade remains largely

68 *Above right* **City Wall, Southampton.** The 14th-century arcade was added in front of a 12th-century merchant's house, the windows of which can be seen.

69 *Right* **Westgate and Merchants' Hall, Southampton.** The Westgate gave access to the medieval quay; the 15th-century Merchants' Hall was re-erected here in the 17th century.

as it was built in the late fourteenth century, in front of the original gate and rounded towers. Records show that in 1378 Henry Yevele, the royal architect, and William of Wynford, Wykeham's architect at Winchester, were commissioned to find masons for work on the Southampton defences. As the north front is in Wynford's style, it is quite possible that he was the designer, just as Yevele may have designed the Westgate at Canterbury. Most of the rough hard stone of which the Bargate and the walls are built – grey with rusty patches – came from the Binstead quarries on the Isle of Wight (p. 114).

It is not far from the Bargate, along the intermittent line of the northern city wall, to the jagged Arundel Tower at a corner of the walled town and, then, round the corner, to a dramatic stretch of wall which once faced open water, built in the fourteenth century against what had been a low cliff – thus strictly a retaining wall. It was made still more impressive when the half-round Catchcold Tower with its machicolated parapet was added in the fifteenth century, and it now holds its own, looking like a huge piece of stage scenery, despite the busy road in front and the 1960s towers to the north. Back to the Bargate, and to High Street leading south. Photographs from early this century ahow that this street had irregular grandeur, its slightly veering alignment punctuated by bay windows and culminated by churches. Bombing was bad, and rebuilding dreadful. But something remains of the old quality. Lloyds Bank of 1927 by Horace Field puts the later buildings to shame. It stands between two coaching inns, the Star with a late Georgian stuccoed front, and the Dolphin of 1775 with two splendid ranges of bow windows, said to be the largest of their kind. Opposite the fourteenth-century tower of Holy Rood church, the ruins of which are maintained as a seamen's memorial, is a vigorous Victorian bank, formerly the National Provincial, designed, like the company's old headquarters in Bishopsgate, London, by the versatile John Gibson.

Holy Rood used to have a spire, lost in the war, which counterpoised that of St Michael's, further west. This, rebuilt and heightened in the nineteenth century as a landmark for shipping, rises from an older tower, supported internally by four austere arches, built soon after the Norman Conquest or even just before. The church faces St Michael's Square, once the fish market, and opposite is Tudor House, given to the town, after being thoroughly restored, as a museum in 1911. The front part was built about 1500 by Sir John Dawtrey of Petworth when he was customs collector (p. 94). Although the external timber details were mostly renewed, old photographs show that the form of the frontage is largely original (except the ground floor), though the half-timbering was then plastered over; it may have originally been exposed. The great hall and a long wing behind are basically older. The garden, extending back to the city wall, has lately been laid out to a Tudor design by Sylvia Lansberg. The final, great, surprise for a visitor is the stone shell of a late Norman merchant's house at the end of the garden, its lower storey well below garden level. The roof and intermediate floor have gone, but a stone fireplace remains *in situ* at first-floor level – one of the earliest of its kind in existence. Another fireplace of similar date, with a stone chimney shaft, nearly unique, was re-erected here from a bomb-damaged house elsewhere. The shoreside frontage to the Norman house was incorporated into the city wall in the fourteenth century, in a way which is described later.

Bugle Street, now the city's best historic street, leads south from Tudor House, with medieval to modern houses making an attractive mixture. Today it is one of the most sought-after places to live in the city, but in Victorian times it adjoined one of the worst slum areas. Historic but hopelessly insanitary houses in nearby Simnel Street were cleared away by a progressive council in the 1890s, and replaced by council dwellings – which were themselves demolished a few years ago. New red-brick many-gabled housing in the jittery style of the 1980s has replaced them, self-consciously picturesque and particularly effective where it faces the city wall. But one small block of 1890s council housing remains, surmounting a fine vaulted medieval undercroft. The tall tower block to the north, dating from 1963, stands on the site of the castle keep. It is now *de rigueur* to condemn all high-rise housing, but this is a sophisticated design, not brutal – the architect was Eric Lyons, better known for his cosy two-storey housing. Down Simnel Street to the city wall again. The busy road outside the wall runs over the site of the original shoreline and the medieval West Quay, where most of the early shipping was moored. The Georgian assembly rooms, long vanished, stood nearby, as did the first baths – the striking swimming baths of 1962 by Lewis Berger, then city architect, stand near their site. This stretch of city wall is wonderfully impressive. When it was built along the hitherto undefended waterfront after the French raid of 1338, the frontages of some of the stone-built shoreside houses, which had been damaged in the raid, were incorporated in the defences. An arcade of blind arches was built in front of them, broad enough to accommodate a walkway on top, with spaces at the heads of the arches for molten lead or missiles to be dropped on attackers. The most exciting stretch is where the outer wall of the Norman house, already described from Tudor House garden, appears behind the arcade, with double round-headed windows – long blocked, now re-opened. But the archway which originally gave access from the house to the quay remains as it was blocked in the fourteenth century, with keyhole-shaped slits designed to take small primitive guns. This may be the oldest extant example of defensive work designed for gun warfare – which eventually made town walls like this obsolete (p. 98).

Further on is the Westgate, fairly modest considering it opened on to the principal quay. The timber-framed building just inside the gate, confusingly called the 'Tudor Merchants' Hall', originally stood in St Michael's Square and was used by cloth merchants. In 1634 it was demolished and re-erected here. On the old site the ground floor was open-sided, like the market halls at Faversham or Titchfield (p. 135), but it was enclosed on re-erection. The city wall continues a little further – partly a Victorian rebuilding on this stretch – and then ends, the next stretch having been lost. A column commemorates the sailing of the Pilgrim Fathers in the *Mayflower* and *Speedwell* in 1620. The *Speedwell* proved unseaworthy, and it was the *Mayflower* alone

70 **Yacht Club and Wool House, Southampton.** The former Yacht Club, 1846, indicates how early fashionable yachting began in the Solent; the medieval Wool House is now a museum.

which finally left Plymouth. This unintended departure from Plymouth is now far better known than the original embarkation at Southampton.

There are several interesting buildings in the only area where the old town faces open water – between the Victorian Eastern Docks and the inter-war Western Docks. The Wool House, built about 1400 as a warehouse, is now a maritime museum. One can stand, under the splendid original roof, amid models of old ships, and look out of the window at a modern liner in port. Next to the Wool House, in effective contrast, is the elaborately stuccoed Italianate façade of what was originally the Royal Southern Yacht Club, built in 1846 when Southampton itself was the hub of fashionable sailing in the Solent, now centred on Cowes. A different note is struck by the sugary entrance to the former Royal Pier, opened in 1833 for the new steamships to France and the Isle of Wight – predating all piers built for pleasure. (Brighton Chain Pier, p. 30, was ten years older, but it too was primarily for berthing.) Later it did develop for pleasure, hence the sugary entrance, which was built in the 1920s, and is likely to be all that remains, as the rest is doomed. Behind a tall block of warehouses facing the front, converted into flats, is another medieval survival – the ruin of a merchant's house of just before 1200, called Canute's Palace by a romantic historian, because Southampton was supposedly the place where he rebuked his courtiers. Yet another fascinating group of buildings lies to the east. The centrepiece is God's House down narrow Winkle Street, founded about 1185 as a hospice for poor travellers and others – an earlier counterpart of the hospital at Portsmouth (p. 100) and the Maison Dieu at Dover. There is nothing left of the medieval buildings except the restored chapel of St Julian, which retains its original fine chancel arch. Its great interest is that services were held there for Walloon and later Huguenot refugees, their descendants, and other French speakers from Tudor times till 1939; even now there is an annual service according to the Anglican prayer book in French. God's House gives its name to the adjoining Gate at the south-east corner of the town, one of the three town gates to survive, and to the impressive God's House Tower, built as a projection from the town walls in the fifteenth century.

Eastward is an area which derives its character from the development of the modern port. The centrepiece is the former Terminus Station, preserving the main classical block of Sir William Tite's station of 1839–40, closed a few years ago (the trains go by another route). Both the station and the nearby streets, developed at the same time, are more Georgian than early Victorian. Oxford Street takes a bend with a series of bow-windowed houses – almost semicircular in the Southampton tradition – making a marvellous interplay of curves. There is another range of bows in Bernard Street to the north, and there are more in Queen's Terrace facing the park. These streets were dilapidated a few years ago; recently the whole area has been uplifted. Adjoining the old station is the former South-Western Hotel, now offices, taking a bold corner opposite the entrance to the docks – an impressive Victorian building of 1867 reminiscent of a French château, rising to a complex roof with porthole windows in the attic. Here people stayed before joining and after leaving liners. Around 1920 an extension, contrastingly classical in Portland stone, was built for the extra clientèle following the

71 South-Western House, Southampton, built as a hotel in 1867 for people joining or leaving liners; the tall extension was added *c.*1920 when Cunard transferred their transatlantic liners to Southampton.

transfer of Cunard liners to Southampton. The road past the entrance to the docks is called Canute Road – perhaps a Victorian engineers' joke, since it follows the old shoreline, those engineers having succeeded in doing what Canute could not do; to cause the sea to recede. A little way along, and up a side street, is the Hall of Aviation, an imaginative addition to Southampton's many museums, commemorating the area's critical role in the early development of aircraft.

The post-war shopping centre, Above Bar, is almost all dispiriting except for the surviving side of Regency Portland Street leading off, the bordering parks, and one good 1960s building with jutting glazed façades on a corner, making a prelude to the Civic Centre. This product of municipal pride in the 1930s, claimed to be the first to use the rather frigid title – combining council offices, Guildhall, law courts, library and art gallery – is a successful spread-out composition in modernized classical style, culminating in a tall tapering tower, which chimes every four hours the tune of *O God our help in ages past.* The words of the hymn (not the tune) were written by Isaac Watts, the greatest English hymn-writer, not excepting Charles Wesley. He lived as a youth in Southampton in the late seventeenth century, the son of a member of the Independent (later Congregational) church. He is commemorated in Watts Park – one of the series of medieval common fields turned into Victorian parks – by a life-size statue, with finely detailed relief panels illustrating his life. Clearly this was by a good sculptor – he was the almost unknown Richard Cockle Lucas, who lived a reclusive life in nearby Chilworth; almost the only other significant work by him is the even better statue of Dr Johnson in the

72 **Carlton Crescent, Southampton,** part of the fashionable development of the 1820s, by Samuel Toomer.

market place at Lichfield. Nearby is Lutyens' impressive Cenotaph, commemorating those who died in the first world war. Opposite is another poignant memorial, in memory of the ship's engineers who went down with the *Titanic*.

Further north is Southampton's 'Regency' area, developed from about 1820 on. The centrepiece is Carlton Crescent, not quite a crescent but a curve with a slight pinch. The houses are austerely classical, in stucco, the most conspicuous being detached, but linked by screen walls, the whole making a fine series round the curve; one, in a key position, breaks out into a bow. Until lately its attribution was unknown; Mr Robert Coles has shown that the scheme was promoted by Edward Toomer and designed by his son Samuel. Toomer also probably designed the exquisite Carlton Lodge on the corner of Bedford Place, a classical composition full of fascinating detail – for instance the locally characteristic sunflower pattern in the arched recesses over the windows, and the big two-storeyed bow on the Bedford Place frontage. Carlton Crescent adjoins the site of the Ordnance Survey Office, where the finest detailed maps ever were produced from 1841 till 1940. Bombs then destroyed most of the buildings, but some survive, including one with the characteristic sunflower pattern. The Ordnance Survey is now in modern buildings on the outskirts of the city.

Finally, in the district of Highfield, east of the Common, is some of the country's finest suburban development of the inter-war years. It was designed by Herbert Collins who, as Mr Robert Williams describes in a recent book, came from London to Southampton after the first world war. Collins was influenced by Sir Raymond Unwin – the greatest housing architect of the day – at Letchworth and Hampstead Garden Suburb, and by Unwin's disciple Louis de Soissons at Welwyn Garden City. Collins' houses are usually in short terraces, of perhaps four or five, very much in an adaptation of the Georgian vernacular style – that of cottages rather than grander town houses. He related his houses with the greatest care to each other and to the subtleties of their setting – to slopes in the ground, alignments of roads, and trees; Collins never removed a good tree unless it were unavoidable. Green spaces, grassed or tree-grown, make focal points. His principles are displayed almost to perfection in his houses of 1922–38 in Orchards Way, Uplands Way, Highfield Close and the adjoining part of Brookvale Road. He designed elsewhere in Southampton suburbs, for instance in Bassett Green (Ethelburt Avenue) and Swaything (along Mansbridge Road) but not with quite the same flair as in Orchards Way. If only more of the huge amount of inter-war and post-war housing had approached Collins' standards in design!

Tenterden

Kent

Tenterden is a long and colourful town, essentially a single street, which narrows in the middle and widens at the ends – at the north end it borders a green, at the south a grassy strip, planted with trees. It began, improbably, as the outlying pasture – the local meaning of *-den* – associated with the distant Isle of Thanet; the first syllable is a corruption of 'Thanet'. The church, dedicated to Thanet's patron St Mildred, has a superb fifteenth-century tower of silver-buff stone from neighbouring Bethersden; it has corner turrets and tall pinnacles; the best of a group that includes Ashford and Croydon. In front of the church, blocking the view of it from the street, except narrowly through gaps, is a row of buildings whose predecessors were recorded in 1279 as encroaching on the highway. It is they that cause the narrowing of the street. The architecture of Tenterden has infinite variety; many buildings are visibly medieval or Tudor timber-framed, others have Georgian fronts, often with tiles (overlapping or mathematical), or, especially, weather-boarding (see colour illus. p. 111). There are tall, distinctive three-storeyed Georgian houses which are probably framed in softwood (not hardwood, which ceased to be used for framing by 1700; the softwood or deal would have been imported, possibly through Rye), and faced with mathematical tiles, feigning brickwork, or boarding. Tenterden became a limb of the Cinque Port of Rye in 1449; this is explained by the fact that the associated hamlet of Smallhythe, about three miles away, was a port on a branch of the River Rother, long since silted. Smallhythe is now a tiny group of timber-framed houses and brick chapel, all rebuilt after a fire in 1516. One of the houses is a museum devoted to Ellen Terry the actress, who lived there.

Titchfield

Hampshire

Titchfield is a surprisingly preserved old town in the developed area between Southampton and Portsmouth, near the mouth of the little River Meon, which till the seventeenth century had a small estuary reaching to the town. There was a market in Norman times, and in 1232 an abbey was founded about three-quarters of a mile to the north. At the Dissolution it was in the hands of Henry Wriothesley, later Earl of Southampton, one of Henry VIII's agents in the disposal of monastic possessions. He converted the abbey into a mansion for himself, with a great stone gatehouse over part of the site of the church, a splendid example in the English tradition with corner turrets. Nearby are two Tudor chimneystacks which are among the earliest examples of decorative brickwork in the area. Close by is a monastic barn with a fine roof, recently restored, now used as a farm shop. There were four earls of Southampton of the Wriothesley dynasty – the third was patron of Shakespeare. The fourth had a London house in Bloomsbury, the development of which he started; it was his heiress who married into the Russell family, bringing Bloomsbury into the possession of the Dukes of Bedford. Titchfield passed to other hands, and the house was ruinous by the mid-eighteenth century. Much of the town is still Tudor or early seventeenth-century in its fabric, with timber-framed and early brick houses, and others with Georgian fronts often concealing older work. There is an attractive pattern of narrow streets converging on the central wide street where, until the nineteenth century there stood a small timber-framed market hall with open-sided ground storey. This was dismantled, partly re-erected elsewhere, and, in the 1960s, re-erected again in the Weald and Downland museum at Singleton, near Chichester. It probably dates from the sixteenth century and provides an early instance of brick-nogging (bricks filling the timber framework) of which there are other examples in the town. The base of the church tower was a Saxon porch which may date from as early as AD 700. Inside there is a great tomb commemorating members of the Wriothesley family. Titchfield became overshadowed by Fareham in the eighteenth century because of the latter's better situation; it now has the status of a village, defiant against the encroaching development.

Tonbridge

Kent

Tonbridge looks at first sight like a modernized Victorian town. This is because the present shopping street developed after the railway came in 1842, to the south of the old town which lies across the River Medway. Tonbridge grew beside the castle, originally built by Richard de Bienfait, one of the Conqueror's barons, sometimes called Richard de Tonbridge. But his descendants took the name of their even more important stronghold of Clare, in Suffolk; the de Clares became one of the greatest feudal families, with estates in Wales and the West as well as Suffolk, Surrey and Kent, until the last of the main line was killed at the battle of Bannockburn. They were great castle builders, and this can be seen at Tonbridge, where the thirteenth-century gatehouse is one of the finest of its kind, with a many-recessed

73 **Tonbridge Castle** was a stronghold of the powerful Clare family; the very fine gatehouse dates from the late 13th century.

74 **Medieval houses at Tonbridge.** The Chequers was a 14th-century hall house with its hall long since subdivided, and a taller 15th-century wing; the house to the right is 15th-century, with striking timberwork probably meant to be exposed (but not blackened).

entrance between massive projecting towers. Little else is left of the castle except the mound of the keep, and part of the outside wall pleasantly bordering the Medway. The old town developed along the route leading north from the bridge, and already by the fourteenth century houses were built backing on to the castle moat. One partly dates from then – the Chequers hotel with subdivided central hall and tall, three-tiered gabled wing. Next to it, Cobleys is a fifteenth-century two-gabled house, also with three jettied storeys. It is disgraceful that other medieval houses on the same side south of the Chequers were demolished a few years ago for street widening. Further up High Street there are brick Georgian fronts, notably the Rose and Crown hotel, 'mellowed to the loveliest colours, chequered plum and blue with mottled orange rubbed-brick dressings' (John Newman; *Buildings of England: West Kent and the Weald*). Further on is Tonbridge School, founded in 1553 by a native who became Lord Mayor of London, and expanded in Victorian times into a public school; the buildings are unremarkable. Pleasant streets with a few colourful buildings lead east around the church, which has a massive medieval tower of the same warm brown local sandstone as the castle gate.

Tunbridge Wells

Kent

Tunbridge Wells was the first place in England, since the time of the Romans, to develop purely as a resort. It had been a remote place with rough commons and a few scattered cottages, far even from a sizeable village. In 1606, so the story goes, Lord North, a young and dissipated courtier, was returning from a stay at nearby Eridge where he had gone to recover his health, when he passed a spring whose waters looked and tasted like those of the then fashionable Belgian resort of Spa – the prototype in name of all such resorts in Britain. He came back a year later, drank the waters and recovered. By 1615 others were following his example, and in 1630 Queen Henrietta Maria came to take the waters after giving birth to the future Charles II. She and her entourage camped on the nearby common. Other early visitors stayed in country houses, lodged in the town of Tonbridge or in nearer villages, or roughed it in cottages. The sheer rusticity of the place appealed to those used to the sophisticated life of London. After the Restoration Tunbridge Wells was much frequented by high society. Catherine of Braganza, Charles II's queen, came several times in the vain hope that the waters might make her pregnant. One of the early pseudo-scientific treatises on the waters, published by a Dr Madan in 1687, said that the waters engendered a 'sweet Balsamic, spiritous, and Sanguineous Temperament, which naturally incites and inspires men and women to Amorous Emotions and Titillations' – suggesting a pattern of behaviour very different from that associated with Tunbridge Wells today. A French visitor, the Comte de Gramont, said that 'the company, though always numerous, is always select; since those who repair there for diversions ever exceed the number of those who go thither for health, everything there breathes with pleasure: constraint is banished, and joy and pleasure are sole sovereigns of the place.' Yet the place was still completely rustic. A grassy promenade was laid out beside the principal spring in 1638. From 1680 plots alongside were leased for development, with strict conditions that the buildings could be used only for shops, places of refreshment or gaming houses, not for residence or lodging. A colonnade was built in front of them – this was the beginning of the Pantiles, so-called from the tiles used for the original paving (but they were flat, not the curved type for which the word is now used). Meanwhile another landowner leased off plots on the slopes of nearby 'Mount Sion', where lodging houses and also cottages for the servicing population were built haphazardly. More houses and cottages were built round the edges of the common half a mile away on 'Mount Ephraim' – the biblical names were said have been given during the period of Puritan ascendancy.

The waters were taken early in the morning, after which the company promenaded, socialized and played games – cards and dice for money were popular. In the evenings there were balls and assemblies, in what were never very grand assembly rooms adjoining the Pantiles. After about 1720 the social life became organized as a more rural variant of that of rising Bath; in 1735 Beau Nash, who had long controlled Bath, took the additional post of Master of Ceremonies at Tunbridge Wells during the summer season. But the Kentish spa did not develop architecturally anything like Bath, and after Nash's death in 1761 (aged 87) it stagnated till the end of the century. Fashion was then being drawn to Brighton. After about 1800 Tunbridge Wells began to attract permanent residents – people of private means, or retired from commerce, the armed services or a colonial background. They built villas round the common, or larger houses in the surrounding wooded country. The social life dwindled, and Tunbridge Wells became a haven of respectability.

From 1825 a landowner employed Decimus Burton to develop the Calverley estate to a varied and remarkable layout including villas, a park, a crescent and the beginnings of a new town centre. The railway of the 1840s helped to consolidate the new centre, and stimulated the spread of villas, mostly solid 'Italianate' with stucco decoration, massive bay windows and conservatories. Hotels opened around the common. Around the end of the century many of the new houses and hotels were gabled with rich red tile-hanging, derived from the vernacular traditions of the Weald. Today's Tunbridge Wells is still very much a nineteenth-century town, except for the Pantiles and scattered houses on Mounts Sion and Ephraim.

The Pantiles is unique. It began to take shape after 1680, when predecessors of the present buildings were put up behind the first colonnade (which has been gradually renewed since then) and on the opposite, lower side. Other buildings were islanded in the space between, making an attractive informal effect of changing levels and interconnecting spaces. None of the existing structures looks earlier than mid-Georgian, but there is great variety in style, building materials and height. Older buildings are faced, following Wealden traditions, with weatherboarding and tile-hanging; Regency and early Victorian ones are stuccoed; later Victorian ones are again tile-hung in the revived tradition. The waters issue behind an early Victorian canopy at one end; at the other end the modest late Victorian pump-room was replaced in 1970 by an all too characteristic development of the time, too heavy, and built of too harsh brick. Nearby is the church of King Charles the Martyr, built in 1676–96, disconcertingly like a puritan chapel outside, but with splendid shallow-domed ceilings within, partly executed by Henry Doogood who worked with Wren. Roads and alleys lead off casually beyond the church, into an area built up piecemeal since the 1680s. Particularly pleasing is Cumberland Walk, a footpath beside which villas rise amid dense and colourful gardens. One is faced in pebbles, presumably brought from the coast; another has ammonite, or spiral fossil capitals which are the trademark of the Amon Wilds of Brighton (page 85). It seems that Brighton

75 **The Pantiles, Tunbridge Wells** evolved from a rustic 17th-century promenade leading to the medicinal spring and was always totally informal, apart from the unifying effect of the colonnade.

builders were at work in the older, quieter resort. But there is no hint of formality in the area except in the fairly modest Bedford Terrace with its ground-floor bows. Going up Mount Sion there is an astonishing variety of domestic building, ranging from Jerningham House of about 1700 to early, mid and later Victorian houses in evolving styles, while down some unexpected lanes and alleys are tile-hung cottages which must date from the first period of expansion.

Decimus Burton's development makes a contrast. The best part, by far, is Calverley Park, an arc of detached villas (one pair is semi-detached) which look over landscaped parkland – the lower part of the park is public, but its upper part and the roadway past the houses are private. The villas, in grey local sandstone are designed individually in variants of classical or simple Gothic themes; each is set back in a garden. It is a marvellous early example of a sylvan suburb, contemporary with the later parts of Regent's Park, and a prototype for the kind of development which culminated in Hampstead Garden Suburb. Next to it Burton designed Calverley Park Crescent, less successful of its kind, but looking impressive end-on, where its bow-fronted terminal façade groups with the arched entrance to Calverley Park, flanked by two classical lodges. Many other buildings by Burton have been removed or altered. He designed a new Gothic church, Holy Trinity, sited prominently; it was closed several years ago, but saved through being converted into an arts centre. The present town centre is a jumble, but there are impressive individual buildings, including a former Congregational church, now a shop, with a splendid Corinthian portico of 1866 closing the view along

Monson Road, a sinuous street with a long first-floor balcony following the curves.

Finally there is Mount Ephraim. Several streets climb from the shopping centre to the end of the common, which is edged by a mixture of Georgian vernacular houses, Regency stuccoed villas, pretentious Victorian former hotels, and colourfully assertive gabled buildings from around the turn of the century. The central part of the Kent and Sussex Hospital, further north, is a striking piece of inter-war architecture of the Art-Deco phase, built in 1934 to the design of the local architect Cecil Burns, who deserves better recognition. Twenty-five years earlier he designed the Tunbridge Wells and Counties Club, facing the common much lower down, in an impeccable Georgian style, excellent of its kind. From the upper reaches of the common there are views right over the town centre to wooded residential areas beyond – still, from such viewpoints Tunbridge Wells seems more rural than urban. Victorian gabled cottages are built against natural rock outcrops. The common itself is well maintained, and seems half-wild in its further recesses, despite being crisscrossed by roads and paths. There is a great deal else for the intrepid explorer to see in Tunbridge Wells, particularly around its Victorian fringes.

West Malling

Kent

West Malling is a surprisingly delightful place – just off the old A20; a short distance from the exit of its motorway successor; and just clear of the extensive housing and industrial sprawl west of Maidstone. It has the classic form of the small medieval town – a long street, wide in one part, narrowed in another by an island block of buildings which separate a parallel lane. Architecturally the dominant style is Georgian, and there is a strange lack of recent intrusive development. Standing in the centre of the town the finest view is southward – up the street, which is wide at first, then closes in on the right, and finally turns sharply to the left. An impressive

76 **West Malling** is a charming small town with a surprising number of fine Georgian houses on its long street.

Map XI **West Malling** is an almost classic example of a medieval one-street town, although its best buildings are Georgian (76). The widest part, where markets were first held, was encroached upon by an island block separating a back lane, King Street (*see colour illus. p. 142*), from the narrowed main street. The map is of 1867.

series of Georgian houses, mainly in dark red brick, compose the frontage as it closes in, with the church spire rising behind. Half a mile further to the south, outside the town proper, is St Leonard's Tower, essentially a small Norman keep, still formidable with its regularly coursed ragstone walls and flat buttresses, but with a ruinous roofline giving it a romantic appearance. It was probably built by Bishop Gundulf of Rochester, who supervised the building of the Tower of London (page 105), to defend the southern approach to his city. It gives a clue to the origin of the town, which the bishop may have founded as a market centre on this route, where it was intersected by the (originally less important) west-east route, later superseded by the A20. It outgrew East Malling, which was of older origin.

The lower, northern part of the main street is narrowed by the island block, with the parallel lane to the west. The street has a series of low-key, mainly Georgian façades, mainly of brick (too often painted), but occasionally weatherboarded, like the one with a Venetian window; this was a small Assembly Room, suggesting the social life of the town's eighteenth-century heyday. Alleys lead through the island block to

Above left King Street, West Malling

Above right High Street and Butter Cross, Winchester

The Deanery, Winchester

the parallel lane, King Street, which has a rougher mixture of old brick fronts, boundary walls of ragstone, former oasts, and timber-framed houses which are, untraditionally, brought out in black and white (see colour illus. p. 142).

Finally, Swan Street leads informally eastward, pass ing the fifteenth-century gateway of Malling Abbey, founded, for nuns, by Bishop Gundulf. The buildings were converted to a house after the Dissolution, but in 1916 nuns (Anglican) returned. Much good medieval work remains, mostly inaccessible to visitors. The last house in the town, going east, is one of the finest, Went House of about 1720, built to a complicated design including patterning in dark and lighter red brick, set back behind splendid iron railings.

Winchelsea

Sussex

Winchelsea was one of the most remarkable examples of town planning in medieval England, and one of the most spectacular failures. The older town of Winchelsea, of which there is no certain record before 1130, had an important trade with France, especially in wine, and, together with Rye, was associated with the Cinque Ports federation. But by then it was already suffering from sea encroachment, culminating in the great storm of 1287 which made it uninhabitable. The old town was important strategically, and in 1280 Edward I had appointed commissioners to prepare a plan for a new town to replace it on a site to the north, a flat-topped promontory with short steep slopes above what was then the tidal estuary of the River Brede. A rigid grid of streets was laid out, with rectangular house plots varying greatly in size, which were offered rent-free for seven years to migrants from the old town and other suitable settlers. The new town – or at least the northern part of it – was occupied between 1288 and 1292. But the estuary soon started to silt; Winchelsea never grew to the intended extent, nearby Rye being better situated, and by the sixteenth century there was no access by ship to Winchelsea. It is difficult to imagine

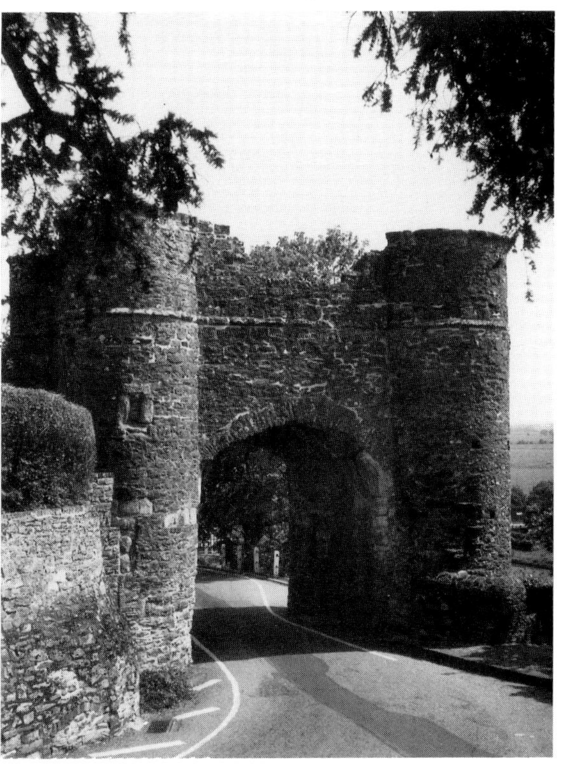

77 *Below left* **Strand Gate, Winchelsea,** one of the gates to the shrunken medieval town.

78 *Below right* **St Thomas, Winchelsea** was built very ambitiously and probably never finished; this view shows an unfinished part, looking towards the completed eastern section.

that there were ever ships where the now narrow and non-tidal River Brede flows to the north-east of the town. Winchelsea simply shrank into a genteel-looking village, which it remains today. It is approached by two routes from the former harbour site, each up a steep slope to a town gate. Strand Gate to the north-east is the more impressive, with its rounded corner towers; Pipewell Gate to the north-west looks less like a town gate since the wall adjoining was either never built or has been demolished. The present town plan – only part of the intended original extent – is a grid of four streets by four, lined, not continuously, by pleasant unassuming houses, usually looking Georgian or later outside. Many are older than their façades suggest; some are partly built in ragstone, and a few have visible medieval features. There are numerous stone-vaulted cellars or undercrofts of the thirteenth or fourteenth century date, like those in Southampton, but they are mostly under later buildings and unsuspected from outside, except where the tops of entrance arches, through which steps led down from the street, are visible; an example is on the corner of Castle Street and Mill Road. The church is the most eloquent memorial of Winchelsea's frustrated prosperity. It was to be of almost cathedral grandeur, but all that we see is the eastern part, with broken walls towards the west. Either it was never finished, or less probably (but according to legend), the western part was destroyed by the French in one of their devastating raids which hastened the impoverishment of the town. What we see inside is a spacious, delicate work of early fourteenth-century Gothic, with lofty arches, windows with flowing, prickly tracery, and elaborate tombs, probably of members of the Alard family – merchants and Cinque Ports magnates who were originally in the old town and helped to found the new.

Winchelsea is remarkable among medieval towns for the straightness, indeed rigidity, of its streets. Of course there had been large planned towns before with grids of streets – Saxon Winchester; Norman Bury St Edmunds; early thirteenth-century Salisbury. But their grids were less regular, with many complexities. Smaller towns, like Romney, Hythe, Newport, Shoreham and, to some extent, Rye had grid plans, but they were also rough and irregular. Most of the numerous early medieval planned towns in England had little more than one or two streets, like Alresford. There was no English medieval parallel to Winchelsea in its rigidity; its main counterparts are in south-west France where Edward I also helped to found new towns. Even if Winchelsea had become fully built up, the straight vistas would probably have been far less interesting than those in more organic medieval towns where nearly every street has a twist, however slight, or a variation in width, helping to define the views along it. But for all that Winchelsea has its own particular charm, with an intriguing mix of medieval, Georgian, Victorian and twentieth-century buildings.

Map XII **Winchelsea** was laid out ambitiously in the 13th century with a rigid grid of streets, contrasting with the looser patterns of earlier new-founded towns like Newport (map VIII) or Petersfield (map IX). The town never developed as intended; the church is incomplete (78); gates survive (77), but the intended town wall may never have been built. The map is of 1872.

Winchester
Hampshire

Winchester is one of the great medieval cities of Europe. Few others retain medieval buildings to compare, collectively, with the cathedral, castle hall, college and hospital of St Cross. These, together with hundreds of others of all dates, make Winchester the most interesting city in the region, not excluding Canterbury.

There was a Roman town, *Venta Belgarum*, alongside a prehistoric site; of this the alignment of the High Street and the line of the city walls remain. It shrank to insignificance for a time after the Romans left. The first church was built in 645, becoming a cathedral in 676, when the kings of emergent Wessex probably had a palace there. King Alfred refortified the city in his struggle against the Vikings. Under him and his successors Winchester became the chief centre of the kingdom of Wessex which in time, through its northward and eastward expansion, became effectively that of England. The city was replanned within the strengthened Roman defences, with new streets leading off at fairly regular intervals north and south of High Street – they do not correspond with the lost Roman pattern of secondary streets, as archaeologists have proved. Under St Ethelwold, bishop from 963 to 984, the cathedral church was reformed as a Benedictine monastery which, like that at Canterbury, became famous for book and manuscript illustration. Adjoining the cathedral to the north was another monastery, the New Minster, and beyond that was St Mary's abbey for nuns. Together they must have formed the most impressive group of buildings in later Saxon England, except perhaps at Canterbury and possibly York. The Saxon cathedral stood north-west of the present cathedral, which was started in 1079, using stone from the Binstead quarries on the Isle of Wight (page 114). The bishopric was the richest in England, and its holders were often politically powerful. Bishop Henry of Blois built the now ruinous Wolvesey Castle as his fortified residence, and founded the Hospital of St Cross. He was deeply involved in the struggle between his brother King Stephen and the Empress Matilda, when much of Winchester was burnt, including the royal palace which stood south

79 Winchester Cathedral. The Saxon cathedral was on the grassy area, left foreground. The present cathedral was started 1079 with stone from the Isle of Wight. The west front was remodelled in the 14th century and the nave soon after by William of Wykeham. The interior is very much grander than the austere exterior suggests.

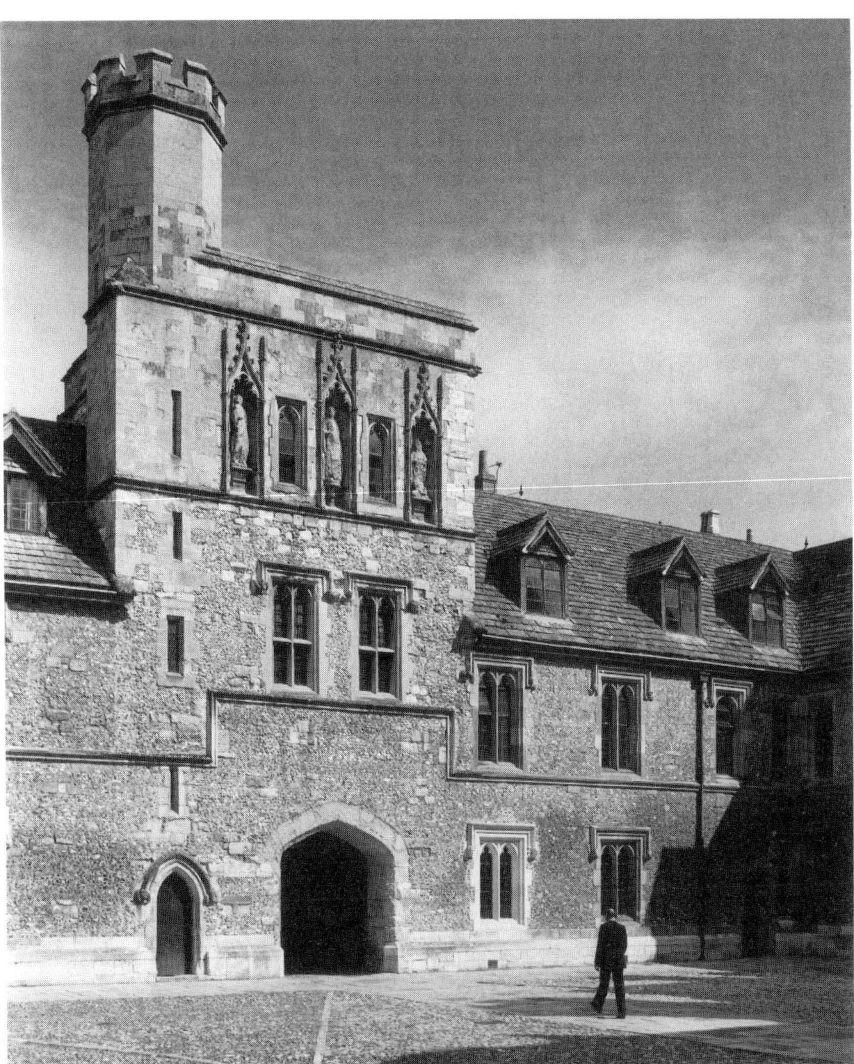

80 Winchester College, founded 1382 by Bishop Wykeham and designed by William Wynford, provided a prototype for many, often much smaller, grammar and public schools.

of High Street, close to the cathedral. But by then the castle had been built on higher ground to the west, partly as a royal residence; here Domesday Book was compiled, and the royal treasury kept till the end of the twelfth century. Henry III built the present Great Hall which is all that survives of the castle – internally the finest medieval hall in England except Westminster Hall. Comparison with Westminster is appropriate, since after the thirteenth century Winchester was no longer a royal residence and Westminster became, indisputably, the centre of the realm. Previously, for about two centuries, the functions and status of effective capital had been shared between Winchester and Westminster.

William of Wykeham, bishop from 1367 and for many years Chancellor of England, remodelled the cathedral nave, to the design of William Wynford – one of the great medieval architects (Henry Yevele is another) whose names are now known through documentary evidence, but who are not yet popularly

81 *Above* **Hospital of St Cross, Winchester.** The back of the brethren's apartments of *c.* 1445 (*see colour illus. pp. 2/3*).

82 *Above right* **High Street, Winchester** follows the Roman line with some distortion in the early medieval period, and has buildings of every subsequent date; the one with a big round-headed window was a Georgian inn; the bank is a conversion of the Guildhall of 1713 – with a statue of Queen Anne and a projecting clock. In the far distance is the medieval Westgate (*see colour illus. p. 142*).

recognized as architects of the calibre of Wren, as they ought to be. Wykeham founded Winchester College, which was at first intended primarily for boys who would pass on to his other foundation, New College, Oxford. But it set the pattern for numerous late medieval, Tudor and subsequent schools, not only large 'public' schools, but also smaller grammar schools in towns all round the country. The main buildings round the two courtyards, with the chapel and cloister, all designed by William Wynford, remain relatively little altered – with many others added in more recent times. Cardinal Beaufort, bishop from 1404, augmented Henry of Blois' Hospital of St Cross, and built the present pensioners' rooms and great hall in collegiate form, adjoining the earlier magnificent church – architecturally one of the most impressive medieval charitable foundations in England (see colour illus. pp. 2/3).

Much of the medieval glory of Winchester departed at the Reformation. Hyde Abbey, on the northern outskirts, which replaced the Saxon New Minster next to the cathedral in the twelfth century, was destroyed, as was St Mary's nunnery. Luckily the cathedral was retained, with dean and canons to replace the medieval monks: parts of the monastic buildings were converted into clerics' houses. The Civil War caused destruction too, both to the cathedral area and to the castle which, after being besieged, was finally 'slighted' (made useless militarily), and eventually cleared except for the Great Hall.

Winchester was already in economic decline before the Reformation. In its twelfth-century heyday its population may have been as much as 8,000 – making it among the largest towns in England. It was an early centre of weaving – the clothiers and weavers mainly operating in the north-eastern part of the city, called the Brooks, where there were many carefully channelled streams used for processing; the River Itchen provided power for fulling mills. Archaeological excavation in this area revealed, *inter alia*, remains of medieval merchants' premises and humbler weavers' homes. The whole of this part of the city became depopulated in the later Middle Ages because of the decline in the weaving trade. Nobody knows fully why the Winchester woollen industry, once so important, should have decayed so early, while that of Salisbury and numerous other places in the West of England, in East Anglia, and elsewhere was expanding so fast. But it did – and this, combined with the loss of Winchester's status as royal capital, the destruction of the abbeys, and the eclipse of the once very important annual St Giles's Fair, led to a reduction in population to about 2,000–3,000 in the early seventeenth century.

Winchester had both a restoration and a renaissance in the later seventeenth century. The cathedral close was reconstructed after the restoration of the monarchy and the re-establishment of the Anglican hierarchy. Charles II decided to build a new palace on part of the castle site, an English version of Versailles, with Wren as architect. It was largely completed, but not fitted, when he died; it was later converted to barracks and finally destroyed by fire. But the building of the palace had a stimulating effect on Winchester which was lasting. Charles stayed there, with his courtiers, on several occasions when the palace was building, and the city became established as a fashionable place to live. Bishop Morley started a new palace adjacent to ruinous Wolvesey Castle – but, like his immediate predecessors, his successors preferred to live in Farnham Castle rather than Winchester itself, and it was not till modern times that Wolvesey Palace again became the permanent home of the bishops. Many other well-to-do people settled in the city, and one of the delights of Winchester is the large number of late Stuart and early Georgian houses, usually of the deep red local brick, sometimes interspersed with grey. Perhaps the city languished a little as a favoured place of residence in later Georgian times, when Southampton became more fashionable, but it had another spurt in early Victorian times – the railway, on the way to Southampton, arrived early; there were trains from London by 1840. But Victorian Winchester never grew substantially. Today, county administration looms large, physically and socially, but Winchester has become once again a desirable place to live in. It is very much on the defensive against being swamped by the development of the burgeoning Southampton–Solent area, and by the traffic heading there. It is visibly conservation-conscious, and walks through its extensive better parts can be an almost continuous delight. Any description of Winchester in a short space must be extremely cursory, and is covered under the following headings: *High Street – Westgate to Eastgate; the Cathedral Close; South of High Street; East of the River; North of High Street.*

High Street – Westgate to Eastgate

The Westgate is best seen from further down High Street, where it still appears to close the street. The effect has been ruined near at hand since the traffic sweeps round one side, leaving the gate to appear to project from the buildings on the other side, a setting that is somehow less satisfactory than that of the Bargate at Southampton, stranded though that is in a complete roundabout. The Westgate is less grand than the Bargate though evidently remodelled at about the same time; the late fourteenth-century outer front is in the same style as that of the Bargate. All around are county buildings, illustrating how the county government developed out of the royal courts at the castle. From the fourteenth century, local justices of the peace sat at Quarter Sessions which were usually held, four times annually, in the Great Hall of the castle – like the Assizes, to which the High Court judges came twice yearly. Serious criminal cases were tried at the Assizes, less serious ones at Quarter Sessions, which also dealt with county business. When elected county councils were set up in 1888, they took on the administrative functions of Quarter Sessions, as well as others. The scope of county government steadily expanded until it reached a peak in the 1960s, and this is reflected at Winchester. Fairly modest buildings in vernacular Tudor or Jacobean styles were built between the restored Great Hall and Westgate in the late nineteenth and early twentieth centuries. In 1959–60 a large new block, based on an inter-war design, was built east of the Westgate – in deep red brick, and in a style which seemed hopelessly traditionalist to the modernists when it was opened, but which is more acceptable today. Later additions in modern styles are less so.

Below the Westgate, High Street steadily takes shape, especially past the staggered crossroads, beset with traffic, where Southgate Street leads off to the right and Jewry Street to the left. The delightful sinuous Georgian shop front of the equally old *Hampshire Chronicle* is a portent of the dense variety of frontages – though often only over shop level – along the rest of High Street, which is mostly now pedestrianized. A great deal is Georgian, with some pleasant bow windows; some is Victorian, like the elaborate building, originally a pub, at the corner of St Thomas Street, by the local architect Thomas Stopher; some is make-believe Tudor, like the façade of the otherwise genuinely Tudor God Begot House. Lloyds Bank is a remodelling of the modest former Guildhall of 1713, with a projecting clock, resembling that at Guildford. Mention of Guildford is appropriate, for in the distance beyond the end of the street, as at Guildford, a green hill rises – here it is St Giles Hill, where the ancient fair was held. The central landmark of High Street is the fifteenth-century Butter Cross, where the street widens (see colour illus. p. 142). It is one of few of its kind surviving – a huge Gothic pinnacle embellished with a host of lesser pinnacles and niches, elevated above steps round which butter sellers are said to have stood, hence the name. It is much restored but lucky to survive at all. The larger and different Cross at Chichester is a slightly later development of the theme. Behind the Butter Cross is a plausibly late medieval house, gabled and jettied, and next is another, probably once like it but plastered and Georgianized – not necessarily less interesting on that account. Nearby is a passageway through to the cathedral area. High Street then narrows; on the right is the Pentice, first the site of the royal palace, then of a mint, then of a drapery market, but by the fifteenth century occupied by merchants' houses. Some are as early, though much altered; two retain original bargeboards on their gables. They all project over the pavement, supported on pillars with modern shops set behind – like the

83 **Eastgate Street, Winchester.** These bowed houses of *c.* 1846/50 take the curve marvellously.

Butterwalks at Totnes and Dartmouth. Here High Street is very busy; property values rise; it then broadens with the Victorian Gothic Guildhall (1871–3) on the right. The widest part – called Broadway – is dominated by the supremely effective statue of King Alfred, arm outstretched, by Hamo Thornycroft (1901). Beyond this the Eastgate stood, demolished like two other town gates for Georgian road improvements. But a later road improvement – the construction of Eastgate Street in the 1840s – resulted in real gain, since the bow-fronted houses on the rounded corner with Broadway, in latter-day Regency style, provide a marvellous interplay of curves.

The Cathedral Close

The Close is south of the cathedral – it developed after the Reformation out of the old monastic precinct – and is approached intricately from the west or the east. The eastern approach is more revealing – beginning in Colebrook Street behind the Guildhall, which has some fine Georgian houses. A path passes a formal watery garden outside the Lady Chapel at the furthest end of the cathedral, and then bends between walls of stone, flint and brick to emerge where the cloister was, now an open grassy space extending irregularly southward, surrounded loosely by cathedral clergy houses, which were either rebuilt or considerably restored in the late seventeenth and early eighteenth centuries, following the depredations of the Civil War and Commonwealth; their history is described in John Crook's *The Wainscot Book*. Some retain medieval parts. The Anglican cathedral close is something not paralleled outside England and Wales: no other country had an established church with an essentially Catholic hierarchy of bishops, deans, canons and other clergy, and allowed them to marry; hence its unique clerical-domestic character; Winchester has one of the most delightful examples. Three vignettes summarize the quality of the Close. First, the view of the Deanery (see colour illus. p. 143) with its exquisite three-arched porch, built for the prior's house which preceded it; its fourteenth-century hall since subdivided, with a plain Georgian end wall; and a long low brick wing behind – built at about the time when Charles II stayed with the Dean while his palace was being built. Second, the cul-de-sac called Dome Alley: four pairs of houses built for canons in the 1660s, with carved brickwork on their gables; the view is closed by the fine Victorian spire of St Thomas' church. Third, at the southern end of the Close, Cheyney Court, with three picturesque timber-framed gables rising above a flinty ground storey. The gables, like the restored windows, look Jacobean, dating from the end of the timber-framing tradition. Nearby is the southern gate out of the Close.

South of High Street

There is a network of little streets south of the middle part of High Street – part of the Saxon grid – with a thick scatter of pleasant, well-tended Georgian houses, and of recent infillings and conversions, reflecting the welcome trend for people to move back to the inner city, from which there has been so much recent depopulation. St Thomas Street is the most typical of these streets, but Southgate Street, wider and busier, has the two best houses. One, the present Southgate Hotel of 1715, has columns and other motifs in carved brickwork. The other, Serles House, set back and now a military museum, is of about the same date but more sophisticated, with a great curved projecting centrepiece, also with brick pilasters, eminently baroque and attributed to the architect Thomas Archer. St Swithun's Street leads down past more Georgian houses and the medieval Close wall to the south gate of the Close, already described. This stands, intriguingly, at right angles to one of the two remaining city gates, Kingsgate, with a miniature church above. Outside is the area dominated by the College; the long and delightful Kingsgate Street runs with a slightly sinuous line and assorted Georgian façades (with some older

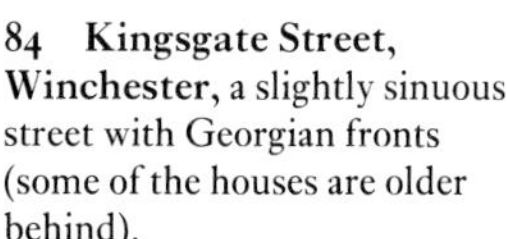

84 **Kingsgate Street, Winchester,** a slightly sinuous street with Georgian fronts (some of the houses are older behind).

85 Chesil Street, Winchester, showing apparently Georgian houses, and one of the city's formerly numerous small churches, St Peter Chesil.

evidence) towards the Hospital of St Cross (see colour illus. pp. 2/3). It is remarkable that both the College and the more distant St Cross should be outside the city wall. College Street leads, from Kingsgate itself, past the entrance to the College and then that to Wolvesey Palace (with the ruined Wolvesey Castle behind) into a delightful area. A path curves past the one remaining length of the city wall, a plain patchwork of flint and occasional rubble stone. On the right is the river.

East of the river

There was always – at least since Norman times – a populous suburb across the River Itchen. It is best seen first across the river, from the path described above. The narrow and strangely unpolluted river is backed by a series of garden walls in a medley of stonework, flint and brick. Behind are long gardens extending to the picturesque backs of houses which face Chesil Street – described shortly – and are on the whole older than they appear from that street. To the right is the picturesque tower of St Peter Chesil church, unusually tile-hung. Such domestic gardens behind street frontages were once very characteristic of old towns; too often now they have become commercial yards or car parks, or have disappeared under development. To reach the front of the houses one crosses the small stone bridge at the end of High Street and its continuation Broadway, with the converted brick and tiled City Mill of 1744 to the north (a youth hostel). Chesil Street is traffic-ridden, but it makes a vignette with the Georgian-fronted houses on the right – whose gardens run down to the river – the two-gabled fifteenth-century Old Chesil restaurant on the left and the little church closing the view. Winchester once had many small churches like this but few survive – many disappeared even before the end of the Middle Ages. The best remaining parish church in the city is nearby St John's – reached along narrow St John's Street, recently revived after decay. The church has a striking thirteenth-

86 **Back of Chesil Street, Winchester,** showing the houses in (85) and the tile-hung tower of the church; many of the houses are older than their fronts suggest. Large gardens, unsuspected from the streets, were characteristic of old towns. In the foreground the River Itchen, and a wall with patchwork materials.

century geometrical window, and from the churchyard there is a good view back over the city.

North of High Street

There is less to see north of High Street, but some of the parallel side streets, of Saxon origin, are interesting. St Peter's Street has fine late seventeenth- and early eighteenth-century houses in brick. Jewry Street with its double twist is full of variety; it is predominantly nineteenth-century, including two parts of what was the prison, of 1804, with grim incised quoin stones on what are now the upper storeys of shops, with a Victorian Congregational church in between. The dominant feature is the old Corn Exchange, now the public library, an inventive classical building of 1838 with a portico recalling Inigo Jones' church in Covent Garden, and recently cleaned walls of creamy brick. It is by Owen Carter, an outstanding local architect, who designed classical terraces and Gothic churches. In contrast is a building further north on the opposite side, fluent with little gables and iron balconies, by Stopher, Carter's successor as the leading local architect. Also striking is the latest building in the street, Sheridan House, by the locally-based architect Robert Adam, in a style inspired by Victorian warehouses, with great brick arches containing shop fronts and first-floor windows – something for which there is no particular precedent in Winchester, but which fits in perfectly.

Worthing

Sussex

Worthing became fashionable when Princess Amelia, sister of the future Prince Regent, visited it in 1798, aged sixteen. In a sense the relationship between the Princess and the Prince symbolizes that between Worthing and Brighton. Worthing was a very small village before the

87 **Park Crescent, Worthing,** an astonishing development of *c.*1830 by Amon Wilds the younger of Brighton, seen from a side archway to the entrance gate. The 'crescent' is sinuous and full of rich stucco details, including ammonite capitals (39).

88 Liverpool Terrace, Worthing, *c.* 1830, a wonderful rhythm of curves.

visitors came. It grew spasmodically after the royal visit, since the land was in varied ownership – as at Brighton the ancient open-field system partly survived, never systematically enclosed, and the strips were built up piecemeal. The railway stimulated further growth, but this was checked by a cholera outbreak in the 1850s, and a typhoid epidemic in the 1890s. It was only in the inter-war years, its sanitary problems solved, that Worthing grew expansively. So it is now a twentieth-century resort retaining a good deal from the Regency period, sometimes grand, often unexpected. There have been some bad pieces of recent development. Starting from the east, Warwick Road with its iron balconies is a good introduction to the town. In Alfred Place leading off, and still more in neighbouring Warwick Place, there are small houses of about 1820 with door canopies like sections of upturned boats – a strange reminiscence of the old village's fishing traditions. The Steine, a space laid out in 1806 in modest imitation of that at Brighton, has a range of houses in creamy-buff brick which caused comment in early descriptions of the town because of its contrast with the pebbles and flints of the traditional buildings, and the increasingly fashionable stucco. More dramatic are Montagu Place and Liverpool Terrace; the former, of 1800–5, has four storeys of bay windows which, with their curved sashes separated by thin mullions, give the impression of almost continuous glazing round the curves on each floor; there is nothing quite like this in Brighton. Liverpool Terrace, of 1826–33, is more substantial, with broader, Brighton-like stuccoed bows, their rhythm emphasized by the balconies at first-floor level. Ambrose Place, to the north, is a charming lower-key counterpart built up piecemeal, so that the houses are all different though consistent, with their balconies and verandahs; one has a bulging bow. But nothing else in Worthing compares with Park Crescent, obscurely set well back from the front, a development by Amon Wilds the younger of Brighton, but more unorthodox than anything he or his father built there. It is entered through a triumphal arch, between smaller pedestrian arches, each flanked by plaster busts in niches. The 'crescent' is sinuous, with busy façades alternately embellished with columns and Amon Wilds' favourite 'ammonite' capitals. The final development in the old tradition is Heene Terrace, facing the sea well to the west, built in 1865 in a Victorian version of the Regency style, with verandahs over porches.

In Worthing's sprawling inland suburbs are two old villages. One, Broadwater, has a fine church; the other, West Tarring remains intact, looking and feeling like a village though hemmed in by modern houses. Besides part of a manor house of the Archbishops of Canterbury, now the church hall, and a fine row of timber-framed houses, containing a museum, there is a winding street which has been skilfully extended in vernacular form with the same twists as in the old part – a sadly rare example of new development unobtrusively in keeping with what is there already.

Select Bibliography

There are numerous books and booklets about individual towns, and this is a selection from those in print or fairly recently published. Older publications are not included; although often interesting and valuable they naturally do not take account of the enormous advances over the last few decades in urban and local history.

In many towns leaflets can be obtained, from bookshops or museums, which indicate suggested walks or trails, with information on interesting buildings and other features. They are usually published by local preservation or civic societies, although some are produced by councils. Such walks or trails often provide the best introductions for visitors to historic towns. Lists of some of the places where they may be available are included under the following county headings.

A detailed bibliography on the history of towns generally is included in the author's *The Making of English Towns*.

Hampshire and the Isle of Wight

Buildings of England: *Hampshire and the Isle of Wight;* Southampton, Portsmouth and adjoining places written by D.W. Lloyd, rest by N. Pevsner

Hampshire's Heritage (published by Hampshire County Council) has material on towns and buildings

Shell Guide: *The Isle of Wight;* P. Hughes

Winchester; B. Carpenter Turner

Medieval Southampton; C. Platt

Buildings of Portsmouth and its Environs; D.W. Lloyd

The Story of Lymington; booklet by R. Coles

The Story of Romsey; booklet by P. Berrow, B. Burbridge and P. Genge

Wayfarers' Winchester; booklet by R. Hubbuck

Titchfield: A History; booklet *ed.* G. Watts

Herbert Collins, Architect (of Southampton); booklet by R. Williams

Portsmouth Papers, a series of historical booklets published by the Portsmouth City Council; among the most relevant are No. 44 (about the Dockyard) by R.C. Riley; No. 8 (about the churches) by R. Hubbuck: No. 32 (about houses designed by T.E. Owen, a local architect) by R.C. Riley

Fortifications of Old Portsmouth; booklet by A. Corney

Walks and Trails for Andover, Fareham, Odiham, Portsmouth (several), Romsey, Southampton and Titchfield

Kent

Buildings of England, in two volumes; *North and East Kent* and *West Kent and the Weald;* both by J. Newman

Shell Guide: *Kent;* P. Hughes

Seventeenth-Century Kent; C.W. Chalklin

Royal Tunbridge Wells; A. Savidge

Rochester: the Evolution of a City; R. Marsh

The Pleasant Town of Sevenoaks; J. Dunlop

The Book of Dartford; G. Porteous

Folkestone: the Story of a Town; C.H. Bishop

Cranbrook: a Wealden Town; booklet by C.C.R. Pile

Sandwich; official guide (good on history and buildings)

Thanet; booklet by J. Hilton (including Ramsgate)

Another Six English Towns; A. Clifton-Taylor – includes Sandwich

Walks and Trails for Canterbury (several), Hythe, Maidstone, Milton Regis, Rochester, Tenterden, Tonbridge and Tunbridge Wells

Surrey

Buildings of England: *Surrey;* I. Nairn and N. Pevsner, revised by B. Cherry

Guildford; R. Chamberlin

Godalming 400; booklet by D. Coombs

Epsom: Town, Downs and Common; booklet *ed.* B.J. Salter

Central Croydon; booklet *ed.* B.J. Salter

Walks and Trails for Dorking, Farnham, Godalming, Guildford, Kingston and Reigate

Sussex

Buildings of England: *Sussex;* a single volume in two parts; West Sussex by I. Nairn, East Sussex by N. Pevsner

The Sussex Landscape; P. Brandon (landscape history including towns)

Shell Guide: *East Sussex;* W.S. Mitchell

History and Architecture of Brighton, and *Fashionable Brighton;* A. Dale

Georgian Brighton, and other historical booklets on Brighton; S. Farrant

A History of Worthing; A.M. Rowland and T.F. Hudson – reprinted from the Victoria County History of Sussex

Horsham; A. Windrum

Petworth today and yesterday; booklet by D. Gundry

Portrait of Arundel; booklet by R. Gardiner

A History of Lewes; booklet by W. Godfrey

Burtons' St. Leonards; booklet by J.M. Baines

Six English Towns; A. Clifton-Taylor – includes Chichester

Six More English Towns; A. Clifton-Taylor – includes Lewes

Walks and Trails for Arundel, Battle, Brighton and Hove (several), Chichester (several), Hastings and St. Leonards, Horsham, Lewes, Rye, Steyning, Winchelsea and Worthing

The black and white photographs are shown in the Index in italic under plate numbers.

Index